KT-551-023

823.009

PALMER,EUSTACE

INTRODUCTION TO THE AFRICA

0435184202 0 001   64

An Introduction
to the African Novel

▼▼

An Introduction to the African Novel

A CRITICAL STUDY OF
TWELVE BOOKS BY
CHINUA ACHEBE, JAMES NGUGI, CAMARA LAYE,
ELECHI AMADI, AYI KWEI ARMAH, MONGO BETI,
and GABRIEL OKARA

EUSTACE PALMER

Lecturer in English
University of Sierra Leone

HEINEMANN
LONDON · IBADAN · NAIROBI

Heinemann Educational Books Ltd
48 Charles Street, London WıX 8AH
P.M.B. 5205 Ibadan · P.O. BOX 25080 Nairobi

EDINBURGH MELBOURNE TORONTO AUCKLAND
HONG KONG SINGAPORE KUALA LUMPUR NEW DELHI

ISBN 0 435 18420 2 (cased)
ISBN 0 435 18421 0 (paper)

© Eustace Palmer 1972
First published 1972

Printed in Great Britain by
Cox and Wyman Ltd
London, Fakenham and Reading

Contents

Preface

I would like to express my gratitude to Kenneth Ramchand for the stimulus which made this work possible; to Paul Edwards who first aroused my interest in African literature and introduced me to a publisher; and to my many students whose participation in tutorials helped me to formulate my views on the African novel.

Introduction

▼▼▼▼▼▼▼▼▼▼▼▼▼▼▼▼▼▼▼▼▼▼▼▼▼▼▼▼▼▼▼▼▼▼

T HE emergence of a very large corpus of African novels in both English and French has been one of the most interesting literary developments of the last twenty-five years. It was perhaps inevitable that the movement towards self-determination, and the emergence into prominence of a powerful, well educated, and articulate élite, would result in a number of works of art designed to express the strength, validity, and beauty of African life and culture. Appropriately, some of the earliest novelists – Tutuola, Camara Laye, and Chinua Achebe – derived their inspiration from traditional lore, indigenous customs, and the oral tradition, in a bid to demonstrate to their readers, African and non-African alike, that Africa has a culture she could be proud of. The earliest novels therefore had a distinctly sociological bias. Partly because of this sociological preoccupation and partly because African literature was a new, and therefore interesting, phenomenon these novels attracted a lot of attention from the Western world. Metropolitan critics and reviewers hailed the new literature with delight as quaint, charming, dignified and different. Social anthropologists and specialists in African studies were equally enthusiastic. However, the more African novels one reads, the more the uncomfortable feeling grows that the literary quality does not always justify the praise. The indulgent policy adopted by many publishing houses associated with African literature meant that although a number of good African novels were published, a number of mediocre and even bad ones got through as well. Nevertheless, reviewers often praised inferior work which would almost certainly have been condemned had it been written by a Western author. For a variety of reasons critics have been reluctant to relegate bad or mediocre African works to the limbo to which they belong. To the African intellectual, however, this attitude is patronizing since it implies that lower standards are permissible, indeed, to be expected, in African affairs. African fiction has been given time to settle, it is proliferating, and finding its way into the curricula of African, European and American schools and universities, and the time has come to establish certain principles of criticism, and to initiate discussion on the relative merits of the various novelists.

It has often been suggested that critics of the African novel should concentrate more on what African novelists are trying to say, and less on the way in which they say it. If this view is accepted, two problems emerge. How does one assess the quality of the novel and the relative merits of one author *vis-à-vis* another? How do we distinguish between novels, and sociological or political documents, which might be saying exactly the same things as the novels in question? Surely what transforms the novel from a political or sociological work to a work of art is the novelist's technique, the devices he uses to shape, explore, define, and finally evaluate his material. Discussion of the novel cannot afford to neglect technique. Not that the importance of the message in African literature should be devalued: African novelists have much to say to their society and to the world.

The message is certainly important, but 'artistic' criticism of technique is not invalid. The well-made novel is a composite of message and technique, and any work which is deficient in either is open to criticism.

Some say that the critical criteria normally applied to European literature cannot be applied usefully to African literature. Since the African writer's experience is markedly different from that of his European or North American counterparts, naturally he will evolve new forms of expression, and consequently his literature should not be measured by an alien yardstick. The African writer's unique experience may lead him to evolve new forms, but not necessarily. Dostoevsky's and Tolstoy's experiences were markedly different from those of Conrad, George Eliot, and other English novelists, but the form of their novels is not entirely alien to English literature. In fact, most African novelists have been quite content to use the established forms of the English, American and Continental novel. From the point of view of form, there isn't much to choose between Achebe and Hardy, Ngugi and Conrad, Camara Laye and Kafka. But even if the form of African novels were different, this would not mean that a different set of criteria should be evolved for their criticism. Within the corpus of English literature there is a wide variety of forms, and yet the same criteria have been consistently applied (by Leavis for example) to novelists as varied as Conrad, Lawrence, James, and George Eliot. The point is that his unique experience has probably led the African novelist to evolve new forms, not new *genres*. Since we are still concerned with the same *genre*, the same criteria should still apply. To allow different critical criteria is to provide loopholes for mediocrities.

What then does one expect of a well-made novel? Arnold Kettle suggested that the essential prerequisites should be 'life' and 'pattern'. If I understand him rightly he is suggesting that a novel should not merely give the feel of life but that the author should manifest a consistent moral attitude and impose some pattern on the chaos of experience. By 'pattern' Kettle refers not only to the abstract details of plot, structure, point of view, style and other aspects of technique, but implies that all these aspects are subsumed under the term 'pattern', for how is the novelist to convey his 'consistent moral attitude' without the aid of technique? When we attack Defoe, for instance, for not manifesting a consistent moral attitude in *Moll Flanders,* it is largely because we are not aware of his use of any techniques which might point to such a moral attitude.

One expects of a good novelist, therefore, that apart from his preoccupation with his message, he should have some concern for the appropriate style and show signs of technical competence. These are the criteria which will be consistently applied in this book. According to these criteria, then, it seems to me that the African novelists whose works, taken as a whole, indicate mastery of their art, are Ngugi, Achebe, Camara Laye, Mongo Beti, Armah, Elechi Amadi, and Gabriel Okara. This does not mean that every novel by each of these writers is a perfect work of art; indeed, the quality of the achievement in almost every case is uneven, as will be evident in subsequent discussion. But each of these authors has shown in some or other of his works that he understands what the novelist's art is about and has striven to master it.

Eyebrows will inevitably be raised because of some significant omissions. The first of these is Ekwensi. Now, while Ekwensi deserves to feature in any historical discussion of the African novel it is my opinion that he has no place in a critical work devoted to the masters of African fiction. Everything that needs to be said about Ekwensi has probably been said by Bernth Lindfors. Ekwensi is certainly the most prolific African writer, and in Lindfors' words:

> At least nine novels, four of them still unpublished, six novelettes for schoolchildren, two collections of folktales, and dozens of short stories have poured from his pen, but not one is entirely free of amateurish blots and blunders, not one could be called the handwork of a careful, skilled craftsman. Ekwensi may be simply too impatient an artist to take pains with his work or to learn by a calm rational process of trial and error. When he is not repeating his old mistakes, he is stumbling upon spectacular new ones. As a consequence, many of his stories and novels can serve as excellent examples of how not to write fiction.*

These may be damaging words but they are essentially true. Ekwensi also mars his work by vulgarizing his style to suit the needs of a mass audience. Although he has been reputed to refer to himself as the African Charles

* Lindfors, B., 'Cyprian Ekwensi: An African Popular Novelist', *African Literature Today 3*, Heinemann Educational Books, 1969, pp. 2–14.

Dickens, his literary affinities are really with fourth-rate American sex-and-crime fiction. His art is that of the sensational thriller and it is imitative rather than imaginative. His characterization is weak, most of his figures being mere puppets or type-characters, usually abstracted from Western films or the pages of cheap thrillers. His pretentious language, far from reflecting the rhythms of African speech, consciously imitates the thriller style. And although his characters usually end badly, it is doubtful whether this is due to any conscious moral concern. Ekwensi hardly ever manifests a consistent moral attitude, his main preoccupation being the sensationalism created by vice. All these weaknesses are clearly present in his most successful novel *Jagua Nana*. Like Defoe's *Moll Flanders*, which it resembles in several respects, *Jagua Nana* gives a very realistic picture of the seamy side of Lagos life. There is certainly a lot of 'life' in the book. But the novelist's task is not merely to convey experience, but also to attempt to clarify and order the chaos of experience, and analyse the nature of man. This is what Arnold Kettle means when he suggests that the novelist should impose pattern on his work and manifest a consistent moral attitude. One would not indict Ekwensi for taking us into the world of prostitutes, pimps, dishonest politicians, organized crime and thuggery, but one can indict him if he fails to take some moral standpoint. In *Jagua Nana* Ekwensi could either have tried to make excuses for his characters and show plausibly that they are victims of their society, or he could have used various techniques, such as irony, to indicate that he disapproves of them. But like Defoe, Ekwensi fails to do either. Indeed, both *Jagua Nana* and *Moll Flanders* confront the student of literature with the same problems. Both are badly constructed. In *Jagua Nana* for instance, the Bagana Scenes during which Jagua incredibly contrives a reconciliation between chief Obafuro and his relatives, make no difference to her relations with Freddie (which was the motivation of the visit) nor do they affect the course of events. This scene, like the scenes with Dennis Udoma, could have been omitted without materially damaging the book. *Jagua Nana* is a string of episodes, not a carefully constructed whole, and quite characteristically the dénouement is brought about by an accident, not the logical culmination of events.

Whatever internal unity the book possesses is imparted by the figure of Jagua herself. What is Ekwensi's attitude towards Jagua? This is central to one's evaluation. There is no doubt that Jagua is an immoral woman. Unlike Moll Flanders, she does not turn to prostitution because there is no other means of survival in a money-conscious man's world. She refuses several offers of marriage from the local boys with whom she has had sexual experience, on the grounds that they are not sufficiently expert.

Jagua is a nymphomaniac with a crazy passion for sex and the bright lights of Lagos. Moll Flanders at least was only kept by one man at a time; Jagua on the other hand is not content with one man. It is doubtful whether she is capable of being in love with anyone. Her 'affection' for Freddie, the only man she seems to have been really fond of, is most probably motivated by a need for future security, and at the end she joins forces with Uncle Taiwo to destroy him. Jagua can also be ill-tempered, vengeful, and unscrupulous. All these faults might have been pardoned if she ever showed signs of remorse. But Jagua only repents when she realizes she is finished in Lagos.

One would expect a serious novelist to show some signs of disapproval of Jagua's conduct, but instead Ekwensi seems to try to persuade the reader to share his captivation with her: there is very little criticism, either of her or of the threat which the dangerous Lagos underworld presents to civilized standards. The quality of Ekwensi's moral vision is weak. The characterization is just as weak. The only fully realized character is Jagua herself, the others being hazy figures whom the reader soon forgets. The style is obviously that of the sex-and-crime school.

Jagua Nana represents Ekwensi at his best, and yet by any standards it is a failure. His other novels are too insignificant to be seriously discussed. Ekwensi surely has a place in any history of African fiction, but not in a discussion of the art of fiction.

Another notable omission is Soyinka. Although he has written only one novel, *The Interpreters,* reviewers and critics who were enthusiastic about its exposure of the state of contemporary Nigeria, might expect to find him discussed in a work devoted to African fiction. Now, there have to be very good reasons for including a one-volume novelist in a critical work. Emily Brontë has to feature in all works on the English novel because of the remarkable achievement of *Wuthering Heights.* Even if Ayi Kwei Armah had not written a second novel he would have had to be included on the basis of *The Beautyful Ones Are Not Yet Born.* However, despite the efforts of notable critics to make a case for it, for me *The Interpreters* does not justify the inclusion of Soyinka. There is no doubt that Soyinka does certain things well: in the first place he has a greater capacity than most African novelists for evoking a scene and presenting it vividly to the reader's imagination. Secondly, his comment on the aimlessness, affectation and 'moral turpitude' of contemporary Nigerian society is pointed and necessary. Finally, he brings to the African novel a poetic quality which some other novelists strive after in vain.

Nevertheless, *The Interpreters'* weaknesses are glaringly apparent. Verbal dexterity and linguistic sophistication almost become ends in themselves. Soyinka rejoices in his power over words but this power is not always related to meaning. Derek Elders surely strikes at the heart of the problem when he refers to Soyinka's style as tedious, and finally aimless virtuousity*. Then there is the problem of the novel's structure. It is surely extravagant praise to describe *The Interpreters* as 'a well-conceived whole' or to suggest that the style of narration gives the novel compactness of structure and a feeling of wholeness of conception†. The dominant impression left by *The Interpreters* is one of a tedious formlessness. The novel's defenders would no doubt be quick to suggest that such criticism stems from an inability to recognize the tremendous skill and artistry underlying the apparent formlessness. They would suggest, as Professor Jones does, that the flashbacks are carefully inserted to throw light on the characters' present situation. Every critic knows that a novel is not necessarily formless simply because it departs from the conventional chronological sequence. Virginia Woolf's *Mrs Dalloway*, Sterne's *Tristram Shandy*, Conrad's *Lord Jim* and Ngugi's *A Grain of Wheat* are all novels whose apparent formlessness disguises the most carefully contrived order. But it would be difficult to make the same claim for *The Interpreters*. Again the comparison is with James Ngugi. Ngugi's flashbacks are always so carefully positioned, and the transitions in time so carefully made, that they build up indispensable pictures of the characters' lives. It is difficult to see any adroitness in Soyinka's use of flashbacks. The novel seems to be just a loose string of impressions or episodes.

Finally, a word about Lenrie Peters' *The Second Round*. Peter's intention in this novel is to demonstrate his hero's alienation from traditional life through exposure to European experience during his fifteen years' absence. The reader is meant to believe that Dr Kawa is ill at ease on his return to Freetown and is forced to move to Bo because the life in the Metropolis nauseates him. However, *The Second Round* is one of those novels in which the novelist has failed to keep his themes clearly before his mind, and pursue them to their logical conclusion. In the novel Dr Kawa's disgust with Freetown cannot entirely be blamed on the city's nature; he must to a very great extent bear the responsibility himself. He is weak and indecisive, certainly one of the most spineless heroes in fiction. If his love affair with Laura ends in disaster, it is not because the environment is inimical to healthy love, but because Dr Kawa conducts this love affair like a boy of ten. As a man in love he is unconvincing. It is little wonder that Laura

* Elders, D., 'James Ngugi: *A Grain of Wheat*', *African Literature Today 1*, Heinemann Educational Books, 1968, pp. 51–53.

† Jones, E., 'Wole Soyinka's *The Interpreters*', *African Literature Today 2*, Heinemann Educational Books, 1969, pp. 42–50.

drifts away from him into somebody else's arms. In fact, Dr Kawa seems quite incapable of having a normal relationship with a woman. Laura, the only girl he really falls in love with, is eighteen, about twenty years his junior, and he is attracted to her out of pity. Dr Kawa is an interesting psychological case:

> What he needed most was an aesthetic love affair. One that was not rooted in the flesh alone. He must fall utterly and tragically in love – take the plunge.*

Dr Kawa's attitude to love is not merely idealistic, it is immature. Unfortunately, conditions in Freetown, rather than Kawa's immaturity are held responsible for his frustration. The plot and structure of the novel are also badly handled. Except that Kawa features in both, the first part, with the affair with Laura, seems to have nothing to do with the second, which deals with Kawa's relationship with the Marshalls. The second section has the makings of a self-contained tragedy, dealing with the Freddie-Clara-Mr Marshall love triangle, but this is unrealized and the effect is marred by the melodramatic scenes in which Clara jumps into Freddie's grave, and young Sonia kills her mother. A number of scenes in the novel are not properly developed, others are irrelevant, and traits attributed to certain characters are not demonstrated. Pretentious language, overworked and rather self-conscious medical imagery, and the inclusion of spurious pieces from Jungian psychology, further induce the impression of mediocrity. Gerald Moore's judgement in *The East African Journal* that it is 'a distinguished and memorable work of the imagination' is astonishing.

There are of course several African writers who have been left out, even though they have written more than one work, because none of their novels seems to be of much significance. The bias of this work is critical and not historical, so I have not felt obliged to include everyone with a prolific output. I have concentrated instead, on the dozen or so novels which seem to be of some importance, and which are gradually finding their way into school and university syllabuses. Although this book is also directed to the general reader, I have mainly had in mind a student readership. Consequently, I have concentrated on detailed discussion, not general remarks (this accounts for the number of quotations from the texts), to demonstrate what is in the text, only bringing in sociological or historical information when necessary. I feel that this is the kind of help that students need. I have also tried, as much as possible, to avoid literary jargon, and to write in language which even a sensitive sixth former will understand.

* Peters, L., *The Second Round*, African Writers Series, Heinemann Educational Books, 1966, p. 39.

1 : James Ngugi

▼▼▼▼▼▼▼▼▼▼▼▼▼▼▼▼▼▼▼▼▼▼▼▼▼▼

WEEP NOT CHILD

JAMES NGUGI'S *Weep Not Child* dramatizes the events of the Mau Mau emergency in Kenya in the nineteen-fifties. A novel with this theme could degenerate into a mere catalogue of political events, and, indeed, politics does tend to loom large. Ngugi partly alleviates the effect of a depressing series of historical and political events, by filtering them through the mind of a central consciousness, Njoroge, the hero of the novel. Furthermore, by concentrating on the members of the Ngotho family he ensures that interest centres not on political matters, but on relationships, and on the effects on the characters of the pressure of events. The novel is not propagandist work solely designed to put the African case against the white settlers: Ngugi's balanced viewpoint takes into account the weaknesses of the Africans themselves as well as of the Europeans.

Political freedom in Kenya became synonymous with repossession of the land, and this struggle is central to the novel. In Kenya land is not only held to be of much greater importance than money or cattle, it clearly has spiritual associations. Ngotho's inspired story about the origin of the land brings out this point:

And the creator who is also called Murungu took Gikuyu and Mumbi from his holy mountain. He took them to the country of ridges near Siriana and there stood them on a big ridge before he finally took them to Mukuruwe wa Gathanga about which you have heard so much. But he had shown them all the land – yes, children, God showed Gikuyu and Mumbi all the land and told them, 'This land I hand over to you. O Man and woman it's yours to rule and till in serenity sacrificing only to me, your God, under my sacred tree.'*

* Ngugi, J., *Weep, Not Child*, African Writers Series, Heinemann Educational Books, 1964, p. 27–28. All further page references are to this edition.

In this story of the creation, Gikuyu and Mumbi, the legendary ancestors of the Kenyans, are the East African counterparts of the biblical Adam and Eve. The land which was entrusted to them by God is seen as part of a covenant between God and his people who are specifically enjoined to rule and till it, sacrificing to him under his sacred tree. Consequently the people see the alienation of the land, and its appropriation by an alien people, not only as God's punishment for their sins, but as an alienation from their God and ancestors. Its recovery is therefore essential.

The spiritual significance of the land explains the reverential awe with which Ngotho treats it. He sees the land as something more than a commercial asset; it is the link with his God and his ancestors. Ngotho moreover makes this land bear fruit, as no one else can. And Howlands, whose chief interest is profit, respects him more than any other African.

It is interesting to compare Ngotho's attitude to the land with that of Howlands. Howlands loves the land in his own way, with the satisfaction of possession and subjugation. Towards the end of the novel Mr Howlands is capable of saying 'this is my land' as a man would say 'this is my woman'. Ngotho on the other hand, reveres his land.

Among the natives themselves, there is general unanimity about the need to recover the land, but no agreement about the means of achieving this end. The members of the older generation know of the prophecy that a leader will one day arrive to lead the people to freedom, and are perfectly prepared to wait for its fulfilment. But the younger, much more militant men, demand immediate action. Ngotho's son Boro, is representative of this group. He is the typical malcontent whose character has been completely altered by the course of events. He was uprooted from his home and his traditions during the most formative years of his life, and taken to the Western world to fight in the Second World War. His experiences there were traumatic; he lost a favourite brother, and his eyes were opened to the sordidness of Western civilization, with all its squalor, immorality, and poverty. Subsequently, he returned home to find that the 'inferior' people had become his masters, and that he was completely alienated from his traditional land. Boro is disillusioned and disenchanted, and Ngotho's policy of waiting for the fulfilment of the prophecy seems to him absurd.

Far from sentimentalizing the Africans, Ngugi *does* show that their problem is made all the more intractable because of their lack of unity. Jacobo, for instance, is quite prepared to betray his people and become Mr Howlands' chief informer in order to retain his material prosperity. There is also a paralysing lack of agreement about the best possible means for achieving the desired ends. Ngugi quite scrupulously analyses the causes of the people's suffering and locates them not merely in the acts of intimidation committed by the whites, but in the Kenyans' personal weaknesses. That this is so will be seen from an examination of the characters of Ngotho and Njoroge.

Ngotho is a truly tragic figure, magnificently impressive at the beginning, degenerating to utter ruin at the end. His catastrophe is caused by a combination of the forces ranged against him, and his own personal weaknesses. There is no doubt about his self-confidence at the start. His home is well-known and respected throughout the village as a place of peace, and his son Njoroge admires him for providing the security and stability that are needed in these difficult times.

However, despite his acknowledged pre-eminence, Ngotho is not a man of action but a traditionalist who would rather wait for the fulfilment of the prophecy than take up arms against his overlords. In this he is clearly contrasted with his son Boro, who is openly scornful of the prophecy and of his father's inaction. Circumstances however force Ngotho to take a stand. A strike is planned and, in spite of his personal misgivings about its success, he gives it his endorsement. At this stage Ngotho's indecision, his most conspicuous weakness, is revealed. The scene in which he and his wife discuss the strike brings this out clearly:

> 'What's black people to us when we starve?'
> 'Shut that mouth. How long do you think I can endure this drudgery, for the sake of a white man and his children?'
> 'But he's paying you money. What if the strike fails?'
> 'Don't woman me!' he shouted hysterically.
> This possibility was what he feared most. She sensed this note of uncertainty and fear and seized upon it.
> 'What if the strike fails, tell me that!'
> Ngotho could bear it no longer. She was driving him mad. He slapped her on the face and raised his hand again. (p. 60)

With unerring feminine intuition Nyokabi lays her finger on Ngotho's doubts, indecision, uncertainty, and fears, and he hits her, not because he resents being challenged by a woman, nor because she is wrong, but precisely because he knows she is so right.

During the strike Ngotho, in a characteristically unpremeditated act, rouses the crowd to physical violence against Jacobo giving no thought to the possible consequences. He is borne on a tide of emotion, quite literally overcome by a sense of the occasion. It is the only occasion in the novel when he acts decisively, but it is a gross miscalculation, and the consequences are disastrous.

The strike marks the beginning of Ngotho's downfall, for from now on he is exposed to a number of humiliations. He loses his job and his house, and has to endure Boro's accusing eye. A practical and calculating activist, Boro blames his father's irrational action for the failure of the strike and its consequences. It is a measure of how far Ngotho has degenerated, when Boro attempts to force him to take the Mau-Mau oath.

Ngotho is further humiliated by the arrest of his wife Njeri and his son Kori when he proves completely incapable of saving them. Finally Ngotho is castrated and literally loses his manhood. The castration is a symbolic culmination of the gradual loss of his manly self-assurance and dignity.

However, like most tragic heroes, before his death Ngotho redeems himself in the reader's eyes. Thinking that Kamau was the murderer of the arch-traitor Jacobo, Ngotho confesses to the murder in order to save his son. It is the greatest act of sacrifice of which the human being is capable – to lay down his life for another – and the old man rises once more in our estimation. Finally, on his deathbed, he rises to his former stature, and even the formerly contemptuous Boro returns to his father's bedside, acknowledges his worth, and, in tears, asks and receives his forgiveness.

The hero of this novel, however, is not Ngotho, but his son Njoroge. It is through his eyes and largely from his point of view that we see the details of the story. Indeed for the most part the story seems to emanate from the consciousness of the hero, which accounts for the novel's apparent simplicity. Ngugi makes a determined effort to keep the reader close to the consciousness of a small, naïve boy; in some early scenes he captures and dramatizes the enthusiasm with which the boy responds to his lessons at school.

Yet although Ngugi is anxious to enlist our sympathy for poor Njoroge, whose aspirations are completely destroyed, our response to the hero should not solely be pity. For Ngugi presents Njoroge as a visionary and dreamer living in a world of illusions, and seeking every possible opportunity to escape from tough reality into phantasies about a bright and better future. Indeed in Njoroge, Ngugi presents us with a portrait of some psychological depth; Njoroge not only dreams, but also shows a stubborn reluctance to grow emotionally and psychologically. The boy who attempts to hang himself at the end of the novel, is not very different from the one who had eagerly looked forward to his first day at school nearly thirteen years earlier.

Ngugi's presentation of Njoroge provides evidence of his intelligent objectivity. He intended to demonstrate that the solution to the country's

problems did not lie in education. It merely gives people an excuse to
shirk the responsibilities of the present, by dwelling on hopes of better
days to come. The young Njoroge embodies this attitude, hence the need
to expose his idealism, and the gap between his dreams and the actual
facts of life.

At the start of the novel Njoroge, a very sensitive, introverted child is
very much tied to his mother's apron strongs. He is also passionately
attached to the idea of education as a panacea for the country's ills, and
he sees himself as destined to play a very important role in the process of
liberating his country:

> Njoroge listened to his father. He instinctively knew that an indefinable
> demand was being made on him, even though he was so young. He
> knew that for him education would be the fulfilment of a wider and
> more significant vision – a vision that embraced the demand made on
> him, not only by his father, but also by his mother, his brothers and even
> the village. He saw himself destined for something big, and this made
> his heart glow. (p. 44)

But Ngugi is perfectly aware that this vision is just day-dreaming and he
seizes the opportunity whenever he can, to laugh at his hero's idealism:

> Njoroge did not want to be like his father working for a white man, or
> worse, for an Indian. Father had said that the work was hard and had
> asked him to escape from the same conditions. Yes, he would. He would
> be different. And he would help all his brothers. Before he went to
> sleep he prayed, 'Lord, let me get learning. I want to help my father
> and mothers. And Kamau and all my other brothers. I ask you all
> this through Jesus Christ, our Lord, Amen.'
> He remembered something else.
> ' . . . And help me God so that Mwihaki may not beat me in class. And
> God . . . '
> He fell asleep and dreamed of education in England. (pp. 49–50)

To a certain extent Njoroge even begins to have delusions of grandeur,
and singles out Old Testament characters such as Moses for his favourite
heroes. He sees himself in the role of a redeemer after finishing his education: 'he would one day use all his learning to fight the white man, for he
would continue the work that his father had started. When these moments
caught him he actually saw himself as a possible saviour of the whole of
God's country. Just let him get learning. Let that time come when he . . .'

Although day-dreaming is a harmless pastime it is no substitute for action. Throughout this novel Njoroge merely dreams, while momentous changes are taking place around him. Both his day-dreaming and his obsession with education are escapist.

Eventually, however, reality catches up savagely with Njoroge, when the consequences of the Mau-Mau Emergency pursue him even to the sheltered school where he had thought he would be immune from violence. But neither his religion, nor his school are effective protectors against the menace of the times. Teacher Isaka and other Christians are hounded to death even while they hold up their Bibles, and Njoroge himself is brutally torn from school and tortured, his piteous cry 'I am only a school-boy, affendi', merely serving to arouse even greater sadism from his tormentors.

Njoroge had not only indulged in visions of an educated life, he had also placed implicit faith in the Bible, and had believed the world governed by equity and justice. From now on, however, he has a number of shocks in quick succession, which reveal the difference between the world as it really is, and the world he had imagined. His ideals are shattered, his illusions exposed, and his family and aspirations destroyed. In desperation he turns to Mwihaki and suggests to her that they should escape to Uganda.

Mwihaki is meant among other things to serve as a foil to Njoroge, to put his day-dreaming and his basic immaturity in perspective. Once, during their childish Romeo and Juliet-like love affair *she* had suggested to Njoroge that they run away, demonstrating her own immaturity at that stage. Njoroge had refused, not because he was more mature and more aware of his responsibilities, but because such a course would have interfered with his visionary plans. Now, several years later, Njoroge puts the same proposal to Mwihaki, who has become his last anchor in a rapidly disintegrating world. But the girl demonstrates how much she has grown since their childhood days by refusing Njoroge's proposal. She is aware of the responsibility imposed upon her as a consequence of her father's death:

> She wanted to sink in his arms and feel a man's strength around her weak body. She wanted to travel the road back to her childhood and grow up with him again. But she was no longer a child.
>
> 'Yes, we can go away from here as you had suggested when — '
>
> 'No! no!' she cried, in an agony of despair, interrupting him. 'You must save *me*, please Njoroge. I love you.'
>
> She covered her face with both hands and wept freely, her breast heaving.

Njoroge felt sweet pleasure and excitedly smoothed her dark hair.

'Yes, we go to Uganda and live — '

'No, no.' She struggled again.

'But why?' he asked, not understanding what she meant.

'Don't you see that what you suggest is too easy a way out? We are no longer children,' she said between her sobs.

'That's why we must go away. Kenya is no place for us. Is it not childish to remain in a hole when you can take yourself out?' . . .

'Yes. But we have a duty. Our duty to other people is our biggest responsibility as grown men and women.'

'Duty! Duty!' he cried bitterly.

'Yes, I have a duty, for instance, to my mother. Please dear Njoroge, we cannot leave here at this time when – No! Njoroge. Let's wait for a new day.' (pp. 150–51)

Mwihaki has developed fully from childhood, through adolescence to emotional and psychological maturity, and realizes that adulthood imposes responsibilities and that escape is too easy a way out. Njoroge, on the other hand, forgets that he has 'two mothers' and that his father on his death bed had asked him to take care of them.

Now that all hope has vanished, Njoroge plans the most final method of escape – suicide. But even here his courage fails him:

This time the voice was clear. And he trembled when he recognized its owner. His mother was looking for him. For a good time he stood irresolute. Then courage failed him.

And later:

But as they came near home and what had happened to him came to mind, the voice again came and spoke accusing him:

You are a coward. You have always been a coward. Why didn't you do it?

And loudly he said, 'why didn't I do it?'

The voice said: 'because you are a coward.'

'Yes', he whispered to himself. 'I am a coward.'

And he ran home and opened the door for his two mothers (pp. 153–4)

This last sentence, which is also the last sentence of the novel, has been taken as an indication of Njoroge's long-delayed growth into maturity and consequent acceptance of responsibility.* But if we follow the leads of the

---

* Ikiddeh, I., 'James Ngugi as Novelist', *African Literature Today 2*, Heinemann Educational Books, 1969, pp. 3–10.

novel, the passage does not seem to sustain this interpretation. The overall
effect here is of cowardice. Njoroge realizes that his failure to commit
suicide, itself an act of cowardice, was not due to a belated awareness of
his duties, but to failure of nerve. There is no justification for believing
that Njoroge would develop into a Mugo or Kihika, for all the evidence
suggests that he will merely continue to be a passive, weak, introspective
and sensitive boy.

One of the major objections usually raised against Ngugi is that he
cannot create credible European characters. This charge is worth in-
vestigating with reference to Mr Howlands. In my view, Ngugi is as fair
to Mr Howlands as he could possibly be, and we have as much information
about him as we need, to know him fully. Indeed, at the start of the novel,
it almost seems as if the author goes out of his way to be fair to Mr Howlands. His own claims to the land, albeit the claims of the conqueror, are
set beside those of Ngotho and fairly balanced. Ngugi also demonstrates
the equal admiration both men have for the land, and his tone of voice in
the relevant passages (p. 35 for example) suggests that he does not despise
Howlands. Moreover, the histories and fortunes of the two men are
strikingly similar. Both of them experienced the First World War, and
ended up disillusioned with Britain. Both feel alienated from Britain
(Mr Howlands now regards Kenya as his home and, if anything, hates
Britain more than Ngotho). Both lost promising sons in the Second World
War. Both are plagued with doubt as to whether their sons – Stephen and
Njoroge – on whom responsibility would now devolve, are adequate for
the task. It is obvious that in this section of the novel at least, Ngugi is
doing his best to elicit the reader's sympathy for Mr Howlands. As Mr
Howlands and Ngotho survey the *shamba* together, we see them as two
men with similar histories and doubts.

Furthermore, it is not entirely true that we are given no inside view of
Mr Howlands as the following passage shows:

> He stood and walked across the office, wrapped in thought. He now knew
> maybe there was no escape. The present that had made him a D.O.
> reflected a past from which he had tried to run away. That past had
> followed him even though he had tried to avoid politics, government,
> and anything else that might remind him of that betrayal. But his son
> had been taken away ... It was no good calling on the name of God for
> he, Howlands, did not believe in God. There was only one God for
> him – and that was the farm he had created, the land he had tamed.
> And who were these Mau-Mau who were now claiming that land,
> his God? Ha, ha! He could have laughed at the whole ludicrous idea,

but for the fact that they had forced him into the other life, the life he had tried to avoid. He had been called upon to take up a temporary appointment as a District Officer. He had agreed. But only because this meant defending his God. If Mau Mau claimed the only thing he believed in, they would see! (pp. 86–7)

This is an inside view of Howlands. Ngugi takes the reader into the mind of the man and exposes his thoughts, not all of which are to Howland's discredit. We see not only his determination to exterminate Mau Mau and make Ngotho pay for the inconvenience caused, but also his reluctance to be involved in anything that reeks of politics, or government, or is in any way connected with the British régime. Like Ngotho and Njoroge, Mr Howlands is also caught in the toils of fate.

Once he becomes District Officer, however, he plays his part to perfection. He seems bent on inventing new tortures with which to plague and then destroy Ngotho and his family. At this point he finally forfeits our sympathy, not because Ngugi is unfair to him, but because he represents a number of particularly despicable white District Officers.

If attention has not been proportionately given to the Africans' suffering in this study, it is because it is quite straightforward, and presents no problems of attitudes or interpretation. Also, emphasis in this novel lies not so much in the record of the people's suffering, but in the way in which these affect character. Ime Ikiddeh has pointed out* that Ngugi shows tremendous power in arousing the reader's sympathy at the picture of Little Mwihaki fatherless and alone, Ngotho humiliated, castrated, and finally destroyed, teacher Isaka cut down even while affirming his faith, and Njoroge reduced to a condition of near-beggary, having seen his father die, his brothers taken off to execution or detention, his home destroyed, and his aspirations shattered. Nevertheless, the author has the events of the novel perfectly under control so that pity does not degenerate into sentimentality.

Ngugi's language deserves special attention. Firstly, its biblical aura is most appropriate for the description of the sufferings of a people in bondage. However, one must face the problem of Ngugi's apparent stylistic ineptitude. Quite a number of his sentences seem not only clumsy, but grammatically wrong, as this for instance: 'One day a European woman came to the school. As she was expected the school had been cleaned and put in good order.' However, instances of such grammatical or stylistic errors are mercifully rare. The real problem of Ngugi's language is that one is constantly irritated by its naïvety and extreme simplicity. He seems

* Ikiddeh, I., ibid.

incapable of constructing sentences of even the slightest complexity, and the result is quite often drearily monotonous. However, one should perhaps add that this simplicity of language and style keeps the reader close to the consciousness of villagers in general, and the small, naïve Njoroge in particular:

> There was a man in India called Ghandi. This man was a strange prophet. He always fought for the Indian freedom. He was a thin man and always dressed poorly in calico stretched over his bony body. Walking along the shops, you could see his photograph in every Indian building. The Indians called him *Babu,* and it was said this Babu was actually their god. (p. 9)

The impression of simple villagers conversing comes out very strongly in the passage. Similarly, when on p. 17 we find the sentence: 'It was sweet to play with a girl and especially if that girl came from a family higher up the social scale than one's own', we can easily believe that this is not Ngugi's opinion but that of the childish Njoroge, who would not realize the inappropriateness of the word 'sweet' in this context. Of course, it is difficult to say for certain that the author was making a conscious attempt to keep the reader close to the minds of simple people: the correspondence may have been quite accidental. However, it is safest to give Ngugi the benefit of the doubt, specially since in *The River Between,* which was actually written before *Weep Not Child,* Ngugi demonstrates a certain mastery of the language, and in *A Grain of Wheat,* his mastery is complete. Indeed, even in *Weep Not Child* he occasionally shows sensitivity towards language: 'This morning he walked along the road – the big tarmac road that was long and broad and had no beginning and no end except that it went into the city.' (p. 31)

The main weakness of *Weep Not Child* is the choice of Njoroge as the central consciousness. Not because Njoroge is too passive and ineffective to be at the centre of the novel's events, but because a young, inexperienced boy is not the best vehicle to demonstrate that an obsession with education as a panacea is escapist. It is in the nature of young boys to dream, and have illusions about the future, and one can hardly expect them to understand the complexity of national affairs. The same tendency in an adult here would have been much more convincing.

One cannot make great claims for *Weep Not Child.* Nevertheless, it is an important work which within narrow limits, has been modestly successful.

THE RIVER BETWEEN

A S A RESULT of the use of the technique of close reading, which is now generally accepted as a means of approaching the English, American and Continental novels, a number of works have yielded meanings richer and more significant than was commonly supposed. There still seems, however, to be a general reluctance to use this critical approach in the study of the African novel, perhaps because of the misguided assumption that they are uncomplex mechanisms scarcely repaying detailed analysis. Criticism of the African novel has been largely characterized by vague generalizations and misjudgements, partly arising from hasty and superficial reading. Typical of this kind of misinterpretation is the view that Ngugi's hero, Waiyaki, in *The River Between,* is a modern, progressive, and idealistic individual engaged in a losing battle against reactionary forces and inevitably 'facing the fate of those wise before their time'. The antagonistic forces in Waiyaki's society are blamed for the catastrophe, and his own faults, which are an important contributor to his downfall are ignored. If such a reading were correct then Waiyaki would qualify for the martyr's halo and his story would just be pathetic; but a close examination reveals that Waiyaki, like Ngotho, is a tragic and an enormously impressive hero, whose downfall is caused not only by the forces ranged against him, but also by his own weaknesses.

Before proceeding with a detailed analysis of the novel it is worth pointing out that *The River Between* is a more accomplished novel than *Weep Not Child.* Indeed it would have been neat and convenient to have been able to plot Ngugi's stylistic development from *Weep Not Child,* through *The River Between* to *A Grain of Wheat,* but actually, although *The River Between* was published second, it was written first. Probably Ngugi delayed its publication because he was dissatisfied with it, and only offered it to a publisher after some polishing and pruning. The argument for a logical stylistic progression would, therefore, still hold.

The advance is most noticeable in Ngugi's control of language. The almost childish simplicity of *Weep Not Child* makes way for stylistic sophistication and an awareness of the complex rhythms of English. Stylistic infelicities, though not entirely absent, occur less frequently. Furthermore, Ngugi's powers of characterization also seem to have developed. Many students of *Weep Not Child* feel that Njoroge fails to come to life, and that this is the novel's main weakness. But as for Waiyaki, he is most convincingly and substantially *there*. We look at him from every angle, from inside and out, so that at the end we feel we really know him, and accept him as credible and convincing. The choice of Njoroge as hero of the earlier novel could be faulted, but that of Waiyaki is unexceptionable, for he is strong enough to carry the novel's message.

Ngugi's treatment of the love affair between Waiyaki and Nyambura in this novel, demonstrates greater sensitivity and skill than his handling of the same kind of relationship between Njoroge and Mwihaki, in the earlier novel. The growing strength of their feelings towards each other, the dilemma in which they find themselves, the choice they have to make between love and duty (in this case synonymous with death and life) is much more powerfully and convincingly evoked than in the adolescent affair in *Weep Not Child*.

In this novel, unlike *Weep Not Child*, Ngugi makes a deliberate attempt to use symbols relevantly. The most obvious is the figure of the Sleeping Lions, the ridges Makuyu and Kameno, facing each other antagonistically, and representing the divisions in Waiyaki's society. Although in the valley the two ridges become antagonists, we are also informed that Waiyaki, who climbs to the top of the Sacred Grove with his father, finds them no longer so: 'they had merged into one area of beautiful land, which is what perhaps, they were meant to be.' In other words, to someone like Waiyaki, who has achieved a wider vision, the antagonisms tend to disappear. The River Honia also functions on a symbolic level. It means 'cure', but it is also the river of life, flowing through the valley of life. It should have been a unifying, life-giving force, but it is actually the symbol of division, keeping the two ridges apart.

Circumcision also has a symbolic value in the novel, though in a different sense to the 'Sleeping Lions' or the River Honia. The importance of circumcision for the people of Kameno lies not in the physical act, but 'in what it did inside a person', as Waiyaki himself is to realize later.* Among other things, circumcision establishes a bond between the initiate and his society and country. For instance, when Waiyaki is circumcised, his 'blood trickled freely on to the ground, sinking into the soil. Henceforth a religious bond linked Waiyaki to the earth, as if his blood was an offering'. (p. 52) Later, Waiyaki himself realizes that circumcision keeps the people together and binds the tribe: 'it was at the core of the social structure, and something that gave meaning to a man's life.' This is obviously true of Muthoni who runs away to be circumcised because she wants to be a woman, 'beautiful in the tribe'. Muthoni is expressing what Waiyaki only

---

* Ngugi, J., *The River Between*, African Writers Series, Heinemann Educational Books, 1965, p. 163. All further page references are to this edition.

realizes later, that only through the ritual of circumcision does one experience full manhood or womanhood, and achieve complete self-fulfilment within the tribe. The novel suggests that circumcision is a life-giving force, which is why it is clearly linked with the River Honia, the river of life. The initiates bathe in the river before the ritual; significantly when Nyambura is secretly longing for circumcision (although she would have died rather than admit it), she turns her gaze towards the Honia, and responds to its life-giving rhythms: 'Nyambura was fascinated and felt attracted to the river. Her breast glowing with pleasure, rose and fell with a sigh: She felt something strange stirring in her bowels.' (p. 26) Later we see how the whole village, old and young, responds to the imminence of the circumcision ritual in a joyous frenzy and even the frigid Waiyaki joins in the dance. The missionaries' failure to appreciate the symbolic importance of circumcision, its life-giving, self-fulfilling function, partly leads to the disasters in the novel.

Remembering that *The River Between* actually predates *Weep Not Child*, we should not overlook the similarities. It is here that Ngugi launches his general theme of the disintegration of indigenous society and the collapse of its morale as a result of the gradual encroachment of the white man. In *Weep Not Child* we see the white man victorious, and the African people carrying on the struggle begun in *The River Between* to keep their traditions and institutions, and expel the invader and all he stands for. The structure of both novels is determined by the heroes' path from initial optimism, through part-fulfilment of their aspirations, to ultimate disaster, caused partly by forces which they are incapable of understanding and controlling. The character groupings are also similar: the Chege – Joshua – Livingstone triangle for instance, matches Ngotho – Jacobo – Howlands; the Waiyaki – Nyambura affair parallels the Njoroge – Mwihaki relationship. There is no parallel in *Weep Not Child* to the Kabonyi – Kamau group, since personal jealousy is almost completely absent from that novel.

At the heart of *The River Between* are rigidly uncompromising attitudes which, for want of a better term, can be best described as 'egoisms': an aggressive concern for oneself and one's views, and a complete contempt for those of others. On the one hand are the traditionalists whose stronghold is Kameno, traditionally the seat of Gikuyu and Mumbi, the legendary ancestors of the tribe. As the repository of the tribe's traditions, its inhabitants are determined to keep Kameno pure in the face of the threatened encroachment by the white man and his new religion. Their leader Chege is descended from a long line of distinguished Gikuyu seers. Like his ancestors, he warns the people of the white man's menace and attempts to make them aware of the need for action. Moreover, he knows about an ancient prophecy foretelling the coming of a saviour from the same line of famous seers, who will lead the people in their endeavour to retain tribal purity and subsequently expel the invader. Chege is thus the embodiment of the Kameno ideology. In his way he is just as rigid in his own egoism as Joshua, the Christian leader, for although he is prepared to send his son Waiyaki to the mission school at Siriana to acquire 'some of the white man's learning', it is merely a tactical ploy, an attempt to fight the opponent with his own weapons. That he is essentially as narrowly traditionalist as his supporters, is demonstrated by his interpretation of Muthoni's death as a punishment on Joshua for forsaking the ways of the tribe.

Makuyu is the stronghold of those who have embraced Christianity and abandoned the tribal rituals, and their leader, Joshua, is as bigoted a religious fanatic as ever existed. In Joshua we see the dangerous consequences of a blind and uncritical acceptance of an alien ideology. Lacking any kind of critical intelligence, Joshua accepts Christianity with a naïvety which is almost comic. Indeed, it is perhaps a mistake to suggest that he accepts *Christianity*, for his brand of Christianity is a gross perversion of the real thing. Like most Christian fanatics Joshua knows his Bible thoroughly, and quotes from it with a proficiency which impresses even Waiyaki, but all his examples and allusions are drawn from the Old Testament, and it is quite obvious that his religion is not the religion of love and mercy preached by Christ, but that of Moses and the Patriarchs – a religion of vengeance and justice untempered by mercy.

The issue which most clearly epitomizes the divisions in this society is circumcision, and on this, as on everything else, Joshua's position is rigidly uncompromising:

> To Joshua, indulging in this ceremony was the unforgivable sin. Had he not been told to take up everything and leave Egypt? He would journey courageously, a Christian soldier, going to the promised land. Nobody would deflect him from his set purpose. He wanted to enter the new Jerusalem a whole man.
>
> In fact, Joshua believed circumcision to be so sinful that he devoted a prayer to asking God to forgive him for marrying a woman who had been circumcised. (p. 35)

And later when the period of circumcision approaches, Joshua prays:

> 'O, God, look at their preparations,

O, God, why don't you descend on this wicked generation and finish
their evil ways? Circumcision is coming.
Fight by me, Oh Lord.'
He felt like going out with a stick, punishing these people, forcing them
on to their knees.
Was this not what was done to those children of Israel who turned
away from God, who would not harken to his voice?
Bring down fire and thunder,
Bring down the flood. (p. 37)

Joshua's religious fanaticism is not just grotesquely comic, it is also destructive. In a very real sense it helps to destroy his two daughters, but over
and above this, Ngugi regards his attitude as basically life-denying. It
has already been seen that circumcision is regarded by the people as
life-affirming; therefore, in rejecting it, Joshua is cutting himself and his
followers from a source of 'life'. We see (on p. 39) how Joshua's brand of
Christianity has stifled the 'life' in his wife: 'however, one could still tell
by her eyes that this was a religion learnt and accepted; inside the true
Gikuyu woman was sleeping.' Partly the awareness of this life-denying
quality of Joshua's religion leads to Nyambura's secret longing for circumcision as a path to 'life', and subsequently to her acceptance of the religion
of love that Waiyaki offers.

These then are the forces ranged against each other; one of the hero's
problems is the tenacity with which each clings to its own position.
The death of Muthoni, who had crossed over from Makuyu to Kameno
in order to be circumcised, precipitates the clash, and consolidates the
existing antipathies. Makuyu sees her death as the consequence of
deserting Christianity, and indulging in the most primitive practices:
Kameno interprets it as a just punishment on Joshua for abandoning the
ways of the tribe. For both sides her death is seen as a call to intensify
their efforts against the opposing faction.

Since Muthoni is such a controversial figure it may be as well to discuss
her significance in the novel at this stage. Muthoni is one of the two people
who span the gap between the warring ideologies, the other being the hero,
Waiyaki. But unlike Waiyaki, she quickly works out her reconciliation
of the two factions. There can be no doubt of the strength of her Christian
conviction, illustrated in her dying words 'tell Nyambura I see Jesus'.
But at the same time she realizes that the tribal rituals, especially that of
circumcision, offer her the best opportunity of achieving complete self-
fulfilment. So she goes away to Kameno to be circumcised. Muthoni is
the first person to see that the two ideologies are not mutually exclusive,

and she is the only one who makes a deliberate attempt to reconcile them. She measures Waiyaki's failure by the very fact of her own conscious attempt, as Waiyaki himself is to realize later:

> Muthoni had tried. Hers was a search for salvation for herself. She had the courage to attempt a reconciliation of the many forces that wanted to control her. She had realized her need, the need to have a wholesome and beautiful life that enriched you and made you grow. (p. 163)

It is obvious that Muthoni finds this wholesome and beautiful life during the process of circumcision, for her ritual dancing is more fully expressive of the will to live and the joy of living than anybody else's. Although she dies shortly afterwards, this is a symbolic consequence, not of the act of circumcision, but of the attempt to resolve the conflict. If anyone meets the fate of those wise before their time, or was destroyed by the reactionary and antagonistic forces in society, it is Muthoni.

The other person with a foot in both camps is, of course, Waiyaki, and it is with him that we shall now be concerned. I wish to demonstrate that in spite of Waiyaki's sterling qualities he does have some significant weaknesses, and that these are just as important in precipitating the catastrophe as his opponent's malevolence and society's backwardness. There may be suggestions of the Christ-like figure in Waiyaki's characterization, but he is no more idealized than Njoroge in *Weep Not Child*.*

On the face of it, Waiyaki seems tailor made to fulfil the prophecy. His qualities of leadership are conspicuous; he possesses drive, initiative, superb intelligence, tremendous enthusiasm, and great organizing ability. Some of these qualities are already indicated in that first memorable scene, where Waiyaki, without lifting a finger, compels the young Kamau and Kinuthia to stop fighting. Even the recalcitrant Kamau is forced to submit to that compelling voice and the mesmeric quality of those eyes. Waiyaki exudes personal charisma, but although outwardly he compels obedience, inwardly he is unsure of himself: 'the boy felt an irresistible urge to fall on Kamau: he pulled a blade of grass and began to chew it quickly, his eyes dilating with rage and fear.' The vacillation which we shall see later, is already present in this early chapter which actually foreshadows much that is to happen in the novel.

These feelings of self-doubt are more strikingly revealed in the Sacred Grove with Chege, where they are explicitly connected with the responsibility entrusted to Waiyaki to arise and save the tribe:

* Ikiddeh, I., 'James Ngugi as Novelist', *African Literature Today 2*, Heinemann Educational Books, 1969. He suggests that Waiyaki is an idealized Christ-like figure.

Waiyaki stood as if dumb. The knowledge that he had in him the blood of this famous seer, who had been able to see the future, filled him with an acute sense of wonder. He could not speak; the only word which escaped him was 'Ha!' His father was still speaking:

'He died here. Our fathers do not know where his grave is. But some say that he was carried up by Murungu.'

Chege stopped and turned slowly to Waiyaki. Waiyaki trembled freely.

'I see you fear. You must learn to fight fear . . . fear . . . It was not only Mugo whom they rejected. When I told them about Siriana they would not listen.'

For the first time, Waiyaki felt really frightened. Unknown terror gripped him. He fought with it.

'No doubt you wonder why I tell you all this.'

Waiyaki wanted to cry out: 'Don't tell me more. I don't want to hear more. No! No! No, Father!' Instead he only whispered.

'Ye-es!'

'Arise. Heed the prophecy. Go to the Mission place. Learn all the wisdom and all the secrets of the white man. But do not follow his vices. Be true to your people and the ancient rites.'

'Father . . .' Waiyaki called out when he recovered from the shock. He felt weak and small. He did not know what he wanted to say.

'You go there. I tell you again, learn all the wisdom of the white man. And keep on remembering salvation shall come from the hills. A man must rise and save the people in their hour of need. He shall show them the way; he shall lead them.'

'But-but-they don't know me. I am a child and they rejected Mugo . . .
(pp. 22–24)

In case it is pointed out that Waiyaki at this stage is a mere child, and his behaviour should not be taken as symptomatic of his later development, it must be made clear that nothing that Ngugi says in this novel about children is irrelevant to their later development, for he is quite deliberately dropping a number of clues to the future. The same uneasiness about his rôle appears in the older Waiyaki.

Waiyaki's doubts about his destiny are intensified by his experiences at Siriana where exposure to Christianity and the white man's ways gives him different values and almost alienates him from his tribe's traditions:

Waiyaki's absence from the hills had kept him out of touch with these things which most mattered to the tribe. Besides, however much he

resisted it, he could not help gathering and absorbing ideas and notions
that prevented him from responding spontaneously to these dances and
celebrations. (p. 46)

It is not that Waiyaki comes to disapprove of his traditional rites;
it is simply that he is a man caught between two cultures, and he can
appreciate the values of both. His tragedy is partly that he is called
upon to be the embodiment of one, and work for the destruction of the
other.

Muthoni's death alerts the missionaries to the need for more vigilance,
and their school at Siriana bars entry to all whose parents do not renounce
the rite of circumcision. Inevitably, the traditionalists are seriously
affected by this move, and under the leadership of Waiyaki they decide
to set up their own 'people's schools'. So almost overnight Waiyaki
becomes a folk hero, easily the most respected man in the community,
the one to whom the people look for leadership and whom they affection-
ately call 'the Teacher'. As we, the readers, observe him, we come to share
the villagers' admiration, for he sets about his task with tremendous energy
and dedication; he infects others with his enthusiasm and can put people
at their ease.

All this is, of course, quite commendable. But one soon becomes aware
that Waiyaki's dedication to education has an uncomfortable ring. His
passion becomes an obsession shutting out all other issues. This is his
own peculiar 'egoism'. 'The idea of education had now come to him like a
demon, urging him to go on, do more.' And later in the same passage:
'he saw only schools, schools everywhere and the thirst that burned the
throats of so many children who looked up to him for the quenching water.
And he wanted to feel all would get this water. He even wanted Joshua
and his followers to come and join hands with him. Education was life.
Let it come.' (p. 112) Taken out of context these statements may seem
favourable but when read in their context, Waiyaki's obsession appears
as a severe limitation.

Waiyaki has assimilated Livingstone's teaching that the boys should
not concern themselves with politics, and he regards education as an end in
itself; but the people of Kameno, whose leader he is supposed to be,
regard it as a means to the much more important end of keeping the tribe
pure, and expelling the white men. Education only makes sense to them
within this context. This is the first hint of a gradual divergence between
the vision and intentions of Waiyaki and the aspirations of the public he
is called upon to lead. The following passage embodies a built-in criticism
of Waiyaki's 'egoism':

And Waiyaki saw a tribe great with many educated sons and daughters, all living together, tilling the land of their ancestors in perpetual serenity, pursuing their rituals and beautiful customs and all of them acknowledging their debt to him. He felt grateful at the thought. Perhaps this was the mission, the mission that the Sent One would carry out. Yes – Waiyaki would strive, strive. He was elated by his thoughts as he beheld this vision of greatness. Waiyaki walked with a brisk step, following the vision. (p. 100–2)

It is typical of Ngugi's art in this novel, that using calm and unruffled prose, he can introduce a damaging irony in an almost off-hand manner. While the element of boyish idealism in Waiyaki is not on a par with Njoroge's immaturity, he nevertheless shows signs of inexperience. Partly Waiyaki's immaturity and naïvety make him oblivious to guile and jealousy in the world; and he incautiously allows himself to be tricked into compromising situations. This simplicity and consequent lack of caution are directly linked with his obsession with education:

If Waiyaki had been fully aware of this faith in him, he might have feared. But he was not. The idea of education had now come to him like a demon, urging him to go on, do more. Even when later he was forced by the Kiama in their extravagant enthusiasm to take an oath of allegiance to the Purity and Togetherness of the tribe, he did not stop to analyse if any danger lurked in such a commitment. Kabonyi did not exist. (p. 112)

This very important passage links the taking of the oath with Waiyaki's obsession and lack of caution. Actually the administration of the oath is a a clever device of Kabonyi's who knows Waiyaki's kind well, and rightly concludes that he will have no time to consider its implications. Furthermore, when he resigns from the Kiama, Waiyaki nominates one of his greatest enemies, Kamau, to take his place; he does it as an act of appeasement, not realizing that he is putting his worst enemies in charge of such an important organization.

Waiyaki neglects the fact that the educational thirst and enthusiasm which he himself has stirred up will have to be given expression and fulfilment at a political level. At one point the level-headed Kinuthia wonders whether Waiyaki knows that the people 'want action now' (p. 135) but only towards the end, when Kinuthia confronts him with this danger, does he realize the truth: 'Oh, there are so many things I did not know. I had not seen that the new awareness wanted expression at a political level. Education for an oppressed people is not all.' (p. 160)

Waiyaki's obsession has, however, more serious consequences. In the first place he underestimates the influence of his enemies and their capacity for subversion. Jealousy is Kabonyi's driving passion and his son Kamau is only a smaller version of the father. In spite of his passionate and almost fanatical championship of whatever cause he happens to be supporting, Kabonyi does not really believe in anything; he is capable of drifting just as easily from one extremist ideology to another. The point is that he seeks pre-eminence; he must always lead, and if his ambition is thwarted he either crosses to the other side or uses every resource in his power to destroy those who stand in his way. Kamau, like his father, does not really believe in the cause for which he is supposed to be fighting. If Waiyaki had not won the competition for Nyambura's hand, Kamau would have been prepared to propose marriage to her, in spite of the force of the oath and, had she accepted, would have deserted the cause and fled with the girl to Nairobi. Jealousy of Waiyaki's success is what motivates Kamau's hatred, not devotion to the cause of the people. Together the father and the son form a formidable opposition. Apart from his age, a powerful factor among Africans, Kabonyi is a compelling orator who can strike certain chords in the hearts of the older people. He is also a skilful politician choosing his grounds of battle carefully, shrewdly assessing his opponent's nature, and deliberately laying traps for him. Kamau, for his part, always seems to be present, unnoticed, at any incident in which Waiyaki is likely to compromise himself.

Most important, Waiyaki's obsession with education leads to the postponement of his plans for a reconciliation between the ridges of Kameno and Makuyu. In fact Waiyaki does not set out consciously to educate his people as a first step towards the reconciliation. He only stumbles on the idea because their rivalry threatens his ambitions in education:

> Another thing was coming into his mind. Every day he was becoming convinced of the need for unity between Kameno and Makuyu. The ancient rivalry would cripple his efforts in education. He also wanted a reconciliation between Joshua's followers and the others. The gulf between them was widening and Waiyaki wanted to be the instrument of their coming together. A word from him in the coming meeting might be a big start. Now was the time to show his stand. This was not a plan but a conviction. It had come like a temptation, at first a faint echo, then becoming a distant possibility and now a need. (p. 104-5)

The fact is that education, not the possibility of reconciliation, remains Waiyaki's god and his primary concern.

Although Waiyaki is regarded as the champion of Kameno, he does not want to be identified with either faction and is committed to reconciliation, but his intentions are never translated into action. Muthoni had shown him the way, and although she had died in the process, we are not supposed to imagine that reconciliation is impossible. If Joshua can make forays into Kameno and persuade some of the traditionalists to join him, Waiyaki ought to be able to persuade them to live with each other and direct their hatred against the white man instead. Moreover, the people demonstrate that they will respond to Waiyaki, in spite of Kabonyi's squalid man-œuvres to alienate them. For instance, at that great meeting when Waiyaki at last speaks up for reconciliation, the people accept his views and are about to murder Kabonyi when Waiyaki stops them:

> 'We are all children of Mumbi and we must fight together in one political movement, or else we perish and the white man will always be on our back. Can a house divided against itself stand?'
> 'No-o-o,' they roared in unison.
> 'Then we must stand together. We must end the ancient rivalry.'
> People seemed moved, and when he sat down they rose and, as if with one voice, shouted: 'The Teacher! The Teacher!' (p. 171)

Obviously then, Waiyaki could have urged reconciliation much earlier. He had great opportunity at the first meeting of the people, which was, in many ways, a dress rehearsal for the final one. He had indeed intended to preach reconciliation then, but failed to do so because he was once more carried away by his enthusiasm for education; we are told at the end that 'with a fleeting feeling of guilt he remembered that he had forgotten to preach reconciliation.' (p. 112) From now on Waiyaki's efforts at reconciliation are a combination of procrastination and self-accusation:

> For Waiyaki the fleeting feeling of guilt at having failed to preach reconciliation was now growing stronger. He had missed the opportunity at a time when he could have made his stand clear. A combination of events, excitement and Kabonyi had made him lose that moment when he had the people from the various ridges under his control. Would such a chance come again? He would bide his time. He would wait for another moment, a moment when he would preach reconciliation, tolerance and unity. Then his work would be done. (p. 125)

And again:

He had wanted to bridge the gap between Joshua and the others. For

what? He had not stopped to answer that question. The feeling that this
was in a way his mission had come to him before the meeting that
marked the height of his glory. And he had been training himself for
this mission: end the Kameno-Makuyu feud and bring back the unity
of the tribe. Yet when the appropriate moment came he had failed.
He had become intoxicated with wonder, anger and surprise and had
lost himself. The moment had come. The moment had passed. Had he
remained calm he would have spoken outright for reconciliation.

'Another time. Next time,' Waiyaki always told himself when these
moments of self-blame came. And in a way he was glad. Education
was really his mission. This was his passion. He needed help and co-
operation from all, even from Joshua and Kabonyi. They called him a
saviour. His own father had talked of a Messiah to come. Whom was
the Messiah coming to save? From what? And where would He lead
the people? Although Waiyaki did not stop to get clear answers to these
questions, he increasingly saw himself as the one who would lead the
tribe to the light. Education was the light of the country. That was what
the people wanted. Education. Schools. Education. He did not see any
connection between what his education mission and what the Kiama
were doing. He just wanted all the people to get learning. And unity was
the answer. But sometimes he was afraid. Joshua and his followers
were now completely identified with the white man. And now, with this
outright boldness of Joshua, this naked challenge, he could not tell
what would happen. What would the Kiama do? He had resigned from
the Kiama, and he did not know what the inner circle, under the
leadership of Kabonyi would be up to . . . (p.115)

I quote this passage at some length because it seems to me to contain the
nucleus of the novel. We have the forces ranged against Waiyaki – the
antagonisms in society, and the Kabonyi–Kamau duet – but we also have
Waiyaki's failure to preach reconciliation and his awareness of that failure.
The self accusation, the obsession with education, the failure to think
out his objectives clearly as far as reconciliation and even education are
concerned, the consciousness of his destiny to lead the people, and the
underestimation of his opponents, leading to the fatal resignation from the
Kiama, are also here.

Waiyaki's failure to preach reconciliation effectively prevents his relationship with Nyambura from being accepted. There is nothing inherently
wrong with the relationship: indeed Ngugi convinces us that it is one of
the most beautiful things in the novel. Furthermore, it is clear that the
brave Nyambura finds in Waiyaki's religion of love the kind of self-fulfilment,

self-realization, and liberation from the destructive influence of her father's religion, that Muthoni had earlier found in circumcision. For Waiyaki, the yearning for something outside himself, which had plagued his soul, is satisfied. What is wrong about the affair is Waiyaki's failure to take the people into his confidence. He could only have done this as part of a conscious plan of reconciliation. At one stage he declares that Nyambura and his love affair are none of the people's business, and in so doing he is expressing the age-old agony of the public figure who wishes to have a private life. As a public man, however, Waiyaki does not have a private life: he has an obligation to the people to explain.

Secondly, had he preached reconciliation at the earlier meeting, there would have been no need for him to take a damning oath banning any kind of relationship with the opposite side. He ought to have seen that such an oath was inconsistent with his policy of reconciliation. And at the final meeting it is the oath which condemns him. For although he wins some success in his now belated attempt to talk about reconciliation, yet he had broken an oath, and for the Kikuyu an oath is inviolable, as the skilful Kabonyi, who plays this trump card at the very end, points out. To the cry of 'the oath' Waiyaki had no answer; nor could he now deny Nyambura. The time for explanations had passed.

Waiyaki's tragedy is that of a commanding personality who, despite the very best intentions, is blinded by his own obsessions, he fails to see the people's aspirations, fails to bring his own into line with them, fails to implement the most important items in his policy, and allows his opponents to exploit his shortcomings. Towards the end of the novel Waiyaki *does* work out what has to be done (p. 162). He realizes that the best elements in both ideologies can be blended. He also realizes what the people want, and pledges himself to work for education – education for unity, unity for political freedom. Had he done this much earlier all would have been well. Now, however, it is too late.

This does not imply that the enmity of Kabonyi and Kamau, and the people's antagonism should be minimized. Waiyaki is embattled against tremendous forces, and had he been perfect he might have dealt with them competently. Had Waiyaki been destroyed by backward and wicked forces, the novel would have been merely pathetic. The element of tragedy lies in Waiyaki's weaknesses, which make him incapable of dealing successfully with his opponents, but do not force the reader to withhold sympathy from him.

Something has already been said about Ngugi's skill in this novel. It now only remains to mention his superb descriptive power, evident for instance in the passage about the Sacred Grove (p. 19), and his evocation of a dream-like atmosphere in the scene where Chege tells his mystified son about the prophecy. Finally, various ironic touches demonstrate that in spite of his normal calmness and compassion Ngugi can be quite tough and unsentimental. For example:

> Joshua was such a staunch man of God and such a firm believer in the Old Testament, that he would never refrain from punishing a sin, even if this meant beating his wife. He did not mind as long as he was executing God's justice. (pp. 35–6)

> Thenceforth nobody would ever be a member of Christ's Church if he was so much as found connected in any way with circumcision rites. The fire in Joshua gave new strength and hope to his followers. The white men in Siriana and other places were behind them. And with them all – God. (p. 68)

> Joshua preached with so much vigour and energy that many later said that he had been speaking with the tongues of angels. Others said that the Angel of the Lord had appeared unto him, while still others said it was Mary who had spoken to him. (p. 114)

If all these examples refer to Joshua, it is because Ngugi's irony is most biting when applied to that fanatic. Nevertheless, Waiyaki himself is often the object of irony. Ngugi's technique is to throw in, almost casually, a damaging ironic statement in the last sentence of an apparently eulogistic passage. This is one of the methods he uses to put Waiyaki into perspective and subjecting some of his actions to criticism.

▼▼▼▼▼▼▼▼▼▼▼▼▼▼▼▼▼▼▼▼▼▼▼▼▼▼▼▼▼▼▼▼▼▼▼▼

A GRAIN OF WHEAT

A GRAIN OF WHEAT is Ngugi's most ambitious and successful novel to date. In the depth of its psychological penetration and the power of its characterization, in the subtlety of its narrative technique, in the density of its texture, and in the sophistication of its language, it exceeds all expectations raised by the two earlier novels, promising though they were. Its complexity of form recalls the involutions of Conrad's *Lord Jim,* on which it seems consciously to have been modelled. Most novels, including African ones, present experience chronologically, with the story moving logically from the beginning, through various complications and problems to the resolution and conclusion. Others ignore this convention, and present experience through a series of impressions, digressions, casual anecdotes, and incidents which are not necessarily presented in chronological order. This is the method of *A Grain of Wheat,* which opens on the eve of Kenya's Independence and ends four days later. But very little in the novel actually happens during those four days; instead the reader is taken back by numerous 'witnesses' to a whole series of events in the past.* This is Ngugi at his most baffling and exasperating, withholding information, supplying it belatedly when he chooses, employing flashback within flashback, 'reflector within reflector, point of view within point of view, cross-chronological jux-taposition of events, and impressions'.† In no other novel of Ngugi, and possibly in no other African novel, is the reader asked to be more alert and to participate more fully. Indeed his rôle is very much like the judge's in a court of law: to sift the evidence, hear all aspects of the case, organize the material, and find out exactly what happened. Our interest is partly in discovering who betrayed Kihika, and why Mugo is such a mysterious character. But also, like the judge in court, the reader is required to keep a delicate balance of sympathy and impartiality in respect of every character.

The title of the novel comes from the book of *Corinthians* (1, 15 : 36–38):

Thou fool, that which thou sowest is not quickened, except it die. And that which thou sowest, thou sowest not that body that shall be, but bare grain, it may chance of wheat, or of some other grain. But God giveth it a body as it hath pleased him, and to every seed his own body.

It refers to the need for continual struggle, suffering, and even death in order that the millennium may be achieved. Even the white man Thompson realizes, albeit belatedly, that 'A man was born to die continually and start afresh'. The legendary Waiyaki's blood had to be spilt in order that the party may be born which would eventually lead the people to the promised land. Similarly, Mugo, Gikonyo, Karanja, Mumbi, and the others, had to undergo their own share of suffering, shame, and guilt before Uhuru, it-self out of all proportion to their meagre efforts, could be achieved.

* For the term 'witnesses' I am indebted to Albert Guerard's analysis of *Lord Jim* in his *Conrad the Novelist,* Haward, 1966.

† Ghent, D. Van, *The English Novel : Form and Function,* Harper and Row, New York, 1953, p. 237.

In this novel, as in his other two, Ngugi is concerned not merely with the wickedness of the oppressors, but with the weaknesses of the indigenous people themselves. He is also interested in contemporary Kikuyu society in a much wider sense than in the other novels. Consequently, the novel has not one, but about five centres of interest – Mugo, Gikonyo, Karanja, Mumbi and the white man, Thompson. It is the eve of Independence, and Uhuru demands unity (*harambee*); those men and women who presumably played heroic roles in preparing for the great day should come together to celebrate and affirm their determination to work for a great and prosperous Kenya. But the eve of Uhuru finds all these characters plagued with guilt, shame and jealousies stemming directly from their activities during the Emergency; and these feelings threaten to mar the spontaneity and totality of their commitment to Uhuru. If they are to participate fully, if they are to be 'free', and if Uhuru is to mean anything to them, they must resolve and reconcile these warring emotions and attitudes, and redefine their relationships with each other. Each is preoccupied with analysing the motives for his actions during the Mau-Mau Emergency, resolving his inner conflicts, doubts and fears, seeking to expiate his guilt and redefining his relationship to the other characters. Each character is painfully groping his way towards self-knowledge. Wangari, Gikonyo's mother, says very succinctly to her son: 'But you are a man now. Read your own heart, and know yourself.'

The task of getting to know the characters is also the reader's. For in this novel the quality of our moral and emotional responses is of supreme importance. It is essentail that we do not judge too hastily, or we might find ourselves being continually tripped up and forced to revise our estimates. At one moment a character may appear despicable, but at the next we might read of an incident which shows him in a favourable light. Ngugi knows that no individual character can be reduced to a simple formula. Consequently, he constantly shifts the narrative focus from character to character, and into all situations which might cast some further light thus forcing a complex response in the reader. We must not merely condemn; we must also be prepared to sympathize.*

A Grain of Wheat then, is partly concerned with moral and emotional responses to a group of varied characters, and it is clear that this preoccupation affects the structure and narrative technique. For the narrative, while being about the present, cannot remain in the present. To induce the reader to make a complex response and to pause before judging, Ngugi withholds information. Had we, for instance, been informed early in the

---

* Conrad, in *Lord Jim*, also shifts his focus from witness to witness, and jumps in time to all sorts of incidents which help throw light on Jim's character and actions.

novel that Mugo was Kihika's betrayer, we should have condemned him automatically and immediately. But by the time the damaging information is given, a steady fund of sympathy has been built up for Mugo. Similarly it is not until Chapter 7* that we are definitely told that Gikonyo returned from detention to find his wife with another man's child. This delayed information explains Gikonyo's coolness to his wife at the start of the novel. Had we been given it earlier, we might have formed the erroneous impression that Gikonyo's response was due purely to masculine possessiveness and vanity. But in a series of flashbacks leading up to Gikonyo's return, his tremendous love for Mumbi is all-too-powerfully demonstrated and we realize that it is precisely this love which explains his hostile reaction to Mumbi's conduct. Early in the novel we might think that Mumbi committed adultery with Karanja, but when we later see that she only capitulated under extreme pressure we are able to understand.

Ngugi seldom intrudes; he seldom tells us what he thinks of the characters; so to form an opinion the reader must pay careful attention to every bit of evidence, every anecdote, digression and incident, looking especially for juxtapositions which modify each other.

For the sake of clarity I would like now to demonstrate how the exploded chronology technique operates in the early chapters. In Chapter 1, page 1, we are in the present with Mugo, a few days before Independence, but on page 9 the narrative shifts back more than twenty years to Mugo's childhood. On page 11 we return to the present, but on page 13, we move even further back to the days before the Party was born, when the white invader was just acquiring a stranglehold on the country. The narrative then moves forward gradually to tell of Kihika's exploits. On page 22 we are back in the present with Mugo and Gikonyo, Warui, and Wambui, the three voices from the Party who had been sent to Mugo at the end of Chapter 1, and whom we had all but forgotten during Chapter 2. The purpose of the flashbacks, so far, is to give us an insight into the origins and purpose of the Party, and Kihika's rôle in it. But we still know very little about Mugo. On page 34 the narrative, leaving Mugo for a while, swings over to Gikonyo and Mumbi. We observe that relations between Gikonyo and his wife are rather strained, but we are given no explanation, although there is mention of a child. The narrative, still in the present, shifts to Karanja and the Thompsons. Then on page 58, there is an almost unobtrusive flashback, an apparent digression, whose purpose is to illuminate the present state of the Thompsons' marriage. It reveals Margery

* Ngugi, J., *A Grain of Wheat*, African Writers' Series, Heinemann Educational Books, 1968, p. 131. All further page references are to this edition.

Thompson's frustration, which drives her into the arms of Dr Van Dyke, and helps to explain the current lack of communication between husband and wife. On page 61 we go even further back to Thompson's undergraduate days, and learn of his former idealism which throws light on his present disillusionment with the state of affairs in Kenya. On page 67, we move back to Gikonyo's past, but on page 69 we return to the present. On page 74 the focus shifts once more to Mugo, and back in time to the speech he made on his return from detention, then it moves forward to the present and Gikonyo. This brings us to the end of Chapter 6. In these first few chapters then, Ngugi has very skilfully introduced the main participants in the drama, giving due weight to each and using flashbacks judiciously to illuminate their present conditions.

Chapter 7 is by far the longest, and it is useful to analyse it in detail, to see more of Ngugi's technique at work. At the end of Chapter 6 Gikonyo was discussing his marital problems with Mugo. His last words were 'God, where is the Mumbi I left behind?' At the beginning of Chapter 8 Gikonyo is still talking with Mugo about his marital problems. So although we have covered some sixty pages, almost nothing has happened in present time. But the reader has been presented with a number of flashbacks concerning either Gikonyo or Kihika.

The chapter begins with a flashback dealing with the social life revolving around the weekly train at Rungei station in the pre-Emergency days. Gikonyo's words: 'Yet the day I missed the train was the happiest in my life' bring us momentarily back to the present, but we are immediately returned to the past and Gikonyo's devotion to his trade as a carpenter. This flashback itself involves a flashback into Gikonyo's babyhood, when his father expelled him and his mother from his house. Moving forward, we are given greater insight into Gikonyo's work and shown the start of the Gikonyo-Mumbi romance. Ngugi lingers on this for some time, demonstrating with great power and subtlety Gikonyo's romantic longing, and the strength of his love which inspires his artistic pursuits. Then there is a shift of focus to Kihika's boyhood and schooldays, demonstrating among other things, not only his bravery, but also a certain idealism, fanaticism, and arrogance, which, on hindsight, helps to alleviate the gravity of Mugo's crime. From there we move forward, not as far as the present, but to the days immediately preceding the Emergency, and the famous race for Mumbi. Gikonyo loses the race, but wins Mumbi, and stays behind to make love with her in the grass. However, the focus now shifts to Karanja and his reactions to the loss of Mumbi. At this stage there is a very important passage which might easily be overlooked, but is essential for an assessment of Karanja. He has a vision:

Everybody was running away as if each person feared the ground beneath his feet would collapse, They ran in every direction; men trampled on women; mothers forgot their children; the lame and the weak were abandoned on the platform. Each man was alone, with God. It was the clarity of the entire vision that shook him. Karanja braced himself for the struggle, the fight to live. I must clear out of this place, he told himself, without moving. The earth was going round again. I must run, he thought, it cannot be helped, why should I fear to trample on the children, the lame and the weak when others are doing it? (pp. 108 – 9)

It is not only Karanja's disillusionment with love, but also this vision of universal selfishness, callousness, and preoccupation with self preservation, that shapes his determination to brace himself for the struggle for life, and compels him to look after his own interests. In the light of this, his subsequent betrayal of the Party can at least be understood, if not condoned. This very important chapter demonstrates the way in which structure is deliberately exploited to modify one's judgement.

The narrative also shifts at this stage to Kihika, to reveal his egoism and lack of romanticism in his love affair with Wambuku. He values Wambuku, not for herself, but for her rôle in relation to himself. Soon however, we return almost immediately to the past, to the declaration of Emergency, and Gikonyo's departure into detention. We now move a few years forward to Gikonyo's release and his anticipation of his reunion with Mumbi: 'His reunion with Mumbi would see the birth of a new Kenya'. But before he is reunited with Mumbi, the narrative moves almost unobtrusively into a flashback within a flashback, demonstrating Gikonyo's suffering during his detention, and his enduring love for Mumbi, the only thing that kept him sane in a situation where men like Gatu lost their grip and committed suicide. Consequently, when Gikonyo confesses the oath to the officer in command, we can sympathize, for we realize that his confession and betrayal of the cause is due, not to weakness or cowardice, but to the strength of his love for Mumbi, and his desire to be reunited with her. The act of confession itself is cleverly withheld until the flashbacks have induced a strong current of sympathy for the man.

The narrative now moves forward to the pivotal scene where Gikonyo finds Mumbi with another man's child in her arms. That man is his archenemy and one-time rival, Karanja. Now we appreciate fully Ngugi's technical skill in withholding vital information until the flashbacks have done their work. For we apprehend the full extent of Gikonyo's shock and disappointment, having seen the strength of his love.

These then are the apparently perplexing chronological and spatial oscilla-
tions of a chapter which, in spite of its length, hardly moves forward in
present time. But it greatly enriches our total understanding of issues in
general, and some characters in particular. *A Grain of Wheat* may at first
appear rambling and disorganized, but like Stern's *Tristram Shandy* and
Conrad's *Lord Jim* this apparent disorder deliberately conceals a carefully
organized plan. Ngugi believes that we should also be alert, always
prepared to look for extenuating circumstances, explanatory factors,
and supporting evidence which will prevent us from making hasty and
wrong-headed judgements. This conviction is borne out by the novel.

The betrayal of Kihika overshadows the novel and I should now like
to examine how Ngugi controls and manipulates our responses towards
the traitor, Mugo. At the start of the novel he is a solitary, mysterious,
and sensitive figure, who thinks everyone's eyes are on him. On his way to
his *Shamba* he passes the house of the old woman with whom he realizes
he has a special bond. His contemplation of the old woman's poverty
reminds him of his earlier poverty. A flashback takes us to his early
childhood. We discover that the premature death of his parents condemned the young boy to a life of the most unmitigated misery,
poverty, filth, and loneliness, with a perpetually drunken aunt, whose
pastime was mouthing obscenities at the young Mugo and poisoning the
atmosphere with the stench of her vomiting:

> She was a small woman who always complained that people were after
> her life; they had put broken bottles and frogs into her stomach; they
> wanted to put poison in her food and drink.
>
> And yet she always went out to look for more beer. She would pester
> men from her husband's rika till they gave her a drink. One day she
> came back very drunk.
>
> 'That man Warui – he hates to see me eat and breathe – that sly-
> smile – he – creeps – coughs – like you – you – go and join him — '
>
> And she tried to imitate Warui's cough; but in the attempt started
> coughing in earnest. Suddenly she held her throat, stood, lurched
> forward and fell; all her beer and filth lay on the floor. Mugo cowered
> among the goats hoping and fearing she had died. In the morning she
> forced Mugo to pour soil on the filth. The acrid smell hit at him.
> Disgust choked him so that he could not speak or cry. The world had
> conspired against him, first to deprive him of his father and mother,
> and then to make him dependent on an ageing harridan. (p. 10)

Ngugi lingers over the details describing them with great realism. The sense of nausea, the acrid smell, the boy's disgust, the coarseness, brutality, filth, and bestial squalor are very powerfully evoked, inducing strong sympathy for Mugo. When the aunt subsequently dies, paradoxically the young Mugo misses her. This in itself emphasizes his loneliness and the hopelessness of his situation: 'Whom could he now call a relation? He wanted somebody, anybody, who would use the claims of kinship to do him ill or good. Either one or the other as long as he was not left alone, an outsider.' Mugo accordingly makes a resolution to earn his living from the soil, and force society to recognize him. For him prosperity and confidence in the future can only be possible with hard work. He cannot afford to be idealistic. Conscious of his earlier squalor he is determined to be a success, and so 'to bury seeds . . . to tend plants to ripeness . . . these were all part of the world he had created for himself and which formed the background against which his dreams soared to the sky. But then Kihika had come into his life.' That last sentence is vital, for it places Kihika's entry into Mugo's life beside the latter's determination to be a success through hard work. We are meant to hold onto it and set it beside the confession. It is both a hint that Mugo might have been implicated in the Kihika affair, and a mitigating explanation.

Mugo next appears in another flashback; this time he is listening to Kihika's speech calling for sacrifice, for suffering, and the shedding of blood in order to liberate the land: 'A day comes when brother shall give up brother, a mother her son, when you and I have heard the call of a nation in turmoil.' Kihika, in other words, stands at the opposite pole from Mugo. While the latter wishes to conserve, to work hard, achieve success, and prosper, the former is talking of sacrifice, reckless, daring exploits which might possibly end in death and destruction:

> Mugo felt a constriction in his throat. He could not clap for words that did not touch him. What right had such a boy, probably younger than Mugo, to talk like that? What arrogance? Kihika had spoken of blood as easily as if he was talking of drawing water in a river, Mugo reflected, a revulsion starting in his stomach at the sight and smell of blood. I hate him, he heard himself say and, frightened, he looked at Mumbi, wondering what she was thinking. (p. 19)

The hatred mentioned here stems not from jealousy, but from fear that Kihika and the kind of action he proposes threaten Mugo's hopes of success and liberation from a life of squalor. Kihika, after all, has never experienced the misery of life as he has, therefore it is easy for him to talk of blood 'as if he was talking of drawing water in a river'. He, Mugo, had experienced suffering and revulsion at the sight and smell of his aunt's excrescences, if not of blood. What right, therefore, had Kihika, a mere boy to talk like that? This episode is contributing to the reader's understanding if not acceptance of Mugo's eventual treachery. After this flashback we return to the present and to Gikonyo's request that Mugo should make the main speech on Independence day. A more thorough villain than Mugo would have braved it, accepted boldly, and played his part to perfection, in order to divert suspicion from himself. But Mugo, visibly racked by emotion, is unable to conceal his confusion. Later, when the confession is made, it is more than likely that the reader will remember this mental torture, this genuine reluctance to play the hypocrite, and hold it in Mugo's favour.

Ngugi manipulates us to respond more sympathetically to Mugo's crime, not only by making points in his favour, but also by giving us an insight into the more unattractive side of Kihika's nature. On page 91, for instance, the focus shifts over to Kihika who fed, we are told, in his younger days, on stories of Mahatma Ghandi and Moses. We see not only his idealism, but also the egoism implicit in his visions of himself as a saint 'leading the Gikuyu people to freedom and power'. We are informed of his immense arrogance and self-preoccupation. 'Even in those days Kihika loved drawing attention to himself by saying and doing things that he knew other boys and girls dared not say and do. In this case it was his immense arrogance that helped him to survive the silence around . . . .' It is already being suggested, therefore, that Kihika is the kind of young man who would engage in reckless exploits and try to involve others in them. There is even a wicked flicker of irony implicit in the fact that the man who could now talk passionately of passive resistance in the Ghandi-Moses tradition, and conjure the vision of thousands of men and women throwing themselves in front of moving trains, will later indulge in the most wanton acts of destruction. It is being suggested, in fact, that our sympathy for Kihika should not be absolute. Reduced sympathy for him must mean a corresponding increase in sympathy for Mugo.

A little later (page 196) Ngugi relates how Mugo selflessly rushed to the defence of the pregnant Wambuku who was being mercilessly beaten by homeguards. Before this, Mumbi had told us about Wambuku's pathetic story; consequently we cannot but be favourably disposed towards anyone who defends her in the trench, knowing fully that such an act would result in his arrest and detention. We subsequently discover that Mugo's motives were not entirely untainted, but we are temporarily sympathetic, and now Ngugi can lead in to Mugo's great confession to Mumbi. But before the confession itself, Mugo gives a moving account of his present suffering. Moreover, his mental torture is partly due to his consciousness of the part he himself played in inflicting this suffering, by his betrayal of Kihika and the entire village. Mumbi is moved to tears and reaches out, desiring to right the wrong and heal the wounded, and so do we.

The confession itself seems to emanate from a mind so tortured and overwhelmed, so obviously losing its grip as a consequence of the pressure of events both present and past, that condemnation seems a totally inadequate response:

> 'I wanted to live my life. I never wanted to be involved in anything. Then he came into my life, here, a night like this, and pulled me into the stream. So I killed him.' (p. 210)

This is the information which has been delayed for so long, but by the time it comes, we have already been manipulated into a position of sympathy for Mugo. Inevitably, we set this confession beside his earlier determination to earn his living and achieve success – a determination which was thwarted by Kihika's entry into his life. Moreover, we have seen that after such an early life of squalor he richly deserves success and recognition. We also set this confession beside an ensuing passage:

> 'Imagine all your life you cannot sleep – so many figures touching your flesh – eyes always watching you – in dark places – in corners – in the streets – in the fields – sleeping, waking, no rest – ah! Those eyes – cannot you for a minute, one minute, leave a man alone – I mean – let a man eat, drink, work – all of you – Kihika – Gikonyo – the old woman – that general – who sent you here tonight? Who? Aah! Those eyes again – we shall see who is stronger – now –' (pp. 210–11)

This is the problem in microcosm. Mugo always wanted to be left alone to earn his living unmolested. The irony of his situation is that the boy who in his loneliness longed for relatives who would either ill-treat or be kind to him, becomes the man who wishes to be left alone, and discovers it is impossible.

To make absolutely sure that the reader makes the correct responses, Ngugi returns to the episodes involving Kihika's murder of Robson and Mugo's actual decision to betray Kihika. It is here that we get the full dimensions of the Mugo problem. We then see that Mugo had escaped the complications of the Emergency, keeping to himself, looking after his crops, his eyes fixed on the future, not because he was unpatriotic or a coward, but because of his determination to succeed and live:

He often heard men talk as they built huts in the new Thabai; but their words did not touch him: what did it matter to him that women were doing men's work, that children were maturing too early? Had he himself not started fending for himself at an early age? Mugo was among the first to finish their huts within the given time. He had done the work, erecting the hut, thatching the roof, mudding the walls, without help from anybody. The hut was his first big achievement. After moving into it, he resumed his daily life: he looked after the crops, his eyes fixed to the future. (p. 213)

If Mugo isolates himself in the new Thabai, it is not because he is a solitary by nature, or because his early loneliness had developed into a chronic condition, but because he realizes that in order to achieve economic prosperity and success, he must remain uninvolved and avoid contacts which would drag him into the complications of the Emergency. This explains Mugo's isolation, and the almost ritualistic precautions he adopts every evening to ensure that he shuts the world out of his hut:

He often fussed over pushing the key into the lock, delaying the final act; the operation gave him pleasure; the hut was an extension of himself, his hopes and dreams . . . . After eating he walked to the door to make sure it was securely bolted. Again he lingered over the bolt admiringly. He was only twenty-five. He possessed nothing, but the future was in his hands. He stretched flat on the bed; it was always good to lie on the bed after a hard day's work in the shamba. He massaged his stomach and belched, vaguely satisfied. Outside the hut were curfew laws. Again these laws did not affect Mugo since, even before 1952, he rarely went out. (pp. 213–14)

Although Mugo still possesses nothing, the future lies within his grasp, and we can sense his feelings of satisfaction with his achievement so far. It is into this life of security and hope, symbolized by the bolted door, that Kihika breaks. Immediately Mugo feels his security slipping, a sudden realization reflected in his anguished cry, 'Do you want to kill me? I have done nothing.' It is at this stage that Kihika appears at his worst, demonstrating not only arrogance and insufferable egoism, but a complete lack of consideration for the feelings of the weak that we have not hitherto suspected: 'I despise the weak. Let them be trampled to death. I spit on the weakness of our fathers. Their memory gives me no pride. And even today, tomorrow, the weak and those with feeble hearts shall be wiped from the earth. The strong shall rule.' This kind of Hitlerite assertion is so empty of all morality and humanity that we do not marvel at Mugo's suspicion that the man is mad. Mugo regards Kihika not only as a threat to his dreams of prosperity, but as a man possessed, rather like a dangerous animal:

> He suddenly stopped speaking, pacing, and for the first time seemed aware of Mugo. Mugo sat rigidly in his seat, staring at the ground, sure that the homeguards would get him tonight. Kihika was mad, mad, he reflected, and the thought only increased his terror. (p. 218)

Kihika then asks Mugo to organize an underground movement in Thabai, an act which would be clearly self-destructive. At this point we must still note his arrogance, egoism, and lack of consideration. Calmly brushing aside Mugo's weak protestations, he assumes that everything has been settled and that Mugo will be their man in Thabai. When he leaves, Mugo realizes that his security and hopes have disappeared with him, and that the bolted door has failed to keep out disaster. Why should he bother to bolt the door? 'It was better to be without a door rather than it should be there and yet bring in cold and danger.' Therefore, in a last gesture of hopelessness, he unbolts the door and goes to bed. Mugo is now caught in a dilemma:

> A few minutes ago, lying on the bed, in this room, the future held promise. Everything in the hut was in the same place as before, but the future was blank. He expected police or homeguards to come, arrest him or shoot him dead. He saw only prison and death . . . . Why should Kihika drag me into a struggle and problems I have not created? Why? . . .
> What shall I do, he asked himself. If I don't serve Kihika he'll kill me. They killed Rev. Jackson and Teacher Muniu. If I work for him, the government will catch me. The white man has long arms. And they'll hang me. My God, I don't want to die, I am not ready for death, I have not even lived. Mugo was deeply afflicted and confused, because all his life he had avoided conflicts: at home, or at school, he rarely joined the company of other boys for fear of being involved in brawls that might ruin his chances of a better future. His argument went like this: if you don't traffic with evil, then evil ought not to touch you; if you leave people alone, then they ought to leave you alone. That's why, now, at night, still unable to solve his dilemma, Mugo only moaned inside, puzzled: have I stolen anything from anybody? No! Have I shat inside a neighbour's courtyard? No. Have I killed anybody? No.

How then can Kihika to whom I have done no harm do this to me?
(pp. 220–1)

Although the thought of the price on Kihika's head helps form Mugo's
decision to betray him, there is no doubt that the main motive is the overpowering urge for self-preservation, the desire for life and success. Can we
then, having been exposed to Ngugi's revelations both before and after
the crucial confession, refuse to extend our understanding and sympathy
to Mugo?

Because of his abnormally alert sensitivity, and his powerful imagination,
Mugo's sense of guilt plagues him all the more relentlessly. His crime
haunts him in a series of nightmarish images; drops of water in his hut
take the shape of icicles pointing at his heart; thick blood seems to drip
from the mud walls. He becomes paranoic, imagining eyes spying on him,
accusing him, and this culminates in his hysteria in the scene with Mumbi.

Gradually he comes to realize that he cannot expiate his guilt by isolation
and his attempt to resolve his conflicts corresponds with his redemption.
It begins with Mumbi discussing with him the affair with Karanja and
her suffering during the days of the Emergency. He also starts to appreciate
how his own destiny relates to others. Hitherto he had flinched from considering the past; through guilty curiosity he returns to the section of
the trench he himself had helped to dig; he realizes fully that the sufferings of Thabai, and of people like Mumbi and Wambuku, were caused by
his betrayal of Kihika. For following the execution of Kihika Thabai was
severely punished as a lesson to all other villagers harbouring terrorists.

The process of redemption and the resolution of conflict does not follow
a straight path, for soon after this, Mugo feels a sudden urge to resume
'that state of limbo in which he was before he had heard Mumbi's story
and looked into her eyes'. However, he now learns the story of the old
woman with whom he had felt a special bond. The story haunts him and he
is troubled 'by what was dead'. He hears Mumbi's voice in his heart,
sees General R's accusing face and realizes he cannot escape from the fact
of his crime: 'Mumbi's voice was like a knife which had butchered and
laid naked his heart to himself.' For one agonizing moment he tries to
evade responsibility and shift it on to the general chaotic nature of things:
'But would it not have happened? Christ would have died on the cross,
anyway. Why did they blame Judas, a stone from the hands of a power
more than man? Kihika . . . crucified . . . the thought flashed through him,
and a curious thing happened.' He sees blood dripping from the walls of
his hut, which brings his guilt and responsibility for his people's suffering
most forcibly to his mind. From now on he no longer tries to evade it,

and when the delegation calls to see him again, he bluntly declines to make the main speech at the Independence celebrations.

We next see Mugo on the day before Independence as he walks alone in the pouring rain. Water and rain are very important symbols in this novel as we shall see later. Here, Mugo's deliberate refusal to take shelter from the rain is an indication of his acceptance of guilt and responsibility, and his readiness to do penance for his crime. Events have been moving rapidly towards a climax. Not only is Mugo's reputation among the other villagers now at its highest, he himself, as we have seen, is more conscious than ever of his guilt, and full of a sense of the past. Appropriately, Mugo realizes on the very eve of Uhuru, that if he is really to be 'free' from the burden of guilt, he must confess. His own conflict will be resolved, his true relationship to the others be defined. Under the magic influence of Mumbi he is gradually led to confession, which, for him, is 'Uhuru'. However, to be complete the confession has to be public; during the Independence celebrations he goes up to the microphone, and although he could with some justification have allowed the public to vent its rage on Karanja, he confidently confesses. The confession is a sign of integrity:

> Why should I not let Karanja bear the blame? He dismissed the temptation and stood up. How else could he ever look Mumbi in the face? His heart pounded against him, he felt sweat in his hands, as he walked through the huge crowd. His hands shook, his legs were not firm on the ground. In his mind everything was clear and final. He would stand there and publicly own the crime. He held on to this vision. Nothing, not even the shouting and the songs and the praises would deflect him from this purpose. It was the clarity of this vision which gave him courage as he stood before the microphone and the sudden silence. As soon as the first words were out, Mugo felt light. A load of many years was lifted from his shoulders. He was free, sure, confident. (p. 267)

It is true that his confidence only lasts for a minute, making way for the sudden fear of being torn to pieces by all those people, and for the laudable, though frightening, consciousness that he is responsible for his own deeds. He has a sudden urge to run away to a new life and is even momentarily tempted to step into the old woman's hut and take shelter from the rain (itself a symbol). But the confrontation with the old woman acts once more as a kind of epiphany, revealing to him the true nature of things and what his course of action ought to be. Abandoning his plan of escape, he walks out again into the drizzle, thus symbolically assuming

responsibility, and demonstrating readiness to do penance after the
momentary lapse. It is significant that when he goes into his hut he
does not even remove his wet clothes:

> Water dripped from his hair, down his face and neck in broken lines;
> water dripped from his coat, again in broken lines, down his legs and on
> to the ground. A drop was caught in his right eyelashes and the light from
> the lamp was split into many tiny lashes. Then the drop entered his eye,
> melted inside, and ran down his face like a tear. (p. 269)

Mugo's regeneration is complete. When General R. and Lieutenant
Koinandu come for him, his response is: 'I am ready.'

Clearly then, Githua's cynical response to Mugo's confession is shown
to be quite inadequate. The true response is Wanjiku's: 'It was his face,
not the memory of my son that caused my tears.' Her concern is rather for
Mugo and his suffering than for Kihika, and with Ngugi's guidance
this should be ours as well.

In this novel the lives and destinies of all are interrelated. No matter
what Mugo does, he cannot avoid the thought of Mumbi, since he betrayed
her brother; Mumbi and Gikonyo have a secret problem to resolve
between themselves; Karanja's life impinges on Gikonyo's and Mumbi's
because of the seduction, and is tied up with Thompson's through the
possibility of the latter's departure; Mugo's life is tied up with all of theirs
since he is regarded not only as a hero, but also as a sage, and therefore
the man who ought to be consulted in the event of conflict. By bringing
their lives to crisis-point, Uhuru helps them to redefine these relationships and resolve the conflicts. We have seen how Mugo succeeds in his
efforts; let us now look at Gikonyo.

Gikonyo is the example of the ordinary man for whom the deprivations
and tortures of the Emergency prove too strong; he claims our sympathy
and understanding as an example of simple, frail humanity. His early life
was not markedly different from Mugo's. Driven from his father's house
in his infancy and deprived of the usual boyhood comforts, he nevertheless
grows up to be an exemplary son and industrious worker. He becomes one
of the few men in his village whose life *is* their job, and the reader senses
and appreciates his skill and his initiative:

> Holding a plane, smoothing a piece of wood, all this sent a thrill of fear
> and wonder through the young man. The smell of wood fascinated him.
> Soon his senses developed sharp discrimination, so that he could tell
> any type of wood by a mere sniff. (pp. 85–86)

He is also an ambitious young man, whose secret desire to acquire wealth and buy a piece of land is linked with his growing love for the beautiful Mumbi.

The treatment of the love affair between Gikonyo and Mumbi is one of this book's greatest claims to excellence. It demonstrates that Ngugi's handling of the theme of love has matured since the rather adolescent days of *Weep Not, Child* and *The River Between*. Gikonyo and Mumbi are two mature people whose love is described in terms of sensations, inner feelings, fears, and jealousies. They seek to communicate their feelings towards each other in terms of motifs and symbols. Gikonyo's early romantic longing is described with great realism as he seeks to express the power of his love through the excellence of his guitar-playing and singing:

> But he found his hands were shaking. He strummed the strings a little, trying to steady himself. Mumbi waited for him to play the tune. As his confidence rose, Gikonyo felt Thabai come under his thumb. Mumbi's voice sent a shudder down his back. His fingers and heart were full. So he groped, slowly, surely in the dark, towards Mumbi. He struck, he appealed, he knew his heart fed power to his fingers. He felt light, almost gay. (p. 91)

On another occasion, Mumbi brings along a panga which needs a wooden handle, and Gikonyo decides to construct the wooden handle as an offering to Mumbi in expression of his love:

> The touch of wood always made him want to create something. But now he felt as if his life depended on giving himself wholly to the present job. His hands were firm. He drove the plane (he had recently bought it) against the rough surface, peeling off rolls and rolls of shavings. Gikonyo saw Mumbi's gait, her very gestures, in the feel and movement of the plane. Her voice was in the air as he bent down and traced the shape of the panga on the wood. Her breath gave him power. (p. 94)

We admire the skill and devotion of the man as he strives after perfection, for only perfection will express his love adequately. And at the end, peace settles in his heart; he feels a holy calm and is in love with all the earth. It seems that Gikonyo's love for Mumbi, as expressed through his art, has a purifying, ennobling force. And his efforts are amply rewarded by Mumbi's unconcealed joy and appreciation when the panga is presented. Clearly then, Mumbi, the most beautiful girl in the village, falls in love with the ungainly Gikonyo rather than the suave Karanja, because of the former's creativity in singing, carving, and playing. When Gikonyo plays, Mumbi's voice trembles with passion; 'she feels the workshop, Thabai, earth and heaven and experiences their unity'. His playing makes her feel at peace with herself and the rest of creation.

Although Gikonyo does not know it, the battle for Mumbi has been won even before the great race to the station, which he and Karanja, in their simplicity, thought would decide the issue. He loses the race but wins Mumbi and consummates his love. In his subsequent married life he finds complete happiness and self-fulfilment: 'Before I was nothing. Now, I was a man.' During the dark days of detention it is only his love for Mumbi and the possibility of the future reunion which keeps him alive and sane. One day before he was taken to detention he had heard Mumbi and Wangari discussing traditional Gikuyu stools, and immediately, and characteristically, Gikonyo had itched to carve a stool as an offering to Mumbi, and as a symbol of his love; it would be a special stool, different from all the others. Now in detention, as his love for Mumbi burns more ardently than ever, he thinks about the stool again, considering possible motifs.

As we have seen, his confession of the oath in order to be reunited with Mumbi can be understood in the light of this overpowering love; Ngugi evokes Gikonyo's bitterness and extreme disappointment when after months of eager anticipation and hopes for a better life in a new Kenya, he returns to find the woman he loves carrying another man's child:

> But now the image of Mumbi moaning with pleasure as her naked body bore Karanja's heavy weight, corroded him everywhere. He recreated the scene in its sordid details: the creaking bed; Karanja's fingers touching Mumbi everywhere; their heavy breath merging into one – and oh, Lord, the sighs, those sighs! He went through a long, continuous shuddering, then tottered towards a small tree by the road and held on to it. But the images did not stop corroding his mind. Karanja on top of Mumbi. He found himself dwelling on irrelevant details, worrying himself, for instance, over whether Mumbi had whimpered with pleasure at the orgasm . . . . Before he could finish the details of the scene, he groaned and emitted a hoarse cry. (p. 138)

He demonstrates his jealousy not only in terms of feelings, but also in his actions towards Mumbi and her son: 'Gikonyo roughly pushed the boy away from the knees, disgust on his face. The boy staggered and fell on his back and burst into tears, looking to the mother for an explanation.'

Yet although his relations with Mumbi are obviously strained, and life ceases to have any meaning for him, Gikonyo's characteristic energy and initiative re-assert themselves, and he becomes one of the most prosperous men in the community. With the approach of Uhuru, however, he is compelled to re-define his relationship with Mumbi and resolve his inner conflict. He engages in a series of long conversations with Mugo, finally leaving, irritated and angry with everyone, including Mugo, and determined to vent his anger on Mumbi. Fortunately, he discovers that she has left his home for her parents'. Events come to a climax on Independence day, during the great final race which Gikonyo once more regards as a race between Karanja and himself for Mumbi. Neither wins the race, for they both fall over a stump of grass and Gikonyo has to be taken to hospital. In hospital he finally reflects and comes to terms with himself, and can resolve his conflict. When he hears the truth about Mugo he exclaims: 'remember that few people in that meeting are fit to lift a stone against that man.' This is a recognition that they were all, in one way or another, guilty of some crime or misdemeanour. Gikonyo is reminded of his own guilt, and is more anxious than most to give Mugo a fair chance. If he is prepared to excuse Mugo's crime, we can expect that before long he will be able to excuse Mumbi's.

> But after Mugo's confession, he found himself trying to puzzle out Mumbi's thoughts and feelings. What lay hidden behind her face? What did she think about Mugo and the confession? He increasingly longed to speak to her about Mugo and then about his own life in detention. What would she say about the steps that haunted him? (p. 278)

And now the desire to carve a stool as an offering to Mumbi recurs:

> Then, as he thought about it, he became more and more excited and his hands itched to touch wood and a chisel. He would carve the stool now, after the hospital, before he resumed his business, or in-between the business hours. He worked the motif in detail. He changed the figures. He would now carve a thin man, with hard lines on the face, shoulders and head bent, supporting the weight. His right hand would stretch to link with that of a woman, also with hard lines on the face. The third figure would be that of a child on whose head or shoulders the other two hands of the man and woman would meet. (p. 279)

The decision to carve the stool not only indicates forgiveness of Mumbi but also the return of his love, and his acceptance of the child.

Mumbi, a relatively simple character, is presented as one of the best people in the village. Unlike the others, she is tortured by no inner conflict, but the approach of Uhuru finds her uncertain about Gikonyo's love for her. Her problem is to resolve the crisis of her marriage and regain her husband's love. This proves no easy task, since Gikonyo obstinately refuses to discuss the child. In her desperation Mumbi turns to Mugo and tells him her story, revealing extenuating circumstances in her affair with Karanja. What originally looked like adultery was really seduction.* In the face of relentless pressure from Karanja, who during the detention days was gradually acquiring more power and wielding it with characteristic ruthlessness, Mumbi's resistance was sure to have crumbled sooner or later. Moreover, Karanja gave her and her mother-in-law genuine assistance, at a time when there was no man in the house, and virtually saved them from starvation and death. Had Mumbi capitulated then, we would have understood. Only when Karanja indicates that Gikonyo is being released from detention and will be returning soon does she, in her extreme joy, allow him to make love to her.

Returning on Uhuru day from the hospital to which Gikonyo has been admitted, Mumbi surrenders her body to the rain and returns home drenched. Her surrender to the downpour is like a cry of pain caused by Gikonyo's continuing harsh treatment. Although she does not want to visit him again, on her mother's advice, she relents. When she next goes to the hospital she discovers that Gikonyo has himself experienced a change of heart. Gikonyo now wants to talk about the child. They have come through a lot of suffering, and what has happened cannot be passed over in a sentence; nevertheless they will open their hearts to each other, and plan their future. When she leaves the hospital she is sad, but she is also sure.

For Karanja, Uhuru means exile. In the new situation there is no place for the traitor Karanja. Karanja's mentality is typically colonial. Convinced of the superiority of the white man, he is elated if he shows him any favours, uses his contact with his white bosses to enhance his prestige among the other natives, and views with apprehension the imminent departure of the British régime. His activities as homeguard and chief are repulsive and damaging. Nevertheless, in conformity with his general practice in this novel, Ngugi does not present him without an element of sympathy. It has already been seen that his own selfishness is partly reaction to his reading of the world as selfish and callous. Furthermore, the instinct for self-preservation makes him join the homeguards. Karanja also arouses

---

* See also Derek Elders' review in *African Literature Today 1*, Heinemann Educational Books, 1968, p. 53.

the sympathy normally extended to the man who loses the contest. On two occasions we share his anguish when he realizes that the woman he loves has been won by his rival Gikonyo, and we must not forget that the desire to be close to Mumbi is one of the factors influencing his decision to join the homeguards, and remain in Thabai. We also pity him for the humiliation he suffers at the hands of the very white men he respects so much:

> 'Yes, yes,' the white man answered quickly, as if puzzled by the question. Panic seized Karanja. He played with his fingers behind his back. He would have loved to suddenly vanish from the earth rather than bear the chill around . . . .
> Karanja stood in the corridor for a while and took a dirty handkerchief to rub off the sweat from his face. Then he went back, his gait, to an observer, conjuring up the picture of a dog that has been unexpectedly snubbed by the master it trusts. (p. 182)

Like the other characters, Karanja goes out and surrenders himself to the downpour, again indicating acceptance of guilt, and readiness to pay the penalty. He thinks back on Kihika's decomposing body hanging on the tree after his execution, which had forced him to think about the meaning of freedom. If freedom and fighting for freedom meant ending up like Kihika, or being separated from Mumbi, he would have none of it. But in longing to be free he had condemned himself to a form of imprisonment, and symbolically, his first job was in a hood. Now the image of the hood recurs, reminding him not only that he betrayed and destroyed his own people, but also that, with the coming of Uhuru, he is not really free in his own land, and he must go into exile.

The Thompsons are the only white characters of any importance in the novel, and the approach of Uhuru gives them an opportunity to resolve their own problems and redefine their relationship. At the start of the novel Mrs Thompson's frustration leads her to make advances to Karanja, just as it had previously sent her into the arms of the repulsive Dr Van Dyke. The reasons for the latent hostility between John Thompson and his wife are not far to seek. In the first place, John was much too absorbed in his work, too engrossed in the daily business of administration, too concerned with promotion. Moreover, life with John was much too conventional. He was always 'correctly dressed, knew how to behave, and never allowed himself to get drunk'. It is the very contrast which the vulgar, disgusting, Dr Van Dyke presents which makes him attractive.

John himself is bitterly disappointed by what he regards as Britain's betrayal in giving Kenya independence. Why, the Duke of Edinburgh himself, the husband of the princess, the symbol of the imperial order, who had actually shaken his hand years ago, would be there to preside over the lowering of the Union Jack. However, John is not simply the reactionary colonialist civil servant *par excellence,* and Ngugi is not entirely hostile to him. His contact with two highly educated Africans at Cambridge had generated a youthful idealism. 'In a flash I was convinced that the growth of the British Empire was the development of a great moral idea . . . . ' Later he is inspired with an even nobler idea of creating one British nation, embracing peoples of all colours and creeds, based on the just proposition that all men are created equal, and he writes a treatise on the subject entitled *Prospero in Africa.* There is not the slightest hint of snobbery or condescension in the scheme he proposes. Rather, the emphasis is on equality. He is influenced by the French policy of assimilation but is also critical of the system as it is practised in the French territories. 'We must avoid the French mistake of assimilating only the educated few. The peasant in Asia and Africa must be included in this moral scheme of rehabilitation.' The weakness of John's scheme lies in his naïve assumption that English civilization and culture can be exported. His disillusionment stems from his naïvety, for life in Africa is very markedly different from what he had imagined when he wrote his treatise in the sheltered cloisters of a Cambridge college. Like Kurtz in Conrad's *Heart of Darkness,* he is forced to reverse his opinions. The optimism of his first experience of Kenya gives way to condescension and contempt, and finally to open hostility:

> In dealing with the African you are often compelled to do the unexpected. A man came into my office yesterday. He told me about a wanted terrorist leader. From the beginning, I was convinced the man was lying, was really acting, perhaps to trap me or hide his own part in the movement. He seemed to be laughing at me. Remember the African is a born actor, that's why he finds it so easy to lie. Suddenly I spat in his face. I don't know why, but I did it. (p. 65)

Subsequently, Thompson, now a camp supervisor, shocks the world by callously beating eleven men to death for taking part in a hunger strike. It is precisely the frustration of his ideals which explains the bitterness he feels on Uhuru eve.

Although Thompson is not presented in as much detail as the Africans, Ngugi tells us as much as we need to know him fully, partly through an analysis of his inner thoughts and struggles. When Dr Lyndt's dog attacks

Karanja, Thompson inwardly wrestles with a paralysing unconscious sadism, which would really have liked to see the dog draw Karanja's blood. We are intended to feel not contempt for Thompson, but pity for a man who is aware of his inner weaknesses and desires, and struggles to suppress them.

For Thompson, Uhuru means leaving Kenya, but before he leaves he and his wife manage to sort out their difficulties. The initiative comes from Margery, who, during a most embarrassing moment at their farewell reception, goes up to her husband and takes his hand. And so, though in Britain they will have to start all over again, Margery, like Mumbi, is sad but certain.

General R. and Lieutenant Koinandu are minor characters, but they too share in the guilt that plagues everyone on Uhuru eve. General R. is a calculating man, unglamorous, unsophisticated, but single-minded. For him Uhuru is incomplete until Kihika's betrayer is found out and punished, and to this end he strains every nerve. But although he seems to personify the public demand for vengeance, he is momentarily reminded of his own terrible and savage murder of the Reverend Jackson Kigondo, who had resembled the father he hated. Lieutenant Koinandu is tortured by the memory of raping the defenceless Dr Lyndt.

All these tensions, doubts, and rivalries come to a climax during the symbolic final race on Uhuru day. The purpose of the race is not just to decide who will win Mumbi, but to find out, as it were, who has been most steadfast in the much greater long-distance event – the struggle for independence. Consequently, it is neither Karanja nor Gikonyo who wins, since both of them in one way or another have betrayed the cause; it is General R., running with his characteristic coolness and deliberation, the man who has persevered with unflinching single-mindedness.

The ominous shadow of the past looms over everyone. No matter how hard each character tries no one escapes the consequences of past actions; as General R. points out to Mugo at the end, 'your deeds alone will condemn you . . . No one will ever escape from his own actions.' Even General R. and Lieutenant Koinandu find themselves plagued by memories, and consequences of his boyish lethargy catch up with Karanja at last. Mugo's redemption dates from his determination to face up to the past. Previously he had tried to avoid the past, believing that life was meaningless, 'with no connection between sunrise and sunset, between today and tomorrow'. As Warui says:

'. . . It's strange in our village, and I cannot stop saying it to myself when I see things that happened one, two three – many years ago, come to disturb a woman's peace and rest. Those buried in the earth should remain in the earth. Things of yesterday should remain with yesterday.' (p. 198)

All these inner conflicts, tensions, guilt, and personality clashes rather mar the dawn of Uhuru. This was the millennium they had all been awaiting, but when it comes 'it was not a happy feeling; it was a more disturbing sense of an inevitable doom'. The people's disillusionment and sense of betrayal is intensified by the behaviour of their local M.P.s, who, basking in their new-found prosperity and power, are beginning to demonstrate the condescension and corruption so typical of African politicians. It is clear that the country is not exactly in the right hands, and the chaos which John Thompson so gloomily forecast is already beginning to make itself felt. The sense of disillusionment of Uhuru day is symbolized by the heavy destructive rain which falls on Uhuru night, accompanied by thunder and lightning, breaking hedges, uprooting trees, damaging crops, and drenching people in their houses.

Nevertheless, in spite of all the disillusionment, the unexpected revelations, and the personal antagonisms, the novel does not end on a pessimistic note. Mugo, having relieved himself of his burden of guilt achieves 'freedom' and goes to meet death willingly; Gikonyo and Mumbi begin a new life; the whole village goes about its business with stoical determination, for there is work to be done. Life must go on. Characteristically, it is Mumbi who points the way:

'I must go now. I'm sure the fire is ready at home. Perhaps we should not worry too much about the meeting . . . or . . . about Mugo. We have got to live.'

'Yes, we have the village to build,' Warui agreed.

'And the market tomorrow, and the fields to dig and cultivate ready for the next season,' observed Wambui, her eyes trying to see beyond the drizzle and the mist.

'And children to look after,' finished Mumbi as she stood up and took her rain-sack ready to leave. Then suddenly she turned round and looked at the two old people, as at aged wisdom which could tell youth the secrets of life and happiness. (p. 275)

The growing assurance with which Ngugi uses symbols and motifs should now be apparent. The dominant symbol is that of water which variously represents consciousness of guilt, attempts at its expiation, or a kind of baptism – re-birth into a new life, as when Mumbi feels an urge to surrender herself to the pouring rain. The artistic motifs – the carved stool and the panga – by means of which Gikonyo tries to express his love, and the passages underlined in Kihika's Bible which are so relevant to the work as a whole, are also worthy of mention.

Ngugi's characterization in this novel can hardly be faulted. One of the reasons why the main characters are all fully-rounded, recognizable people, is that we are given an unusually full account of their innermost thoughts. Indeed, in this novel Ngugi frequently makes use of techniques we have come to associate with stream-of-consciousness or interior-monologue. Finally, tribute must be paid to Ngugi's superb descriptive technique and impressive prose. We may take this passage as an example:

Only Mumbi felt she could understand, because she knew the man's hands and fingers on her body; she knew the man's power as his limbs fixed her helpless to the ground. And her body would wait, wings beating in readiness. Those were the moments one experienced terror and tenderness; and she wanted him too, now exulting in her woman's strength for as the man swooned into her, it was her tenderness and knowledge that saved him and gave life back to him. (p. 119)

A Grain of Wheat is a profoundly satisfying work of art. Ngugi has clearly attained maturity and produced a novel which can stand unashamedly with some of the more lasting English works of fiction.

2: Chinua Achebe

▼▼▼▼▼▼▼▼▼▼▼▼▼▼▼▼▼▼▼▼▼▼▼▼▼▼▼▼▼▼▼▼▼

THINGS FALL APART

CHINUA ACHEBE'S first novel, *Things Fall Apart* is unquestionably his best. Never again was he to demonstrate such mastery of plot construction, such keen psychological insight, and such an ability to hold his themes steadily before his mind and pursue them convincingly to a logical conclusion. *Things Fall Apart* derives its strength from the quality of the author's perception of the social forces at work in an ancient and proud society, and from his admirable knowledge of human psychology shown in the development of Okonkwo's character. There are distinct affinities between the work of Achebe and that of Hardy. Both show a keen awareness of the movement of social forces and their effect on the destiny of ordinary people. Okonkwo's story, like Tess's, is not merely a personal tragedy; a once proud and stable society is destroyed by the encroachment of an outside force, morally inferior, but economically and technologically superior. Okonkwo, like Tess, personifies his society at the moment when it is most severely threatened. Both novelists make use of the supernatural, but whereas Hardy always bangs his fatalistic drum and attempts to suggest that fate is to blame, contrary to the concrete experience of the novel, Achebe intelligently relegates the supernatural to the background and shows tragedy to be consequent on the interaction of social forces and human character.

The theme of the novel is stated clearly on page 160: 'He has put a knife on the things that held us together and we have fallen apart.' With the arrival of the white man and his new religion and administration, traditional society's cracks and weaknesses, hitherto concealed by the common fear of the ancestors and the gods, break open and the once-stable community collapses. In order to impress on the reader the tragedy of its collapse, Achebe devotes great skill in evoking his society as it used to be; and this is one of the reasons for the novel's enduring appeal. Those who open this novel hoping to find a description of noble savagery where the tensions of modern Western society do not exist, are likely to be disappointed. Umuofia society is proud, dignified, and stable, because it is governed by a complicated system of customs and traditions extending from birth, through marriage to death. It has its own legal, educational, religious, and hierarchical systems, and the conventions governing relations between the various generations are as elaborate as any to be found in a Jane Austen novel. Here is the account of the trial scene in which the elders settle a marital dispute:

'*Umuofia kwenu!*' shouted the leading *egwugwu*, pushing the air with his raffia arms. The elders of the clan replied, 'Yaa!'

'*Umuofia kwenu!*'

'*Yaa!*'

'*Umuofia kwenu!*'

'*Yaa!*'

Evil Forest then thrust the pointed end of his rattling staff into the earth. And it began to shake and rattle, like something agitating with a metallic life. He took the first of the empty stools and the eight other *egwugwu* began to sit in order of seniority after him . . .

When all the *egwugwu* had sat down and the sound of the many tiny bells and rattles on their bodies had subsided, Evil Forest addressed the two groups of people facing them.

'Uzowulu's body, I salute you,' he said. Spirits always addressed humans as 'bodies.' Uzowulu bent down and touched the earth with his right hand as a sign of submission.

'Our father, my hand has touched the ground,' he said.

'Uzowulu's body, do you know me?' asked the spirit.

'How can I know you, father? You are beyond our knowledge.'

Evil Forest then turned to the other group and addressed the eldest of the three brothers.

'The body of Odukwe, I greet you,' he said, and Odukwe bent down and touched the earth, The hearing then began.'*

And after the litigants have been heard:

'We have heard both sides of the case,' said Evil Forest. 'Our duty is not to blame this man or to praise that, but to settle the dispute.' He turned to Uzowulu's group and allowed a short pause.

'Uzowulu's body, I salute you,' he said.

* Achebe, C., *Things Fall Apart*, African Writers Series, Heinemann Educational Books, 1962, pp. 81–82. All further page references are to this edition.

C

'Our father, my hand has touched the ground,' replied Uzowulu,
touching the earth.

'Uzowulu's body, do you know me?'

'How can I know you father? You are beyond our knowledge,'
Uzowulu replied.

'I am Evil Forest. I kill a man on the day that his life is sweetest to
him.'

'That is true,' replied Uzowulu.

'Go to your in-laws with a pot of wine and beg your wife to return
to you. It is not bravery when a man fights with a woman.' He turned to
Odukwe, and allowed a brief pause.

'Odukwe's body, I greet you,' he said.

'My hand is on the ground,' replied Odukwe.

'Do you know me?'

'No man can know you,' replied Odukwe.

'I am Evil Forest, I am Dry-meat-that-fills-the-mouth, I am Fire-
that-burns-without-faggots. If your in-law brings wine to you, let your
sister go with him. I salute you.' He pulled his staff from the hard earth
and thrust it back.

'*Umuofia kwenu!*' he roared, and the crowd answered. (pp. 84–5)

The dignity of the scene (which is not eroded by our knowledge that the
egwugwu are actually human beings) is evoked by details such as the formality of address, the ritualistic repetition of conventional statements, the
leading *egwugwu*'s deliberate pause for effect before addressing each group,
and the terrible attributes which he claims to possess. Equally powerful
is the description of the wrestling contest:

Dusk was already approaching when their contest began. The drums
went mad and the crowd also. They surged forward as the two young
men danced into the circle. The palm fronds were helpless in keeping
them back.

Ikezue held out his right hand. Okafo seized it, and they closed in.
It was a fierce contest. Ikezue strove to dig in his right heel behind
Okafo so as to pitch him backwards in the clever *ege* style. But the one
knew what the other was thinking. The crowd had surrounded and
swallowed up the drummers, whose frantic rhythm was no longer a mere
disembodied sound but the very heart-beat of the people.

The wrestlers were now almost still in each other's grip. The muscles
on their arms and their thighs and on their backs stood out and twitched.
It looked like an equal match. The two judges were already moving

forward to separate them when Ikezue, now desperate, went down quickly on one knee in an attempt to fling his man backwards over his head. It was a sad miscalculation. Quick as the lightning of Amadiora, Okafo raised his right leg and swung it over his rival's head. The crowd burst into a thunderous roar. Okafo was swept off his feet by his supporters and carried home shoulder-high. They sang his praise and the young women clapped their hands:

> 'Who will wrestle for our village?
> Okafo will wrestle for our village.
> Has he thrown a hundred men?
> He has thrown four hundred men,
> Has he thrown a hundred Cats
> He has thrown four hundred Cats.
> Then send him word to fight for us.' (pp. 45–6)

The cynical may dismiss passages like this as nothing but sociological information, but for the sensitive it surely evokes the feel of life in Iboland before the advent of the white man. One can feel not just the excitement and the physical movement of the wrestling but the very rhythms of life in the pounding of the drums and the resilience of the prose. The frantic ryhthm which Achebe likens to the very heart-beat of the people, is echoed in the prose. Or look at the formal, almost ritualistic way in which Nwakibie and his wives drink Okonkwo's palm-wine:

Anasi was a middle-aged woman, tall and strongly built. There was authority in her bearing and she looked every inch the ruler of the womenfolk in a large and prosperous family. She wore the anklet of her husband's titles, which the first wife alone could wear.

She walked up to her husband and accepted the horn from him. She then went down on one knee, drank a little and handed back the horn. She rose, called him by his name and went back to her hut. The other wives drank in the same way, in their proper order, and went away. (pp. 18–19)

From such descriptions the reader gains a sense of an alien, but nevertheless strong, self-assured, and civilized society.

There is a school of social anthropologists who rhapsodize over traditional African society seeing it as a welcome antidote to the materialism and commercial technology of Western society, with its morbid preoccupation with worldly possessions, status symbols, rapid promotion, and all the trappings of the rat-race. Such anthropologists are likely to have second thoughts on reading *Things Fall Apart*, for this society is just as competitive, just as materialistic, and just as concerned with status as any to be found in the Western world. This is a society in which a man's prestige is in direct proportion to the number of yams he has in his barn, the number of huts he has in his compound, the number of his wives and children, the 'titles' he has taken, and the number of human heads he has to his credit. Indeed, the struggle for the acquisition of titles is the equivalent of modern technological society's rat-race, and like the latter it can be an expensive, soul-destroying process in which the weak and the introverted are easily left behind. Modern technological societies (e.g. the U.S.A.), tend to evaluate a man according to his own achievement rather than his ancestry. This is exactly the situation we find in Umuofia, where ' . . . a man was judged according to his worth and not according to the worth of his father.' As in any modern, competitive, and acquisitive society, age is respected, but achievement is revered.

The apparent prosperity of this society is overshadowed by the ever-brooding presence of danger, fear, and death. There was the fear of evil and capricious gods and magic, the fear of the forest, and 'of the forces of nature, malevolent, red in tooth and claw'. It is fear, especially the fear of the gods and of evil, that motivates the many acts of apparent brutality in this community. Umuofia society reacts with tremendous speed and ruthlessness to expel from its midst anything which it considers a threat to its security or which might bring down on its head the wrath of the gods. Twins are taken from their parents and abandoned alive in the evil forest; *Obanjes* (wicked children who, when they die, enter their mothers' wombs to be born again, only to die again) are mutilated at their death, dragged by the ankle on the ground and buried in the evil forest; those who suffer from the swelling sickness, an abomination to the earth goddess, are not allowed to die in the village, but are taken to the evil forest, tied to trees and abandoned to die and be devoured by birds of prey; suicides, also an abomination to the earth goddess, are buried like dogs in the evil forest; *Osus,* who are consecrated to the service of the gods, are denied all contact with other human beings, and at death are buried by their kind in the evil forest. The most monstrous injunctions of the gods are obeyed without question, whether it be the execution of an innocent boy, the virtual abduction of a mother's only child, or the expulsion of a man from his fatherland for the accidental shooting of his kinsman.

It is a mark of Achebe's intelligent objectivity, that conscious though he is of the strength and stability of traditional Umuofia society, he is not blind to its brutality. He does not merely record these instances of savagery without implying any judgement, for he carefully leaves clues and hints, structural as well as textural, as comments on the nature of the society he describes. For example, after the expulsion of Okonkwo and the destruction of his property, Obierika's viewpoint is given:

> Obierika was a man who thought about things. When the will of the goddess had been done, he sat down in his *obi* and mourned his friend's calamity. Why should a man suffer so grievously for an offence he had committed inadvertently? But although he thought for a long time he found no answer. He was merely led into greater complexities. He remembered his wife's twin children, whom he had thrown away. What crime had they committed? The Earth had decreed that they were an offence on the land and must be destroyed. And if the clan did not exact punishment for an offence against the great goddess, her wrath was loosed on all the land and not just on the offender. (pp. 113–14)

A thorough understanding of Umuofia society is essential for an understanding of the character of the hero, Okonkwo. One of the signs of this novel's excellence is the brilliance with which Achebe has demonstrated the interrelation between sociology and psychology, between environment and character. *Things Fall Apart* is a novel of character and environment, but in a slightly different sense than the novels of Hardy. In Hardy's novels a character's destiny depends on social circumstances. But in Achebe's case environment *is* character. Okonkwo is what his society has made him, for his most conspicuous qualities are a response to the demands of his society. If he is plagued by fear of failure and of weakness it is because his society puts such a premium on success; if he is obsessed with status it is because his society is preoccupied with rank and prestige; if he is always itching to demonstrate his prowess in war it is because his society reveres bravery and courage, and measures success by the number of human heads a man has won; if he is contemptuous of weaker men it is because his society has conditioned him into despising cowards. Okonkwo is the personification of his society's values, and he is determined to succeed in this rat-race. When we first meet him he possesses all the various symbols which are the marks of success; he is a wealthy farmer with two barns full of yams, and three wives. He had demonstrated his prowess in war by bringing home no less than five human heads and he had taken two titles.

Achebe's treatment of Okonkwo's subsequent development shows his subtle understanding of human psychology. He cleverly links Okonkwo's present temperament not only with the values of his society, but also with

his revulsion against everything his father had stood for. Bitterly ashamed
of the father who committed the unpardonable sin of dying without taking
any titles, Okonkwo comes to associate failure and weakness with him.
His character is partly determined by the negative need to be everything
that his father was not. Of course we admire his determination, his
tremendous strength, energy and resilience. He somehow reminds us of
Tulliver in George Eliot's *Mill on the Floss*, a tower of strength, a creature
of powerful emotions, broadchested, expansive, strong, and awesome like
the mill or the horse, and capable of scattering his enemies before him with
one wave of his little finger.

Fully conscious of his own worth, Okonkwo manages to exude an outer
self-confidence. Nevertheless, the reader is uncomfortably aware of hidden
insecurity, or even a feeling of inferiority. Unlike other men who would
have quietly assumed their superiority, Okonkwo, dogged by the memory
of his father, is afraid of being considered weak or of being overtaken by
ruin or failure:

> But his whole life was dominated by fear, the fear of failure and of
> weakness . . . Okonkwo's fear was greater than these. It was not external
> but lay deep in himself. It was the fear of himself, lest he should be
> found to resemble his father. (pp. 12–13)

This fear which dominates all his actions, contributes to his subsequent
catastrophe. It also explains the restlessness, overabundance of nervous
energy, vile temper, fierce emotionalism and the predisposition to violence
we discern in his character:

> When he walked, his heels hardly touched the ground and he seemed to
> walk on springs, as if he was going to pounce on somebody. And he did
> pounce on people quite often. He had a slight stammer and whenever
> he was angry and could not get his words out quickly enough, he would
> use his fists. He had no patience with unsuccessful men. (pp. 3–4)

Okonkwo rules his household with a heavy hand, bullying his wives,
intimidating his son and ill-treating the young Ikemefuna. He treats
unsuccessful people like dirt. Thinking it weakness to show emotion
openly, except it be the emotion of anger, Okonkwo becomes a cold
dehumanized person, always itching for activity and work as an outlet for
his restless energy. In a sense Okonkwo is presented as a life-denying force.
He is always associated with death, whereas his father, with all his faults,
is associated with life. By his constant nagging and bullying he stifles the

life in his son Nwoye, who develops into a sad-faced youth. Always charged and tense as a loaded cannon, Okonkwo seems to be impelled by some ungovernable inner force, and one expects his fiery temper and nervous energy to find an outlet in violent action, or that he will plunge headlong into self-destruction. Indeed the self-destructive impulse is very marked in his character, even if he is not aware of it himself. The killing of his kinsman, though not deliberate, is really much more than an accident. It exemplifies his predisposition to violence which at last finds an outlet, and is the climax to a cumulative process. First, Okonkwo commits sacrilege by beating his youngest wife during the week of peace. On this occasion he has a plausible excuse, the girl being clearly in the wrong. But during the yam festival he unjustifiably beats another wife, and when she makes some disparaging remarks about his skill in hunting, he shoots at her and almost commits murder. Okonkwo's violence is impelling him towards increasingly serious and senseless acts. After this, he impulsively and mercilessly cuts down the innocent Ikemefuna, against the advice of Ezeudu. His accidental killing of Ezeudu's son is the most serious of a number of acts motivated by his temperamental violence and restlessness, which are themselves the consequence of his fear of failure and of weakness.

There are those in Umuofia society who refuse to be involved in the rat-race, and consequently opt out. One of these is Okonkwo's father, Unoka, whose modern counterparts are possibly to be found in the legions of beatniks and bohemian artists. Although Unoka is presented as unindustrious and cowardly, our response to him should not only be condemnatory. We would be failing to appreciate his very human qualities which Okonkwo would have been the better for possessing. Unoka has an artistic imagination; he is both actor and musician. Generous and impulsively good-natured, he loves good food and good fellowship, lives for the day and is in harmony with the forces of nature:

He was very good on his flute, and his happiest moments were the two or three moons after the harvest when the village musicians brought down their instruments, hung above the fireplace. Unoka would play with them, his face beaming with blessedness and peace. Sometimes another village would ask Unoka's band and their dancing *egwugwu* to come and stay with them and teach them their tunes. They would go to such hosts for as long as three or four markets, making music and feasting. Unoka loved the good fare and the good fellowship, and he loved this season of the year, when the rains had stopped and the sun rose every morning with dazzling beauty ... Unoka loved it all, and he loved the first kites that returned with the dry season, and the children who

sang songs of welcome to them. He would remember his own childhood,
how he had often wandered around looking for a kite sailing leisurely
against the blue sky. (pp. 4–5)

The remarkable evenness of the prose reflecting Unoka's inward serenity,
is the surest indicator that he has Achebe's approval. He is seen to possess
a certain humanity, warmth, and generosity of outlook, that his son conspicuously lacks. Who would expect Okonkwo to show open love for
children or to be nostalgic over his childhood? When Unoka makes music
it is meaningful music, reflecting sorrow and grief. He belongs to that class
of artists who believe that they should live for their work and not prostitute
the integrity of their art to a sterile materialism. In this he is unlike the other
musician Okonye, who, in spite of being an artist, is fully involved in the
rat-race, and is about to take the Idemili title, the third highest in the land,
with all the attendant expense. As far as Umuofia society is concerned,
Unoka's death from the swelling sickness is similar to his life: both are
shameful disasters. But in reality, both his life and his death are a comment
on the materialism and brutality of his society. That this is so, is authenti-
cated by the simple effectiveness of the touching last sentence on Unoka:
'Such was Unoka's fate. When they took him away, he took with him his
flute.'

Achebe handles the catastrophe itself, the killing of Ezeudu's sixteen-
year-old son, with great skill, generating an appropriate sense of drama
which is heightened all the more because the event is completely unexpected. Suddenly, from his exalted position as one of the most influential
men in his society, Okonkwo is reduced almost to a nonentity. But this is
the judgement of the society which he embodies, and whose values he
accepts and endorses. It was a shrewd masterstroke of Achebe's to make
the most cruel punishment of Umuofia society rebound on the man who
most personifies it. By killing a kinsman, Okonkwo has commited a crime
against the all-powerful and unrelenting earth goddess, but the crime is of
the 'female' sort, since it was committed inadvertently, and Okonkwo's
punishment is banishment for seven years.

It is a mark of the novelist's superb artistic sense that he makes
Okonkwo's absence from his fatherland coincide with the white man's
arrival and establishment. Achebe thus ensures that the most significant
developments take place at a time when Okonkwo is impotent to influence
their course, and by the time he returns, the new *status quo* has been so
firmly entrenched that it is obvious he is fighting a lone battle, and is
doomed to failure. During his exile in Mbanta Okonkwo sets about the
task of redeeming his fortunes with characteristic energy, but there is no

doubt that he is a man in decline. The authority and influence he wielded in his fatherland do not obtain here, and although his advice, tendered with characteristic vehemence and conceit, is politely heard, it is not accepted. Even within the family unit he has to concede precedence to his aged uncle. Increasingly Okonkwo becomes an isolated figure counselling a campaign of violence and combat in the old style, while the men of his motherland are thinking of a gentler and more realistic approach to the Christians. This isolation becomes even more marked on his return to Umuofia.

With the exile of Okonkwo to Mbanta, the stage is set for the confrontation between traditional Umuofia society and the outside forces threatening it. Umuofia is incapable of dealing successfully with the threat, not only because the alien force is militarily stronger, but also because of the weaknesses in traditional society. The inhumanity of this society makes it vulnerable, and leads eventually to the disunity which the missionaries are able to exploit so skilfully. The first sign of the white man's presence takes the form of a military outrage – the extermination of the entire village of Abame as a reprisal for the murder of a missionary. The incident demonstrates that the white men have brought not only a religion, but also a ruthlessly efficient government. As the whole history of the colonialist exploitation of Africa proves, the missionaries are merely the advance guard of the administrators and other visible signs of colonialism. Nevertheless some of them behave with decency and courtesy, and minister to a vital need:

> The missionaries had come to Umuofia. They had built their church there, won a handful of converts and were already sending evangelists to the surrounding towns and villages. That was a source of great sorrow to the leaders of the clan; but many of them believed that the strange faith and the white man's god would not last. None of his converts was a man whose word was heeded in the assembly of the people. None of them was a man of title. They were mostly the kind of people that were called *efulefu*, worthless, empty men. The imagery of an *efulefu* in the language of the clan was a man who sold his matchet and wore the sheath to battle. Chielo, the priestess of Agbala, called the converts the excrement of the clan, and the new faith was a mad dog that had come to eat it up. (p. 130)

The secret of the new faith's success is precisely that it offers a refuge to all those whom the clan, for a variety of reasons, regard as outcasts. If the clan had not been so callous towards its underdogs, the white man's religion would not have taken hold. As it is, it is the *Osus*, the parents of twins, and all those held in contempt because they have, taken no titles who flock to the missionaries' banner. One of these is Okonkwo's own son, Nwoye, who had seen his best friend cut down in his youth to please the whims of a merciless god. He is also plagued by the fear that he might not measure up to the exacting demands of a society which puts such a premium on courage and prowess in war:

> It was not the mad logic of the Trinity that captivated him. He did not understand it. It was the poetry of the new religion, something felt in the marrow. The hymn about brothers who sat in darkness and in fear seemed to answer a vague and persistent question that haunted his young soul – the question of the twins crying in the bush and the question of Ikemefuna who was killed. He felt a relief within as the hymn poured into his parched soul. The words of the hymn were like drops of frozen rain melting on the dry palate of the panting earth. (p. 134)

Furthermore, Mr Brown, the first missionary, is a man of outstanding goodness and courtesy, who spares no efforts in educating the people and caring for their welfare in every way. The success of the mission station sounds the death knell of traditional society. The sense of impending doom is conveyed by one of the elders during Okonkwo's farewell party in Mbanta:

> 'An abominable religion has settled among you. A man can now leave his father and his brothers. He can curse the gods of his father and his ancestors, like a hunter's dog that suddenly goes mad and turns on his master. I fear for you; I fear for the clan.' (p. 152)

Achebe loses no opportunity to satirize the English administrators. He exposes their presumption in dispensing justice based on total ignorance of local laws and customs. The irony is most biting when directed against the posturing District Commissioner who intends to include the episode of Okonkwo's suicide as a chapter in his projected work: *The Pacification of the Primitive Tribes of the Lower Niger.*

As long as a reasonable person like Mr Brown is in charge of the mission station, co-existence is possible between the new religion and traditional society. But with the advent of the fanatical Mr Smith a conflict becomes inevitable, and it coincides with Okonkwo's return to his fatherland.

It is part of Okonkwo's tragedy that he is blind to the fact that time has not stood still during his absence. He knows that he has lost his place among the nine masked spirits who administer justice in the clan, but he hopes that, given the same conditions for success as existed hitherto, he could quickly make up for lost ground. He makes elaborate plans to ensure that his return will be marked by the people. Unfortunately, while Okonkwo has been living in the past the clan has undergone a silent but profound change. There are even a good many who are prepared to accept the change, for although the new religion may still seem lunatic, it has brought with it trade and prosperity, and the possibility of contact with the outside world. Failing to appreciate the new situation, Okonkwo continues to talk the only language he understands, the language of force and of war, but as Obierika's corrective comments indicate, it is a language devoid of reason and realism, and Okonkwo's isolation from informed and responsible opinion in the clan continues.

Mr Smith's lack of tact undermines the basis of co-existence so carefully laid by Brown, and brings church and clan once more into collision; Okonkwo, still thinking in terms of war and the old days 'when a warrior was a warrior' welcomes the deterioration in relations. But the District Commissioner, acting with characteristic speed, imprisons and humiliates the elders of the clan, including Okonkwo, releasing them only after the payment of a heavy fine. A great meeting is called to decide on the clan's action and Okonkwo brings down his war gear, fully convinced that the meeting will end in the declaration of war.

The meeting itself recalls the earlier 'trial meeting' in which Okonkwo had taken his place as one of the spirits of the clan who administer justice, but where that meeting had the confidence and authority of stability and coherence, this one is marked by gloom stemming from an awareness of the impending disintegration of the clan:

> 'All our gods are weeping. Idemili is weeping. Ogwugwu is weeping, Agbala is weeping, and all the others. Our dead fathers are weeping because of the shameful sacrilege they are suffering and the abomination we have all seen with our eyes.' (pp. 182–3)

A court messenger arrives to stop the meeting, and Okonkwo, impelled by the destructive force within him, kills the man with his matchet. But even while committing the deed he realizes its futility, for the men of Umuofia would not go to war. Disillusioned, and aware that he is the only representative of a once-proud order, he commits suicide. With the death of Okonkwo, an old order passes. His death symbolizes the destruction and collapse of the clan, a fact which is brought forcefully home to us when the District Commissioner, the representative of the new order, commands the elders to leave Okonkwo's house and they obey without a murmur. Achebe deplores the passing of the old order and its replacement by another which is only noticeable for its ignorance and conceit, but he, unlike Okonkwo, accepts the process as inevitable. However, he affirms Okonkwo's solid worth at the end even while demonstrating his refusal to accept change.

One of the charges usually brought against *Things Fall Apart* is that an inordinate proportion consists of sociological information. Indeed, this is a charge often levelled against the African novel as a whole. Critics object not only because such information makes the novel tedious, but also because the novel form ought to exist in its own right, not as a sociological document, but as a medium for the treatment of personal relationships. *Things Fall Apart* does rely heavily on sociology, but it is neither didactic nor tedious. What, according to all the rules, should have been a dull work, is actually a powerfully achieved work of art. The solution of the mystery surely lies in the relevance of the sociological information to the themes of the novel and the way in which this information is handled by the author. Traditional society is regarded almost as a character in its own right since what we are witnessing is the destruction of an entire way of life. It is therefore necessary to insert more sociological information than would normally be found in other novels. The first part of the novel consists largely of descriptions of incidents which might be termed 'sociological' – incidents such as Enzima's illness, the *ogbanje* and the *iyi-uwa*, the trial, the wrestling, and the funeral ceremonies. But as we read on we are aware, not of mere sociological information, but of a society powerfully evoked.

Sociological information is given to convey the 'feel' of life. Achebe captures the sense of occasion and the tension in the activities of everyday life, so that we feel 'we were there'. Let us take a typical scene:

> In the morning the market-place was full. There must have been about ten thousand men there, all talking in low voices. At last Ogbuefi Ezeugo stood up in the midst of them and bellowed four times, '*Umuofia kwenu*,' and on each occasion he faced a different direction and seemed to push the air with a clenched fist. And ten thousand men answered '*Yaa!*' each time. Then there was perfect silence. Ogbuefi Ezeugo was a powerful orator and was always chosen to speak on such occasions. He moved his hand over his white head and stroked his white beard. He then adjusted his cloth, which was passed under his right arm-pit and tied above his left shoulder. (p. 10)

In scenes such as this we see ordinary men and women engaged in traditional activities, in the very business of living. One of the reasons why

the scene in this passage comes to life is that Achebe devotes some attention
to the description of Ezeugo's gestures and movements. The same technique can be seen in another 'sociological' scene:

> Okonkwo brought out his snuff bottle and offered it to Ogbuefi Ezenwa,
> who sat next to him. Ezenwa took it, tapped it on his knee-cap,
> rubbed his left palm on his body to dry it before tipping a little snuff into
> it. His actions were deliberate, and he spoke as he performed them.
> (p. 105)

This is the prelude to yet another 'sociological' scene – the marriage scene;
Achebe does more than convey the friendly custom of snuff-taking among
Ibos. This, and the ensuing scene are presented in terms of dialogue,
deliberate gestures, and movements, and are therefore fully 'realized'.
Indeed, scenes like these do not bore or annoy the reader because of the
superb skill with which Achebe handles them. The incidents are related
in such a way that we feel their relevance, and they are dramatically
evoked in such powerful prose that their reality is enacted, and we do not
stop to question either their relevance or their authenticity. We only have
to contrast Achebe's technique with that of an inferior novelist, Flora
Nwapa, the author of *Efuru*, to see how skilful he is. Miss Nwapa's
sociological descriptions, which are almost always irrelevant, are often pre-
faced by some comment like this: 'They organized themselves in groups and
sang from door to door. Their song went like this . . . ' And then follows an
Ibo song or an elaborate recipe for some kind of soup. The introductory
comment, 'their song went like this' detaches the song or whatever follows
from its context, and it becomes purely sociological information. Achebe's
sociological passages always emerge quite naturally and unobtrusively out
of the living situation in the novel.

The need for sociological detail to create a sense of society dictates the
novel's construction. The first part may appear sluggish, with a number of
apparently irrelevant digressions, while the second moves with astonishing
rapidity and is much more unified. This is necessary, for Achebe is not
concentrating on action in the first part, but on the evocation of Ibo society
which requires the description of episodes some of which, like Ezinma's
illness, or the trial scene, could even be transposed elsewhere, without
materially damaging the story.

No study of Achebe's work would be complete without mention of the
use of proverbs which is such a distinctive feature of his style. In a sense,
Achebe could not avoid using proverbs since they are highly prized in the
society he has set himself the task of portraying. He tells us himself that the

art of conversation is highly regarded among the Ibos and 'proverbs are the palm-oil with which words are eaten'. Here are some examples:

(a) The sun will shine on those who stand before it shines on those who kneel under them. (p. 7)
(b) When the moon is shining the cripple becomes hungry for a walk. (p. 10)
(c) Let the kite perch and let the eagle perch too. If one says no to the other, let his wing break. (pp. 17–18)
(d) An old woman is always uneasy when dry bones are mentioned in a proverb. (p. 19)
(e) A child's fingers are not scalded by a piece of hot yam which its mother puts into its palm. (p. 61)
(f) Eneke the bird was asked why he was always on the wing and he replied: 'Men have learnt to shoot without missing their mark and I have learnt to fly without perching on a twig.' (p. 183)
(g) I cannot live on the banks of a river and wash my hands with spittle. (p. 150)

Achebe uses the proverbs as vivid illustrative analogies. In (d) for instance, in imagining the uneasiness of the old woman we are thus made aware of Okonkwo's discomfort at the mention of anything relating to his father. The proverbs are always appropriate, allowing a speaker to make his point tactfully and concisely. The concentration of meaning and evocative power of the proverbs impart a poetic quality to Achebe's prose. They are also invaluable rhetorical devices, seeming to state basic truths. Proverbs do not merely convey a quaint charm, nor are they only part of the elaborate conventions of Ibo society, they have a very important rôle to play in conversation and are an indispensable aspect of Achebe's style.

Finally, a word about Achebe's use of language. Though normally his style is terse, unpretentious, and concise, it can on occasion glow with radiance and serenity. He also uses the rhythms of his prose to reflect such movements as the wrestling contest, or Okonkwo's powerful breathing while asleep. There has been some discussion about whether the African writer should use standard English, or a form of language which more faithfully reflects the culture and status of the people he writes about.* Normally Achebe uses standard idiomatic English, but he departs from this norm for Ibo statements or bits of conversation which would look odd in idiomatic English. It should be remembered that African novelists

* Chukwukere, D. I., 'The Problem of Language in African Creative Writing', *African Literature Today 1*, Heinemann Educational Books, 1968, pp. 15–26.

are writing for an African as well as a European audience and the language must be recognizably part of their way of life. So one should not, for instance, expect Achebe to translate the *egwugwu*'s words, 'Uzowulu's body, I salute you' into some such phrase as 'Good afternoon, Uzowulu,' for such a translation would leave out such things as the implied relationship between Uzowulu and this ancestral spirit. Moreover, the sense of dignity, partly evoked by the formal address, would be eroded. Similarly, when Ekwefi, in reply to a question about Okonkwo's attempt to murder her, says, 'I cannot yet find a mouth with which to tell the story', her sense of utter horror is conveyed much more forcibly than by some translation such as 'I cannot find words to describe it'.

Things Fall Apart assuredly deserves its universal fame, for in this, his first novel, Achebe demonstrates the awareness of social forces, psychological penetration, powers of characterization, and expertise in the use of language, which we normally expect in much more experienced novelists.

▼▼▼▼▼▼▼▼▼▼▼▼▼▼▼▼▼▼▼▼▼▼▼▼▼▼▼▼▼▼▼

NO LONGER AT EASE

ACHEBE'S second novel, *No Longer At Ease*, is greatly inferior to his first in range of conception and intensity of realization. The understanding with which he conveyed his people's predicament, the mastery of plot, and keen psychological insight seem to have deserted him. Achebe is still preoccupied with the social forces at work in his society, particularly the clash between the old and the new. But this time the new force is not an alien religion or administration, but the attitudes of the young, urbanized Nigerian who, having been liberated from the taboos of tribal life through exposure to other values, now comes to question the traditions and beliefs of his ancestors. At the same time, Achebe demonstrates that this modern Nigerian is ill-at-ease in a society which is no longer recognizably his own, and which consistently fails to conform to his idealized picture.

The quotation from T. S. Eliot with which Achebe prefixes the novel refers to the disenchantment which is one of its major themes. Like the three Magi, Obi returns from an alien country to discover that the assumptions of his elders, and the traditional society of which he was once a part, no longer coincide with his view of life. At the same time he is adrift in decadent, modern Lagos. He lacks the resourcefulness necessary to handle this predicament satisfactorily, he is crushed by the clash and ends in tragedy.

No Longer At Ease is not about the break-up of traditional society – a theme which had been exhaustively and powerfully treated in *Things Fall Apart*. Indeed, the various kinds of society presented here are consolidating themselves, rather than disintegrating. After the traumatic experiences presented in *Things Fall Apart*, the two ways of life seem to have achieved a *modus vivendi* and it is up to the individual to use his personal resources to withstand the demands made on him by both. The traditional way of life represented by Obi's home village and the Umuofia Progressive Society is strong and durable. It has its own culture and values, and can draw on its recorded wisdom for support. It is not a dying society. There seems, therefore, to have been a shift of emphasis between the first novel and the second; the issue is no longer the decay of one society in the face of a superior one, but the clash between the two, and the effect of this clash on the new intellectual élite. Appropriately, the hero of the new novel is the grandson of Okonkwo, the hero of the first.

Characteristically, Achebe is as aware of the strength of traditional Ibo society as he is of its weaknesses, and the quality of his prose reflects the ambivalence of his vision, holding the balance very skilfully between admiration and gentle mockery. On the one hand, this society is self-sacrificing, closely-knit, and very much concerned with questions of morality. They tax themselves to collect money to send some of their brighter young men and women to study in England, and on the eve of Obi's departure (he is the first beneficiary of the scholarship fund) they gather in his home to offer their best wishes and advice:

'I have heard of young men from other towns who went to the white man's country, but instead of facing their studies they went after the sweet things of the flesh. Some of them even married white women.' The crowd murmured its strong disapproval of such behaviour. 'A man who does that is lost to his people. He is like rain wasted in the forest. I would have suggested getting a wife before you leave. But the time is too short now. Anyway, I know that we have no fear where you are concerned. We are sending you to learn book. Enjoyment can wait. Do not be in a hurry to rush into the pleasures of the world like the young antelope who danced herself lame when the main dance was yet to come . . . '

The gathering ended with the singing of 'Praise God from whom all blessings flow'. The guests then said their farewells to Obi, many of them repeating all the advice that he had already been given. They shook hands with him and as they did so they pressed their presents into his palm, to buy a pencil with, or an exercise book or a loaf of bread for the journey, a shilling there and a penny there – substantial presents in a village where money was so rare, where men and women toiled from year to year to wrest a meagre living from an unwilling and exhausted soil.* (pp. 10–12)

Certainly there is gentle raillery here at the Umuofians' cultural and racial introversion, naïvety and long-windedness, but there is also admiration for their high moral principles and selflessness.

However, in spite of the strengths, the weaknesses do appear. Indeed the very selflessness ought to be qualified, for when the Umuofians give Obi the scholarship, they have an eye on their own interests: they ask him to study law in order to help them settle their land cases. They are blind to the real purpose of education, seeing it not as a means of developing the individual in accordance with his own aptitudes, but as a tool to help consolidate the clan and protect its interest against the claims of others. Therefore, Obi's decision to read English (that most useless of subjects as far as Umuofians are concerned) precipitates the first clash and at the same time registers his defiance of the assumptions of his society. On Obi's return they make it perfectly clear that they expect him to use his newly-acquired influence as a senior civil servant on their behalf, such as finding jobs for members of the society: 'We are not going to ask him to bring his salary to share among us. It is in little things like this that he can help us. It is our fault if we do not approach him. Shall we kill a snake and carry it in our hand when we have a bag for putting long things in?'

The members of the Umuofia Progressive Society fail to realize that by educating Obi they gave him the opportunity to acquire ideals which were bound to be more liberal than theirs. They also fail to realize that they have transformed him into one of the élite, and that he will need to live up to his status, a status of which they themselves are proud. But on his return they calmly try to retribalize him. The Umuofians are strangely inconsistent about modernity. On the one hand they expect the newly returned Obi to be dressed in a European suit and to speak pompous English, and they are horrified when he turns up in his shirt sleeves and speaks simple English; they take tremendous pride in Obi's car, and greet him with

* Achebe, C., *No Longer at Ease*, African Writers Series, Heinemann Educational Books, 1963, pp. 10–12. All further page references are to this edition.

thunderous applause when he attends one of their meetings in it. But on the other hand they take the strongest exception to his liberalism. The inconsistency is, however, quite easily explained, if we appreciate that Umuofia society is principally concerned with its own interests. They expect Obi to dress like a European, not because they now accept European values, but because it adds to their glory. Similarly, for one of their members to be seen driving 'a pleasure car' boosts their prestige. They will not consider the other aspects of modernity which imply coming to terms with modern Nigeria:

> Obi admitted that his people had a sizeable point. What they did not know was that, having laboured in sweat and tears to enrol their kins-man among the shining élite, they had to keep him there. Having made him a member of an exclusive club whose members greet one another with 'How's the car behaving?' did they expect him to turn round and answer: 'I'm sorry, but my car is off the road. You see I couldn't pay my insurance premium.' (p. 98)

One feels the pathos of Obi's situation all the more forcefully because on his return from England he seems such an exemplary young man. He returns full of love and admiration for his country, partly because he has idealized Nigeria during the long months of frustration in England. During his first meeting with the Umuofia Progressive Society Obi takes great pride in his countrymen and their traditional ways, and compares them favourably with Englishmen. Back home he finds vitality, neighbourliness, and the art of conversation carried to its highest peak.

At first Obi refuses to identify himself with the new Nigeria, behaving instead in genuine humility and sincerity. He is not a philanderer like Joseph and Christopher, nor is he as extravagant as the latter; he is not a parasite fattening himself on his country's labour like the Honourable Sam Okoli. On the contrary, he has the highest principles and states these bluntly whenever the opportunity arises. He is genuinely against bribery, corruption, incompetence, and nepotism, although there is a suggestion that Obi's ideals are much too theoretical and that he is bound to be disappointed.

Since, however, Umuofia society is determined to make the most im-possible demands on him and to force him to conform to their own standards, a clash is inevitable, and the struggle crystallizes in the dispute over his proposed marriage with Clara, an Osu. No other issue could have exposed the narrow-mindedness of traditional society or the hasty tactless-ness of the modern man more completely. Achebe's artistic touch is sure.

It is when we examine the attitudes of various people to Clara and the problem of the Osu, that we discover how much Obi is in advance of his age and society. Christopher and Joseph are both modern young men, but they are horrified at the prospect of Obi's marriage with an Osu. The normally peace-loving Mrs Okonkwo threatens to commit suicide if Obi marries Clara during her life-time, and Mr Okonkwo, who in his day had rebelled against his own father and tradition, has now become so set in his ways that he fails to see that Christianity is opposed to all forms of discrimination.

In an uncharacteristic display of anger Obi questions the right of his society to interfere in his personal affairs, and he refuses to accept the offer to defer payment of the loan. Almost all his problems can be seen to stem from this.

Having cut himself free from the pull of traditionalism, Obi still fails to achieve complete freedom because he is now firmly in the clutches of decadent, modern Lagos. The scenes presenting modern Lagos are by no means as compelling as those associated with traditional Ibo society in *Things Fall Apart,* but there is enough to suggest the squalor, and to contrast the grim reality with the dream that Obi had once harboured:

> On the other side of the road a little boy wrapped in a cloth was selling bean cakes or *akara* under a lamp-post. His bowl of *akara* was lying in the dust and he seemed half asleep. But he really wasn't, for as soon as the night-soil-man passed swinging his broom and hurricane lamp and trailing clouds of putrefaction the boy quickly sprang to his feet and began calling him names. The man made for him with his broom but the boy was already in flight, his bowl of *akara* on his head. The man grinding maize burst into laughter, and the woman joined in. The night-soil-man smiled and went his way, having said something very rude about the boy's mother . . . During his first winter in England he had written a callow, nostalgic poem about Nigeria . . . He recalled this poem and then turned and looked at the rotting dog in the storm drain and smiled. 'I have tasted putrid flesh in the spoon,' he said through clenched teeth. 'Far more apt.' At last Clara emerged from the side street and they drove away. (pp. 16–17)

The juxtaposition of dead dogs, putrefaction and *akara* certainly brings out the degradation, but the passage brings out another characteristic quality of modern Lagos. In spite of the filth there is real fellow-feeling and neighbourliness, the name-calling is good humoured and without any trace of bitterness. It is as though the inhabitants of Lagos have decided to suffer cheerfully together, and this stoicism elicits the reader's sympathy. Furthermore, there is no doubt that Achebe responds more to the vitality of Lagos than to the elegant Ikoyi. For in spite of 'its luxurious bungalows and flats and its extensive greenery, Ikoyi was like a graveyard'.

As part of his portrayal of Lagos society Achebe also demonstrates the aimlessness of people like Christopher, Joseph, Bisi, Clara, and the Honourable Sam Okoli, and their preoccupation with sex, cars, and entertainment. To Obi's credit, he is different. Nevertheless, the problems of living in Lagos prove too much for him. Obi must play his part in the modern city and acquire all the various trappings of success, but at the same time he is traditionally expected to play his part in the extended family system which obtains in many parts of Africa. Consequently, he has to pay the instalments on his car, refund twenty pounds a month to the Umuofia Progressive Union, pay his income tax, his insurance, and his electricity bill, but at the same time he has to send his parents ten pounds a month, pay his younger brother's school fees, and shoulder a large part of his mother's funeral expenses. We watch in sympathy as financial blow after financial blow falls on him with agonizing rapidity. Inevitably, faced with the necessity of making two ends meet, he succumbs to the very bribery and corruption he had so volubly denounced on his return. At the start of the novel everyone wonders why Obi did it; the novel provides the answer to their questions. Achebe demonstrates that forces in both modern and traditional Nigeria destroy Obi.

As in *Things Fall Apart*, Achebe's insight into the working of social forces shapes this novel. The novel derives its interest largely from this social analysis. But *No Longer At Ease* has flaws. Firstly, the hero is weak and insufficiently realized. Obi Okonkwo was probably conceived as a Jamesian 'central consciousness' around whom all the events of the novel should revolve. The other characters matter only in so far as they throw light on his predicament. But for a central consciousness he is too uninteresting and vaguely portrayed. Rather than determining the course of events, Obi allows events to overtake him, and is merely borne along by the force of circumstance. A tragic hero should possess impressive qualities. Since Obi Okonkwo merely succumbs to the forces against him, he falls short of tragic stature; nor is he a martyr, since he is crushed for betraying his principles, not for championing them.

Although Obi figures frequently enough in the novel, his personality remains hazy. Achebe must take the blame, for he always seems to come between the reader and his creation. The 'omniscient author convention' does not imply that the hero's activities and thoughts should be presented at second-hand; novelists like Jane Austen and James Ngugi show that the 'omniscient author' can allow a story to emanate from the consciousness of the hero or heroine. The fact is that in this novel, events are clearly *told* by Achebe even when he is relating the hero's thoughts and actions. Let us look at a typical passage:

> He spoke about the wonderful welcome they had given him on his return. 'If a man returns from a long journey and no one says *nno* to him he feels like one who has not arrived.' He tried to improvise a joke about beer and palm-wine, but it did not come off, and he hurried to the next point. He thanked them for the sacrifices they had made to send him to England. He would try his best to justify their confidence. The speech which had started off one hundred per cent in Ibo was now fifty-fifty. But his audience seemed highly impressed. (p. 81)

If this speech had been reported as if it were coming direct from Obi's consciousness, we might have felt more of his embarrassment at the failure of that joke about beer and palm wine, of the mental agony involved in finding words to express his thoughts, and of the growing incoherence reflected in the hybrid nature of the speech towards the end. As it is, we are much more aware of Achebe reporting the speech, than of Obi making it.

The failure to take us close enough to Obi's consciousness is the basic cause of our ignorance of the mainspring of the hero's actions and this, in its turn, results in a number of psychological implausibilities in the novel. Was it really necessary or plausible, for Obi to be roused to such uncontrollable anger at the meeting of the Umuofia Progressive Society? One is even more doubtful about the question of bribery. Is it possible that the idealistic Obi would have succumbed so easily to temptation? Although his financial position was desperate, and many a nobler man before him has been unable to resist temptation, one would expect, at least, an agonizing inner struggle. But there is no such inner torment. He merely sinks deeper into corruption, and continues to take bribes even after his financial position has improved. These implausibilities are not confined to Obi. For instance, we know that Obi's father had in his own day rebelled against tradition in favour of Christian principles. Yet he seems to have a mental block about extending these same principles to the Osu – Clara. Would the tender-hearted Mrs Okonkwo, on her death-bed, really threaten to commit suicide if Obi were to marry Clara? These seeming implausibilities stem from inadequate explanation of decisive thought processes, and they seriously weaken the novel.

Another major flaw is the imperfect blending of the two main themes.

Achebe wishes to show that Obi's love affair with Clara is destroyed by his society's conservatism. However, Achebe does *not* demonstrate that social forces are to blame. At home Obi is questioned about his relationship with Clara. Although his father expresses complete disapproval, it is obvious that he will be won over in time, since he himself had once been a rebel. Mrs Okonkwo's objections are more serious, but although she threatens to kill herself if Obi were to marry Clara during her lifetime, she does not extract a promise from him not to marry the girl after her death; indeed she virtually gives him permission, provided he waits until she is dead. Obi is intelligent enough to realize all this, and states the position plainly to Clara on his return to Lagos. But Clara responds in the most unreasonable way; she chooses precisely this moment to break off the engagement, the very moment when, for the first time, the prospect of marriage seems possible. Perhaps Clara is repelled by Obi's weakness and indecision or annoyed that he rates his family's feelings higher than his affection for her. But she had always known that Obi's family would have objections to the marriage, and she had, on an earlier occasion, volunteered to break off the engagement precisely for this reason. Must Obi disrupt his relationship with his family now, when she herself had earlier been unwilling to come between them and Obi? Did she expect that Obi's trip to his hometown would result in an immediate change of heart by his parents? Her motives for breaking off the engagement are obscure. Clara's conduct is implausible and we are given no insight into her feelings, which might explain it. The affair is destroyed, not by the clash between the old and the new, but by Clara's unreasonable behaviour.

The third major weakness of the novel is structural. *No Longer at Ease* is too episodic to form a coherent whole. We saw in our study of *Things Fall Apart* that although some of the scenes were not causally related and could be transposed without materially affecting the novel's meaning, yet each was absolutely necessary in the presentation of Okonkwo and his society. With *No Longer At Ease,* some of the scenes are not only transposable, but are also irrelevant. For instance, the relevance of the episode involving Obi, Christopher and the Irish girls is not immediately apparent. Perhaps it demonstrates the attitude of missionaries in modern Nigeria, but it has little to do with Obi's story. Similarly the haphazard arrangement of the scenes describing modern Lagos result in a blurred picture, by no means as powerful as the picture of traditional Umuofia society presented in similarly unrelated episodes, in *Things Fall Apart.*

Furthermore, in the novel Achebe fails to give due weight to some very important events. He ought, for instance, to have demonstrated Obi's gradual descent into bribery and corruption, for this is one of the most momentous things which happen. Instead, he hastily summarizes this in two pages. The conclusion of the novel, which leaves the impression that Achebe was in a hurry to finish it, is also unsatisfactory.

Finally, Achebe does not seem to have been able to resist melodramatics, for example, Obi's outburst at the meeting of the Umuofia Progressive Society, or the scene in which Clara returns Obi's ring.

What gives this novel its interest is Achebe's social concern and his terse, ironic, lucid, unpretentious style. His scintillating wit, which is itself the index of his objectivity and maturity of outlook, is everywhere apparent. We have already noted the skill with which he holds the balance between admiration and mockery in his treatment of Umuofia society. His statements are often loaded with ironic meaning. Let us take the welcome address presented by the Secretary of the Umuofia Progressive Union as an example:

He rose, cleared his throat and began to intone from an enormous sheet of paper.

'Welcome Address presented to Michael Obi Okonkwo, B.A. (Hons), London, by the officers and members of the Umuofia Progressive Union on the occasion of his return from the United Kingdom in quest of the Golden Fleece.

'Sir, we the officers and members of the above-named Union present with humility and gratitude this token of our appreciation of your unprecedented academic brilliance . . . '

He spoke of the great honour Obi had brought to the ancient town of Umuofia which could now join the comity of other towns in their march towards political irredentism, social equality and economic emancipation . . .

Needless to say, this address was repeatedly interrupted by cheers and the clapping of hands. What a sharp young man their secretary was, all said. He deserved to go to England himself. He wrote the kind of English they admired if not understood: the kind that filled the mouth, like the proverbial dry meat. (pp. 31–32)

Achebe's satiric style is most economical, making his points effectively, while leaving a lot unsaid. Here is how Mr Stephen Udom prepares for the reception he expects on arrival at Lagos:

There was no such crowd for the MV *Sasa*, and it was quite clear that Mr Stephen Udom was deeply disappointed. As soon as Lagos had been sighted he had returned to his cabin to emerge half an hour later in a black suit, bowler hat and rolled umbrella, even though it was a hot October day. (p. 30)

Occasionally in this novel Achebe once more displays that evocative flair which was so evident in *Things Fall Apart*. In that brilliant first chapter, for instance, we have a powerful presentation of Umuofia society. There is a touch of satire combined with respect for the most durable things in this community. It is almost the novel in microcosm.

No Longer At Ease lacks the unity, thematic clarity, and powerful characterization of *Things Fall Apart*. Nevertheless, Achebe analyses the problems confronting the young man in modern Nigeria with realism and intelligent objectivity. He wisely refrains from resolving the dilemma, implying that these two forces, the old and the new, will continue to exert a pull on the educated élite, and that they will need all their individual resources to come through unscathed.

▼▼▼▼▼▼▼▼▼▼▼▼▼▼▼▼▼▼▼▼▼▼▼▼▼▼▼▼▼▼▼▼▼▼▼▼

A MAN OF THE PEOPLE

THEMATICALLY *A Man of the People* belongs to the same tradition as *Things Fall Apart* and *No Longer at Ease*. Having examined the strains and stresses in indigenous Ibo society in the wake of the colonialists' advance, and the problems facing the educated classes in modern Nigeria, in *A Man of the People* Achebe shows what the Nigerians make of their country when the imperialists leave. The result is a scathing denunciation of the political corruption of the new governing classes and of the cynicism of the masses. This largely explains the enormous popularity that the novel has enjoyed; for Achebe gives expression to the disgust that most Nigerians in particular and Africans in general have felt with the mess that their elected representatives had made of their countries. The novel achieved a certain topicality since its publication in 1966 almost coincided with the Nigerian military coup. Stylistically, however, *A Man of the People* is very different from the earlier novels. Firstly, it is a first person narrative; secondly, it is that rare bird in the corpus of African literature – a comic novel. After the tragic grandeur of *Things Fall Apart* and the pessimism of *No Longer At Ease*, it is refreshing to turn to a novel which occasionally stirs a belly laugh. One of the puzzles of African literature is that our verbal humour never seems to carry through to our writing. Perhaps we take ourselves and our leaders far too seriously to expose them publicly in a comic novel, although we are quite prepared to caricature them in private. However, African intellectuals are becoming more ready to laugh at aspects of their society – witness the publication of four satirical novels: *A Man of the People, Mission to Kala, The Interpreters,* and *The Beautyful Ones Are Not Yet Born.*

A Man of the People is a satirical, first-person narrative. This poses certain technical problems, for Achebe simultaneously uses the narrator Odili to laugh at certain institutions and people, and he laughs at Odili himself. The true subject of this novel is not really political corruption, but the corrupting power of privilege, position, and money. The hero is not Chief Nanga (The Man of the People), but the narrator, Odili. The interest lies not so much in Chief Nanga's corrupt activities (which are only barely sketched in), but the process whereby the supposedly idealistic Odili gradually succumbs to the temptations of political success and starts to resemble, in attitude at least, Chief Nanga himself.

Achebe needs great technical virtuosity and control to use Odili both as his mouthpiece against corruption, and to expose Odili's own susceptibility to corruption. He must look through Odili's eyes at society, but also stand apart from him, observing him critically. It is in this stylistic virtuosity that the achievement of *A Man of the People* lies.

Initially, the halting clumsy sentences, the grammatical errors, and the inept punctuation of *A Man of the People* seem most uncharacteristic of the author of *Things Fall Apart* and *No Longer At Ease.* Then it gradually becomes apparent that this is not Achebe's style, but Odili's. The stylistic infelicity is a device to show up the gap between the author and his hero. Quite deliberately, the language has been vulgarized to indicate the indiscipline of Odili's mind, all the more culpable in a university graduate. Let us compare a passage from *No Longer At Ease* with one from *A Man of the People.*

Here is a passage from the former novel:

'Take it away,' she croaked. In the effort to give orders she forgot about the glass of milk. It tilted in her unsteady grip and spilt on her neat floral dress. She went to a seat in the corner and sank in, groaning and croaking like old machinery gone rusty from standing in the rain. It must have been her favourite corner, because her parrot's cage was directly overhead. As soon as she sat down the parrot emerged from its cage on to a projected rod, lowered its tail and passed ordure, which missed the old lady by a tenth of an inch.*

This is prose of a fairly high order, using powerful imagery and detail – the tilting glass of milk, the image of rusty machinery, the parrot ejecting ordure. Also without pretentions to sophistication the prose works fluently and with precision. Here, in comparison is a passage from *A Man of the People*:

A common saying in the country after Independence was that it didn't matter *what* you knew but *who* you knew. And, believe me, it was no idle talk. For a person like me who simply couldn't stoop to lick any Big Man's boots it created a big problem. In fact one reason why I took this teaching job in a bush, private school instead of a smart civil service job in the city with a car, free housing, etc., was to give myself a certain amount of autonomy. So when I told the Minister that I had applied for a scholarship to do a post-graduate Certificate of Education in London it did not even cross my mind to enlist his help. I think it is important to stress this point. I had had scholarships both to the secondary school and to the University without any godfather's help but purely on my own merit. And in any case it wasn't too important whether I did the post-graduate course or not. As far as I was concerned the important thing was going to be the opportunity of visiting Europe which in itself must be a big education.†

The punctuation here is inept; there are grammatical errors such as 'who you knew,' and stylistic infelicities – 'bush, private school,' 'civil service job' and 'free housing, etc.' As the novel progresses, addiction to digressions, cheap moralization, unnecessary parentheses, explanations, and extraneous comments emerge:
'When I read this I was in tears – and I don't cry all that easily.'
or
'It was not until after many encounters that Chief Nanga managed to extract from her that her husband (apparently a very jealous man) had put some juju on her breasts to scare her into faithfulness . . .'
    For the novelist writing in the first person and yet wanting to expose his hero's weaknesses, the most effective device is irony, and in this novel

* Achebe, C., *No Longer at Ease*, African Writers Series, Heinemann Educational Books, 1968, p. 35.
    † Achebe, C., *A Man of the People*, African Writers Series, Heinemann Educational Books, 1966, p. 19. All further page references are to this edition.

Achebe shows consummate skill in its use. At times it becomes a double-edged weapon. Examples of irony can be found on almost every page, but a few will suffice here. During Chief Nanga's visit to Odili's school at Anata, he is determined not to remind the Minister that they had once known each other, implying that he takes no pride in the acquaintance; and when the Minister is introduced, he holds out his hand stiffly. But as soon as the Chief recognizes and embraces him, he is obviously beside himself with delight. He basks in reflected glory and the increase in his prestige in Anata. Similarly, after they have made love together, the American woman, Jean, takes Odili on a tour of Lagos to show him the contrast between the squalor in which the ordinary people live, and the opulence and greed of the governing classes, a contrast that Odili had himself noted and deplored. Now, however, that he is confronted with it, he is inwardly enraged at the lady's nerve, and wonders what right she has to comment on his country's inequalities. He is contemptuous and sceptical of the woman's professed love for Africa, and is convinced that in America she would not be found near a black man. Yet in spite of his contempt, a few minutes later he asks her whether he could see her again.

The following passage deserves careful examination:

The talk, as I said, was very good. My closeness to the Minister gave everything I said heightened significance. And – I don't know whether this happens to other people, but the knowledge that I am listened to attentively works in a sort of virtuous circle to improve the quality of what I say. For instance when at a certain point the conversation turned on art appreciation I made what I still think was a most valid and timely intervention . . .

It was then I had my flash of insight.

'Did you say she was shaking her fist?' I asked. 'In that case you got her meaning all wrong. Shaking the fist in our society is a sign of great honour and respect; it means that you attribute power to the person or object.' Which of course is quite true. And if I may digress a little, I have, since this incident, come up against another critic who committed a crime in my view because he transferred to an alien culture the same meanings and interpretation that his own people attach to certain gestures and facial expression. This critic, a Frenchman writing in a glossy magazine on African art said of a famous religious mask from this country: 'Note the half-closed eyes, sharply drawn and tense eyebrow, the ecstatic and passionate mouth . . . '

It was simply scandalous. All that the mask said, all that it felt for mankind was a certain superb, divine detachment and disdain. If I met a

woman in the street and she looked at me with the face of that mask
that would be its meaning. (pp. 55–56)

The passage not only exposes Odili's arrogance and conceit, but his
essential empty-headedness. He who had originally expressed so much
distaste for the Minister, revels in the respect given to him because of his
closeness to Nanga. The French critic said nothing about the meaning the
mask conveyed, and merely described the look on its face. It is Odili who
tries to explain what the mask 'felt for mankind', and there is nothing in
the critic's description which conflicts with what Odili tells us about its
meaning. The passage certainly directs some irony against the pundit at
the party, and more generally against all those ignorant critics who make
wrong-headed judgements about African art, but Odili's hypocrisy, conceit, and woolly thinking are also exposed.

When Chief Nanga opens the writers' club exhibition, Achebe turns his
ironic focus from Jalio, the president of the club, to Chief Nanga, and then
to Odili himself. At the start Odili greets Jalio, a former schoolmate, but
the latter, with incredible snobbery, merely takes his hand, for he does not
remember Odili's name, and does not seem to care. But Odili, piqued at the
rebuff, reverses his former high opinion of Jalio and his work. The Minister
then lectures Jalio on being improperly dressed for the occasion, which
is certainly a comment on the kind of false virtues Nanga endorses,
but there is also criticism of Jalio's affectation in thinking that now he is a
famous writer, he ought to adopt an *avant-garde*, bohemian style of dress.
However, Chief Nanga's lecture is delivered in such a school-masterish
tone, that any intelligent man would recognize and deplore its tactlessness
and bad taste. But Odili informs us: ' . . . my sympathies would certainly
have stayed with him [Jalio] but I must confess I was a little pleased to see
him deflated.'

There are, of course, occasions when Achebe uses Odili quite straight-
forwardly as a mouthpiece, without directing any irony against him:

As I stood in one corner of that vast tumult waiting for the arrival of the
Minister I felt intense bitterness welling up in my mouth. Here were
silly, ignorant villagers dancing themselves lame and waiting to blow
off their gunpowder in honour of one of those who had started the
country off down the slopes of inflation. I wished for a miracle, for a
voice of thunder, to hush this ridiculous festival and tell the poor
contemptible people one or two truths. But of course it would be quite
useless. They were not only ignorant but cynical. Tell them that this
man had used his position to enrich himself and they would ask you – as

my father did – if you thought that a sensible man would spit out the juicy morsel that good fortune placed in his mouth. (p. 2)

There can be no doubt here that Achebe endorses Odili's scorn for the ignorant cynicism of the Anata villagers. Generally, in this novel Achebe wields his craft with mastery, not only in revealing the corruption in Nigeria, but also exposing the flaws in Odili's character, and indicating the gap between author and hero.

The subject of this novel is the corrupting power of privilege, which ruins Odili, once so high minded and idealistic. The process of corruption begins with that first meeting with Chief Nanga, and our hero's unexpected boost in prestige. This sudden emergence into prominence, with the realization that his proximity to one in high office can be exploited to his own advantage, goes to Odili's head, and destroys whatever ideals he might have had. From now on his judgements cannot be relied upon. He deceives himself in believing that his ideals are unchanged. For instance, he had mentioned to the Minister that he intended to apply for a scholarship to do a post-graduate course in education. He carefully informs us, however, that he had not wished to solicit the Minister's assistance, since he was not prepared to sell his soul for the privilege of going to Europe, and it was the Minister himself who reintroduced the subject after the reception. So far we believe him, but from now on one is unconvinced about his decent high-mindedness. His assertion that he had avoided catching the Minister's attention, and that the Minister's subsequent proposals were inoffensive, is astonishing. Let us look at these proposals:

> He invited me to come and spend my holidays with him in the capital and while I was there he would try to find out from his Cabinet colleague, the Minister of Overseas Training, whether there was anything doing.
>
> 'If you come as soon as you close,' he said, 'you can stay in my guest-room with everything complete – bedroom, parlour, bathroom, latrine, everything – self-contained. You can live by yourself and do *anything* you like there, it's all yours.' (p. 20)

Odili is intelligent enough to realize that the Minister intends using undue influence to get him the scholarship. How can he, who supposedly loathes selling his soul, see nothing offensive in the Minister's proposal? Those luxurious apartments, acquired by the corruption which 'started the country off down the slopes of inflation' are obviously put at his disposal for immoral purposes. The truth is that Odili seizes the chance and, worse, gloats triumphantly over the unfortunate Mr Nwege who, quite justifiably, asks him whether he still thinks an introduction to the Minister un-necessary. We endorse Mr Nwege's sneer.

Odili accepts the Minister's invitation and makes his way to the capital, Bori, determined to use the opportunity offered to continue his liaison with Elsie, the pretty girl he had met at University. When we next see him he is basking in the voluptuous luxury of the Minister's house:

> When I lay down in the double bed that seemed to ride on a cushion of air, and switched on that reading lamp and saw all the beautiful furniture anew from the lying down position and looked beyond the door to the gleaming bathroom and the towels as large as a *lappa* I had to confess that if I were at that moment made a minister I would be most anxious to remain one for ever. And maybe I should have thanked God that I wasn't. We ignore man's basic nature if we say, as some critics do, that because a man like Nanga had risen overnight from poverty and in-significance to his present opulence he could be persuaded without much trouble to give it up again and return to his original state.
>
> A man who has just come in from the rain and dried his body and put on dry clothes is more reluctant to go out again than another who has been indoors all the time. The trouble with our new nation – as I saw it then lying on that bed – was that none of us had been indoors long enough to be able to say 'To hell with it'. (pp. 41–42)

Once he has enjoyed material comfort Odili is perfectly prepared to defend the Minister against those critics (who presumably at one time included himself) who idealistically believed that ministers should resign voluntarily from office, on points of principle. Gradually, but surely, Odili begins to share the Minister's point of view. As if this were not all, he also comes to share the point of view of the crowd he had once detested, and to endorse their cynical morality. The views he expresses here are not very different from those he had attributed to the crowd – and treated with such withering contempt – on page two. Later, we see how Odili enjoys the deference and respect accorded to him when he turns up at the hos-pital in the Minister's chauffeur-driven Cadillac, and exploits it:

> In our country a long American car driven by a white-uniformed chauffeur and flying a ministerial flag could pass through the eye of a needle. The hospital gateman had promptly levered up the iron barrier and saluted. The elderly male nurse I beckoned to had sprinted forward with an agility that you would think had left him at least a decade ago. And as I said earlier, although it was against all the laws of the hospital

they had let me into the female nurses' quarters and woken up Elsie to see me. (p. 63)

However, Odili's attitude to women most clearly indicates his similarity to the Minister. Odili's lechery, always conspicuous, is considerably intensified at Bori. While Chief Nanga goes off to sleep with Agnes, the elegant young lawyer, at twenty-five pounds a time, he stays behind and sleeps with Jean, the beautiful wife of an American expert. The characteristic coarseness with which the Chief discusses women infiltrates Odili's speech, and he begins to talk about them in derogatory terms himself. He even swops tales of conquest with Nanga, and refers to the comparatively innocent Elsie, as a 'good-time girl'. It is this 'woman palaver' which causes the final clash between him and the Minister, for while Odili is patiently waiting for the Minister to go to his own room, so that he can sneak upstairs and make love to Elsie, Nanga outwits him, and slipping calmly to the girl's room, seduces her.

When Odili turns to politics, it is not out of high-minded idealism. Unlike Max and the others, he is not primarily motivated by the desire to rid the country of parasites, and to expose their corruption to the world. If he once felt this it disappeared long ago. His primary motive in entering politics is revenge, and he returns to Anata not only to contest Nanga's seat, but also to seek out the Chief's intended parlour-wife, and 'give her the works'. Nor do his ideals return once he gets involved in the political fight. On the contrary, he gloats with such proprietary satisfaction over party funds and the party car, that the reader wonders how far he would degenerate if he were elected and appointed a minister:

I returned to Anata with a brand-new Volkswagen, eight hundred pounds in currency notes and assurances that more would be forthcoming. I would have driven straight to see Edna but the shining cream-coloured car was covered in a thick coat of red dust and splattered with brown mud from the long journey, so I decided to go home and have it washed first. Then I drove in style to her place only to be told she had gone to see her grandmother in another village. (p. 113)

If in the later sections of the novel Odili remains unattractive in spite of the Minister's blatant corruption it is largely because the reader senses that he himself is tarnished. Indeed, Odili probably ranks as one of Achebe's most unpleasant characters. He is lecherous, egoistic, vulgar, shallow-minded in spite of his college education, and ready to criticize others, including his best friend Andrew Kadibe, and Edna, whose simple and genuine letter he dismisses contemptuously as having come 'straight from one of these so-called letter-writers'. He is conceited, tactless, and immature. His insincerity and lack of warmth are demonstrated again and again, but pre-eminently in the scene where Mrs Nanga, with commendable sincerity, discusses the cultural problems facing her and the children, while Odili can only make patronizing stock responses.

Faced with such an opponent, it is hardly surprising that Chief Nanga does not seem quite as repulsive and self-seeking as we had been led to expect. Indeed, it is one of the paradoxes of this novel that the Chief, who was supposed to be the embodiment of corruption and ministerial incompetence, is actually a very charming and captivating man. Achebe himself is aware of the problem, and so is Odili, who on one occasion is forced to admit that the Chief is a man of considerable charm, although he is later to regard this charm as 'the most daring assault of counterfeit affability'. Partly, Achebe wishes to show that the politician's threat is all the more menacing because he can be so charming and human. Nanga is an expert in the art of public relations; recognizing the need to keep in touch with the people and their traditions, he even makes it a rule for his children to visit his village once a year, lest they forget their indigenous customs. He is unashamedly African; his genuineness enables him to overcome several natural handicaps. Odili himself refers to Nanga as the only man who could confess his ignorance about his country's greatest author, and still transform a potentially embarrassing situation into a splendidly humourous one. Scorning all pretentions to intellectualism, Nanga confidently names the books and the authors with whom he is acquainted – Michael West and Dudley Stamp. Indeed, at the book exhibition while everybody else, including Odili and Jalio, is being affected and hypocritical, the Chief is the only person acting genuinely. Chief Nanga is a man of great ebullience and generosity. There is one moment when we sympathize with him as we contemplate the demands made on a man in his position:

'You see what it means to be a minister,' said Chief Nanga as soon as his visitor left. His voice sounded strangely tired and I felt suddenly sorry for him. This was the nearest I had seen him come to despondency. 'If I don't give him something now, tomorrow he will go and write rubbish about me. They say it is the freedom of the Press. But to me it is nothing short of the freedom to crucify innocent men and assassinate their character . . .' (p. 74)

However, in spite of his obvious charm, there is evidence of Chief Nanga's corruption throughout the novel. We know of the blocks of luxury flats he has built out of his share of the bribe offered for an important government contract: we know that he presses for the construction of a certain road because he has already ordered a fleet of buses to ply the route. The contrast between the luxurious life he lives out of his ill-gotten gains and the squalor of the people around him is insisted on:

> The surprises and contrasts in our great country were simply inexhaustible. Here was I in our capital city, reading about pails of excrement from the cosy comfort of a princely seven bathroom mansion with its seven gleaming, silent action, water-closets! (p. 46)

When he realizes Odili's determination to contest his seat, Nanga first attempts to buy him off with the offer of a scholarship, and when that fails, arranges for the young man to be beaten up. With incredible ruthlessness he orders the village of Urua's waterpipes to be removed as a punishment for supporting Odili's candidature. The second half of the novel introduces a sinister streak in the Minister's character, that the first half hadn't led us to expect.

Chief Nanga's corruption is only a tiny manifestation of the much more widespread corruption that plagues Nigeria, where a lawyer finds it impossible to get a telephone installed in his home because he is not prepared to offer a bribe, and knows no 'big-gun'. Here we have the full horrors of an African election campaign, including victimization of the opposition parties, bribery, violence, and ruthless exploitation of the mass media. Through the disgust of Max and his idealistic colleagues at the existing state of things, we fully appreciate the administration's misdeeds.

However, one of the weaknesses of this novel is that all evidence of corruption is stated rather than demonstrated, and so we do not always feel its force. We are *told*, for instance, about Chief Nanga's block of flats and about the fleet of buses. Even later where the Chief's corruption is apparent, we are *told* by Odili's father of the offer of the scholarship. How much more effective to actually see Chief Nanga making the offer! When Chief Nanga rebukes Odili shortly afterwards, the effect is different:

> 'Look at him. He doesn't even know what is happening; our great politician! You stay in the bush here wasting your time and your friends are busy putting their money in the bank in Bori. Anyway you are not a small boy. I have done my best and, God so good, your father is my living witness. Take your money and take your scholarship to go and learn more book . . .' (p. 133)

D

Chief Nanga appears at his worst because his own words condemn him. When he addresses the political rally and abuses Odili, we see him in action, with his vices demonstrated rather than reported. But the sinister quality which emerges in these two scenes is something we have not been prepared for by the earlier scenes where statement replaces demonstration.

Achebe gives the impression that the vices of Chief Nanga and his kind partly result from the ignorance, cynicism, and indifference of the people themselves, Odili's father, who looks on politics as a lucrative profession, being a good example. One of the village elders is even more cynical:

> The village of Anata has already eaten, now they must make way for us to reach the plate. No man in Urua will give his paper to a stranger when his own son needs it; if the very herb we go to seek in the forest now grows at our very back yard are we not saved the journey? We are ignorant people and we are like children. But I want to tell our son one thing: he already knows where to go and what to say when he gets there; he should tell them that we are waiting here like a babe cutting its first tooth: anyone who wants to look at our new tooth should know that his bag should be heavy . . . ' (p. 141)

A Man of the People caught the world's imagination because of its thoroughgoing exposure of corruption in Nigerian society. The novel is also agreeably humorous and witty. But, on balance it seems to be an inadequately structured artistic whole, and to have certain weaknesses.

Firstly, the narrator–hero lapses too readily into digressions. In Achebe's defence, this is probably deliberate, in order to indicate the hollowness of Odili's mind. Also, in telling his own story, Odili is recollecting things rather haphazardly, and he relates them as they occur, even if this means breaking the thread of the narrative. By capitalizing on Odili's digressions, Achebe can give the impression of the 'talking voice' telling its own story. Let us take as an example the section where Odili introduces us to his girl, Elsie. He regrets that his outlook is hampered by hindsight, but this remark is irrelevant to the portrait of Elsie which follows; he merely piously hopes that being aware of the danger, he has managed to keep it at bay. Why, in that case, does he mention it at all? Odili then tells us that Elsie was, and still is, the only girl he met and slept with on the same day. After this he relates (quite logically so far) how he met Elsie and seduced her. Then he tells us that Elsie was one of those girls who emitted loud cries of 'Ralph darling', 'in the heat of the thing'. An explanation follows but then Achebe tells us about the reaction of the student next door who started to call him Ralph from that day. As if this were not enough he informs us that the student's name was 'irre', short for irresponsible, and another anecdote illustrating 'irre's' irresponsibility with women follows. We learn how 'irre' succeeded in seducing a female undergraduate who had seemed so inaccessible that she was called 'unbreakable'. Only after this do we manage to get back to Elsie. The passage demonstrates Odili's butterfly mind, which flits from subject to subject, anecdote to anecdote.

This technique may convey the impression of haphazard reminiscing, but it is disastrous for the work as a whole. It affects the internal unity of individual scenes: the reader's attention is continually distracted from the central point. Take the scene in Bori for instance, where the American couple Jean and John pay a surprise visit to the Chief's house. For most of this scene our attention is engaged by a conversation between Odili and the naïve American, John. But without any warning Odili changes tack, and informs us that 'memorable events were always flying around his [Chief Nanga's] stately figure'. This particular 'memorable event' turns out to be Jean's desire to go to bed with Nanga in broad daylight, if it were possible. But before we have taken this in, Odili suddenly changes the subject to the young man who comes to offer his services as a cook; it is on this note that the Chapter ends, bearing no relation to its beginning. Why does Achebe make this abrupt transition from John's conversation with Odili, to Jean's flirtation with Nanga, only to leave it in mid-air? Why does he make an equally abrupt transition to the unrelated incident of the cook?

One unfortunate consequence of Odili's 'grasshopper' mind is that he never dwells long enough on a scene, to bring it to life for the reader. There are a number of 'unrealized' scenes in this novel. Jean's dinner party and the opening of the writer's club book exhibition had great potential for vivid description. In the former especially, Achebe could have made much more skilful use of dialogue. But as we have it, Odili's digressions diffuse the effect. The latter scene exposes people's attitudes, but it lacks vividness, and apart from the imposing presence of Chief Nanga, one fails to visualize it. One of the few exceptions is Odili's early morning walk after Chief Nanga's seduction of Elsie, where Odili's mental state forces him to pay attention to all the sordid details which make the scene come to life:

Soon my nose began to run and as I hadn't brought a handkerchief I blew it into the roadside drain by closing each nostril in turn with my first finger. As dawn came my head began to clear a little and I saw Bori stirring. I met a night-soil man carrying his bucket of ordure on top of a battered felt hat drawn down to hood his upper face while his nose and mouth were masked with a piece of black cloth like a gangster. I saw

beggars sleeping under the eaves of luxurious department stores and a
lunatic sitting wide awake by the basket of garbage he called his possession. The first red buses running empty passed me and I watched the
street lights go off finally around six. I drank in all these details with the
early morning air. It was strange perhaps that a man who had so much
on his mind should find time to pay attention to these small incon-
sequential things . . . (pp. 79–80)

Achebe's weak detail partly accounts for Chief Nanga coming through as
attractive in spite of his alleged corruption. The fact is that very few scenes
actually demonstrate the Chief's corrupt activities, and Odili, in his haste
to pass on to other things, hardly ever dwells on the details of the Chief's
irresponsibility. Weakness of characterization is another fault. Odili and
Chief Nanga are the only two characters who come to life, the former
because of Achebe's irony, and the latter because he is a representative of a
well-known type in Nigerian politics. All the other characters hover for a
while on the edge of one's interest and then disappear, so that one finds
it almost impossible to distinguish between Edna, Elsie, and Agnes, or
between Odili's father and Edna's father.

Increasingly, *A Man of the People* looks like a tract for the times in which
Achebe's dominant preoccupation is the exposure of the evils of his
country's political system. But he is so full of his didactic mission that he
fails to create situations, characters, and a plot which can convincingly
carry the message. Consequently, the political intention is always obtrusive,
especially in the last sections of the novel, where Achebe becomes more of a
journalist than a novelist. One is disappointed not to see more of the process
whereby law and order broke down. The conclusion of the novel is also
unsatisfactory, for if Chief Nanga deserved to end on the rubbish heap,
Odili did not deserve much better.

The weaknesses of *A Man of the People* should not blind us to its merits,
although it is a flawed work, it is a necessary and an important one.

3 : Camara Laye

▼▼▼▼▼▼▼▼▼▼▼▼▼▼▼▼▼▼▼▼▼▼▼▼▼▼▼▼▼▼

THE AFRICAN CHILD

THE REACTIONS which Camara Laye's *The African Child* has so far elicited are symptomatic of the wrong-headed assumptions on which the criticism of African Literature has been based. Some African critics of *The African Child* deplore Laye's failure to deal with the anti-colonial struggle. One might as well condemn Jane Austen for not dealing with the French Revolution. Surely the novelist is at liberty to choose any theme within the area of human experience. He should not be expected to deal with some political or sociological phenomenon simply because he belongs to a certain nationality, race, or tribe. On the other hand, the enthusiasm of Western commentators seems to be based less on literary considerations than on a response to its portrayal of traditional African society. When William Plomer, for instance, describes the work in his introduction to the Fontana edition as 'clear, fresh and direct' it is obvious that he is talking not about the literary quality of the book, but the novelty of a society alien to his experience. So both the African detractors and the Western enthusiasts are basing their judgements on purely sociological or ideological considerations. Although the picture of traditional society presented in *The African Child* is fascinating, the work's artistic merit is doubtful.

Broadly speaking, Laye has two main preoccupations in this work. Firstly, he traces his growth from innocence to maturity against the background of traditional society; this ends with his uprooting and transplantation first to Conakry, and then to Paris. Laye's second preoccupation, which has not always been noticed, is to suggest the superiority of traditional life to modern technological society.* This leads Laye to idealize traditional life, associating it with peasant soul-harmony and noble savagery

---

* See Ramchand, K. and Edwards, P., 'An African Sentimentalist: Camara Laye's *The African Child*', *African Literature Today* 4, Heinemann Educational Books, 1970, pp. 37–53.

in the manner of Rousseau, to ignore its defects, and lay the blame for the disappearance of magic, miracles, and peasant innocence on Westernization. The first theme is carefully worked out and powerfully demonstrated; the second is suggested in an inflated and self-conscious commentary, and rhetorical questions, and constitutes a weakness in the book.

The treatment of the theme of innocence begins quite appropriately in the vivid first episode, in which the young Camara Laye plays with a venomous snake rather as if it were an attractive toy: 'I was laughing, I had not the slightest fear, and now I know that the snake would not have hesitated much longer before burying his fangs in my fingers if, at that moment, Damany, one of the apprentices, had not come out of the workshop.'* The change of tense reflects the child's growth into awareness and corresponding loss of innocence. As the passage continues, the boy's experiences are powerfully communicated in compelling prose, with a tremendous amount of detail to convey his thoughts and actions. He discovers the significance of his father's magical pots; he experiences first childish, and then adolescent love; he submits to, and then rebels against the brutality of his elders at school; goes through the rituals of initiation and circumcision; learns self-sufficiency, suffers the pain of parting and the death of friends.

The appeal of *The African Child* largely derives from Camara Laye's powerful portrayal of traditional life. He is at his best drawing inspiration from the memory of traditional rituals, which he communicates with clarity exactly as they would have struck the young boy's mind. Any unity and coherence in this book comes not from the author's deliberate attempt to relate character, scene, and setting, but from the force of traditional society. The reason why excerpts from *The African Child* are found frequently in anthologies is that it is made up of a number of self-contained episodes together forming a coherent picture of a dignified society.

The most memorable is the episode describing the making of gold. The episode derives its power from four main factors: the incorporation of the gold-making process into the larger myth of creation, the detailed account of the various activities and reactions of the participants, the evocation of a sense of community, and the numerous human touches with which Camara Laye intersperses the description. Throughout, Laye insists on the creation of a thing of beauty out of mud and chaos, and the impression of the creative process is reinforced by an aura of ritual:†

---

* Laye, C., *The African Child*, trans. Kirkup, J., Fontana, 1959, p. 11. All further page references are to this edition.

† See Ramchand and Edwards, loc. cit.

But what else could they have been, if not magical incantations? Were they not the spirits of fire and gold, of fire and air, air breathed through the earthen pipes, of fire born of air, of gold married with fire – were not these the spirits he was invoking? Was it not their help and their friendship he was calling upon in this marriage of elemental things? Yes, it was almost certainly those spirits he was calling upon, for they are the most elemental of all spirits, and their presence is essential at the melting of gold.

The operation that was going on before my eyes was simply the smelting of gold; but it was something more than that: a magical operation, that the guiding spirits could look upon with favour or disfavour; and that is why there would be all round my father that absolute silence and that anxious expectancy. (p. 26)

The praise-singer, inspired by the goldsmith's efforts and 'intoxicated by the joy of creation' is himself impelled into creative activity and composes his most powerful songs. The episode comes alive, like all that is best in Camara Laye, because the details are consistently kept before our eyes. Starting with the laborious task of collecting the gold out of mud we move on to the praise-singer and the detailed reaction of Laye's father to him; the preparation, the actual smelting, the incantations, the religious concentration of all present, the hammering and moulding of the gold into beautiful patterns, and finally the dance of victory and the general rejoicing are all set out. We notice the realistic human touches which make the scene part of general human experience. Laye's father, for instance, beaming with pride at hearing his deeds and his fame related, succumbs to the flattery and agrees to do the work for the woman; Camara Laye is himself proud to hear of the deeds of his ancestors. The woman's reaction is also vividly portrayed, from her uncertainty about what she really wants, her anxiety to have the work done as soon as possible, her feverish excitement as the work progresses, to her final cry of joy on seeing the finished product. Then of course there is the all-too-human response of Laye's mother, anxious about the effects of such work on her husband's health. We also notice that the process of making gold pulls the entire community into a kind of small village festival, and all present – apprentices, relatives, friends, neighbours, and praise-singer – play a part in the process.

The episode of Konden Diara shows the same signs of Camara Laye's skill, powerfully evoking the mystery and the boys' terror. During the initiation ceremony itself Camara Laye skilfully changes from the past-continuous tense to the present tense, (the only time when the present tense is used extensively in the work) to communicate the immediacy of the boys' experiences. Consequently, the whole narrative at this point seems to emanate out of the young boy's consciousness, foreshadowing Laye's similar achievement in *The Radiance of the King*. In the circumcision ceremony a sense of community vividly demonstrated in the goldsmith episode, is again created. Once more Camara Laye characteristically refuses to flinch from the unpleasant details; he describes the cut, the bandage, the unsavoury smell of blood, the touch of fever, the pain, the cleaning of the wounds, and the final healing, thus forcing the reader to live through the scene through the boy's eyes.

These three episodes – the goldmaking, Konden Diara, and the circumcision – show Camara Laye at his best. I have deliberately left the rice-harvesting episode till last, because although it was obviously intended by Camara Laye to be as functional and important as the other three, it lacks their power, and shows signs of the stylistic weakness so apparent in the second section of the work. Although the past-continuous tense is still used, and there is enough detail to keep the general scene before our eyes, there is a tendency to use rather empty stock-phrases (spinning, glittering sickles, irresistible alacrity, etc.) to describe the feats of the reapers:

> The young men used to toss their glittering sickles high in the air and catch them as they fell, shouting aloud for the simple pleasure of hearing their own young strong voices, and sketching a dance step or two on the heels of the tom-tom players. I suppose I should have done well to have followed my grandmother's advice and to keep a safe distance from those lively jugglers. But there was such a vivid freshness in the morning air, such scintillating vivacity in their juggling feats, in the spinning sickles that in the rising sun would blaze and flash with sudden brilliance, and there was such irresistible alacrity in the rhythm of the tom-tom that I could never have kept myself away from them. (p. 46)

The sense of community which was so powerfully demonstrated in the goldsmith and circumcision episodes has to be asserted, because we do not really experience it: 'then my uncle Lansana or some other farmer – for the harvest threw people together and everyone lent a hand in each other's harvesting – would invite them to begin work.' In any case since Camara and his uncle are yards ahead of the others we experience their separateness not their belonging. A certain tendency to idealize also comes through:

'In our December, the whole world is in flower and the air is sweet:

everything is young and fresh; the spring seems linked with the summer, and the countryside that for so long has been drenched in rain and shrouded in baleful mists now lies radiant; the sky has never seemed so blue, so brilliant; the birds are ecstatically singing; there is joy all round us – its gentle explosions are echoed in every heart. It was this season, this beautiful time of the year, that was stirring me so deeply, and the beat of the tom-tom and the festive air of our little procession moved me also. It was the best time of the year, the summer and all it stands for, all it holds and cannot hold – for how could it contain so much profusion? – and it made my heart leap with joy.' (pp. 46–47)

This passage is in fact a stereotyped description – a conventional evocation of the beautiful spring scene, of the rebirth and rejoicing in nature after the apparent 'death' of winter. It is as old as literature itself, and is powerfully celebrated by Chaucer in the famous opening lines of the Prologue to *The Canterbury Tales*.

Let us once again reiterate Laye's two aims in this work. On the one hand he presents a powerful picture of traditional society, showing his own growth within this society from innocence to maturity, and eventual transplantation. On the other hand he superimposes the view that this society, beautiful and dignified itself, has been spoiled by 'progress.' This view is not always borne out by events, and the flaws in the novel can be traced to this second preoccupation. In the first place it leads to a confusion in the point of view. We know that the mature Camara Laye is telling the story, but all the events are intended to be seen through the young boy's eyes, as he lives through his various experiences. At his best, Camara Laye uses the past-continuous tense and a wealth of detail to achieve this difficult technical feat. For instance:

This workshop was the main building in our compound. That is where my father was generally to be found, supervising the work, forging the most important items himself, or repairing delicate mechanisms; here it was that he received his friends and his customers, so that the place resounded with noise from morning to night. Moreover, everyone entering or leaving our compound had to pass through the workshop, so that there was a perpetual coming and going, though no one ever seemed to be in a hurry . . . (p. 13)

But at times the adult narrator and the preterite tense come between us and a direct presentation, and the voice of the adult Camara Laye superimposes his interpretation on the boyhood experiences:

Ah what was the right path for me? Did I know yet where that path
lay? My perplexity was as boundless as the sky, and mine was a sky,
alas, without any stars . . . . I entered into my mother's hut, which at
that time was mine also, and went to bed at once. (p. 20)

Camara Laye cannot seriously pretend that these thoughts went through
the young boy's mind on this occasion. Surely, this is the mature Camara
Laye expressing the much later dilemma of choosing between a traditional
and a cosmopolitan life.

The difference between the two points of view can be seen even more
clearly in his treatment of magic. In the early scene describing the magical
snake there is no note of apology for its magical qualities or the supernatural.
The reader is held spellbound by Mamadou's account of his meeting with
the snake, and no embarrassing questions are asked about its truth. But
this is because the episode is narrated from the point of view of the young
boy, and the more worldly-wise adult does not interpose. When, however,
we come to the account of his mother's gift of magic it is clear that the
adult narrator has taken over, and the effect is different:

I hesitate to say what these powers were, and I do not wish to describe
them all. I know that what I have to tell you will perhaps be greeted
with sceptical smiles. And today, now that I come to think about them,
even I hardly know what to make of them. They seem to me incredible;
they *are* incredible. Nevertheless, I can only tell you what I saw with
my own eyes. How could I disown the testimony of my own eyes?
(p. 58)

Why this self-conscious hesitation to talk about the gift of magic when the
snake episode had been related without any apology? The reason is that the
older Camara Laye feels he has to convince one of the validity and superiority of traditional ways: if such a tough-minded and sophisticated man,
obviously susceptible to doubt, is convinced of the reality of these experiences, then they must be true. This is part of the idealizing tendency
present in the older Camara Laye's comments. When we come to the
secret of the bombax tree the adult Laye explains away a mystery which the
young Laye had taken for granted. He is still anxious to leave the impression that since he is tough and unsentimental about superstition, the
mysteries he does believe in must be valid.

Ramchand and Edwards recognize this deliberate idealizing tendency:

. . . the work's pervasive nostalgic effect is deliberately created by the

imposition of the older man's mood upon the child's experiences . . . .
Laye wishes to insinuate the same criticism of European civilization
that Rousseau and his followers made. But the trouble is not so much
that Camara Laye should use these stereotypes, as that he fails to go very
far beyond them. The cause of the failure lies, at least partly, in the
author's concern to record the doctrine and no more, rather than to
evoke a life in excess of the doctrine but in which that doctrine might
be explicit.*

There is an irritating nostalgia associated with the older Laye's comments:
'But we were singing! Ah! how happy we were in those days!' There is
nothing inherently wrong in nostalgia about a way of life which one valued,
but it is quite another matter to ascribe its passing to the impact of Westernization, growing technology, or progress. These factors may well be
responsible for the disappearance of traditional civilization, but the fact
must be demonstrated; it is not enough just to say so. However, as Ramchand and Edwards suggest, this is all that Camara Laye does. The following passages are instructive:

> That past is, however, still quite near: it was only yesterday. But the
> world rolls on, the world changes, my own world perhaps more rapidly
> than anyone's; so that it appears as if we are ceasing to be what we were,
> and that truly we are no longer what we were, and that we were not
> exactly ourselves even at the time when these miracles took place
> before our eyes. Yes the world rolls on and changes. (pp. 62–63)

And again:

> But at the moment of writing, is there any part of the rite that still
> remains?
> The secret . . . . Do we still have secrets? (p. 92)

Critics like Gerald Moore,† have been led to lament the passing of a
'vanishing world so rich in dignity and human values' and to deplore the
formality, sterility, and fragmentation of modern Western society as
contrasted with the innocence of Laye's, by vague comments such as the
above, not by any imaginative or factual demonstration. When we look at
the actual details of Laye's society we wonder whether idealization has
not taken over from reality.

* Ramchand and Edwards, op. cit., p. 42.
† Moore, G., *Seven African Writers*, Oxford University Press, London, 1962,
p. 26.

Some of my students, in a recent tutorial discussion, knowing perfectly the implications of the term 'romance', used it in connection with *The African Child*. The entire work seemed unrealistic to them. This nostalgic picture of peasant soul-harmony and noble savagery, uncorrupted by the vices of modern technological society seemed alien to their own experience of life in Africa. They did not just object to Laye's idealization; they questioned his sincerity. These charges should be taken seriously.

The picture of school life in Chapter VI flagrantly contradicts the impression of a lyrically happy childhood and a united and happy community, given elsewhere. At the school there is nothing but cruelty, exploitation, irresponsibility, and incompetence; jungle law prevails at Kourousa School, where the older boys beat up the younger; the parent of one of the younger boys beats up his aggressor; Camara Laye's father beats up not only his son's aggressor, but the headmaster as well, in the presence of his boys and staff.

Could Camara Laye's childhood have been as happy in Kourousa as he suggests, with such a stern mother, rigidly insisting on table manners, and searching her son's hut at night to see whether he is sleeping with girls? How is it that Camara Laye consistently manages to escape the punishment handed out to the children at Tindican who neglect their duty? Surely his childhood has been idealized, for example in the stereotyped 'happy' picture on page thirty-six; 'Then more or less reassured, she would take my hand, and we would walk to the village, and with my hands in theirs we would all – my granny, my uncle and myself – make our entry into the village.'

In spite of his idealization of village life, Camara Laye does not really want to make his future there. There is a curious contradiction reflected in some of his own comments. During his childhood visit to Tindican Camara Laye is nostalgic about the loincloths of his playmates, wishing that he did not have to go about in a townsman's shirt and shorts:

So I would have gladly given up those schoolboy garments which were only suitable for town wear; and, in fact, I would very soon have discarded them if I had had anything else to put on, but those were the only clothes I had with me, and no others were given to me; ... (p. 42)

Having earlier expressed a preference for his playmates' loincloths Laye wishes to discard his schoolboy's clothes; but he does not do so even though a loincloth is one of the easiest things to improvise. Similarly, impressed by the peasant harmony he sees at Tindican, he thinks about becoming a farmer like the rest of his relations, but later he expresses the

general contempt for workers prevalent in his society: 'Now I was ambitious. But I would never realize my ambitions by becoming a manual
worker; I had no more respect than most people for such workers.'

Camara Laye's memory of the kind of life his people lived enabled him
to recreate it with power and imagination. When he confines himself to this
territory, his art is at its best. But when he steps outside the narrative, and
attempts to superimpose a philosophy, then his weaknesses are apparent.
He resorts to stereotypes and self-conscious questioning, shattering the
impression of immediacy. He starts stating instead of demonstrating, for
instance:

> Our husbandmen were singing, and as they sang, they reaped; they were
> singing in chorus, and reaping in unison: their voices and their gestures
> were all harmonious, and in harmony; they were one! – united by the
> same task, united by the same song. They were bound to one another,
> united by the same soul: each and everyone was tasting the delight,
> savouring the common pleasure of accomplishing a common task. (p. 51)

In this passage, the reapers remain very distant from us; Camara Laye
tells us about the sense of community; he does not show us.

It is generally agreed that the second section of the novel about life in
Conakry is inferior to the first. This is probably inevitable, since the author
can no longer draw on traditional society for inspiration. The deterioration
in quality partly reflects the effect on the boy of being uprooted and
transplanted. In the first section the picture of a stable society gave coherence, but now the narrative becomes a string of episodes. Statement
replaces demonstration more obviously than ever, and idealization and self-
conscious commentary become paramount. Finally, the point of view is
most confused. Look at the three episodes constituting the second section.
First, his description of his first sight of the sea:

> And then, I saw a sea . . . .
> I saw it all of a sudden at the end of an avenue. I stood a long time
> looking at its vastness, watching the waves that kept rolling in after one
> another and finally were broken against the red rocks of the shore.
> Far off there appeared, in spite of the mist that hung around them,
> some very green-looking islands. It seemed to me the most astonishing
> spectacle I had ever seen; from the train, at night, I had only glimpsed
> what it was like; I had formed no idea of the vastness of the ocean, and
> even less of its movement, of the kind of irresistible fascination which
> comes from its inexhaustibly endless movement. Now that the whole

spectacle lay before me it was only with difficulty that I dragged myself away from it. (p. 124)

Here statement makes do for imaginative presentation, Camara Laye does not manage to create a sense of wonder, and those of his fellow-townsmen who had also never seen the sea would get no idea of what it is like from this description. We also see the now-habitual stock-phrases and clichés – 'astonishing spectacle,' the 'vastness of the ocean,' 'irresistible fascination' and 'inexhaustibly endless movement.'

The love affair with Marie takes the process of idealization to its furthest extreme. This is an exemplary affair with no sinister motives; they were never tempted and they never fell:

> My uncle would leave his gramophone and records for us, and Marie and I would dance. Of course we would dance very circumspectly: ... Need I say that, in our shyness, we desired nothing better? But would we have danced together if it had been customary to dance in one another's arms? I hardly know what we would have done. I think we would have abstained, although, like all Africans, we have dancing in our blood.
>
> But we did not only dance. Marie would take her exercise-books out of her satchel and ask me to help her . . . .
>
> Marie loved me, and I loved her, but we never gave the sweet, the awful name 'love' to what we felt. And maybe it was not exactly love, though there was something of that in it. What was it? What could it be? It was certainly something big, something noble: a marvellous tenderness, and an immense happiness. I mean unalloyed happiness, a pure happiness, a happiness still untroubled by desire. (pp. 135–36)

Laye resorts to empty stock-phrase and clichés – 'marvellous tenderness,' 'immense happiness,' 'unalloyed happiness' and 'pure happiness' to demonstrate the strength of his love.

Finally there is the death of Check, whose illness it appears is completely stereotyped. The sense of urgency, the anxiety, and pain it must have caused his relatives and friends, who included Camara Laye himself, are hardly enacted. Instead we are told about the relays at the bedside and that: 'all we could do was to take Check's hands in ours and press them hard so that he would not feel all alone in his pain, and say to him, There, Check! . . . There! . . . Be brave . . . it will pass.' The deathbed scene recalls similar scenes in the novels of Dickens: Check first drops into a deep sleep, his face wreathed with smiles; then he wakes up and begins to dictate his last wishes telling those present to whom they should give his banjo, to whom his books and so on; then his voice grows fainter, he says his final good-bye and dies, true to form, as the dispensary clock strikes twelve: imagination and inspiration both seem to have deserted Laye. He resorts to negative ways of expressing feelings and emotions: 'I feel as if I were living through those days and nights again and I do not believe I have ever spent more wretched ones.' Or: 'It seems to me that there was nothing, in all those years, to surpass it; nothing in all those years of exile that meant more to me.' Or: 'Oh! it was a terrible parting! I do not like to think of it.'

I have tried to show at some length the weaknesses of *The African Child*. This does not mean that it has no virtues or that I have been blind to them. Traditional life and values are powerfully evoked, and Camara Laye's stern mother, and indulgent and compassionate father skilfully drawn. These give the work a peculiar charm. But we should not be blind to its flaws – the over-idealization, confused point of view, the propensity for assertion, rather than demonstration, the self-conscious questions and comments, and the addiction to clichés, stock-phrases, and stereotypes, all of them associated with Camara Laye's attempt to impose a philosophy which he has not substantiated.

▼▼▼▼▼▼▼▼▼▼▼▼▼▼▼▼▼▼▼▼▼▼▼▼▼▼▼▼▼▼

THE RADIANCE OF THE KING

CAMARA LAYE'S *The Radiance of The King* richly deserves world-wide acclamation. A work of compelling power and unusual beauty it is obviously the product of a superb intelligence and marks a great advance on *The African Child*. On a literal plane it elucidates the painful process through which the white man adjusts to the new African *status quo* in which he is no longer the boss. But there is more to this complex novel.* To get to its heart, this novel must be seen as an allegory, a visionary statement of an eternal truth. Obviously the major problem posed by such a novel is to blend the literal with the symbolic, and make

* See Brench, A. C., 'Camara Laye: Idealist and Mystic', *African Literature Today 2*, Heinemann Educational Books, 1969, pp. 11–31. He sees Clarence's story only as a quest for assimilation, and fails to appreciate the allegory.

both convincing. Laye has accomplished with brilliance a task much more difficult than any other African novelist has undertaken.

The Radiance of The King is unique in several ways. While the other early African novelists – Achebe and Ekwensi – follow the traditions of their immediate imperialist masters, Camara Laye has based his work not on French authors, but on the Czechoslovak novelist, Franz Kafka. The form of *The Radiance of The King*, like that of Kafka's novels, is the quest – the search for identity, self-realization, and self-fulfilment. Also, to Laye's credit, at this early stage in the development of the African novel, he makes a clean break from stock themes: the clash between the old and the new; the decay of traditional life and values; the impact of westernization; the progress of urbanization, and the evils of colonialism. We have already seen this preoccupation in Achebe's novels. It was probably inevitable, since the early African novelists were on the whole members of an intellectual élite particularly conscious of the changes taking place in their society. Naturally the African novel has needed its period of infancy. But it must grow up, and abandon its sociological preoccupations in favour of such fundamental human problems as love, death, temptation, sin, guilt, and self-sacrifice – the stuff of personal relationships. Signs of such maturity have appeared only recently, but Camara Laye pointed the way as early as 1956 with *The Radiance of The King*, a novel which deals with the individual and his quest for salvation and purification. Laye's novel can properly be described as metaphysical rather than sociological.

The Radiance of The King is also unique among African novels in having a white man as its hero. Camara Laye, reversing the process of most of his compatriots, shows the white man at the mercy of black men, lost and bewildered in a culture that he does not understand. The choice of a white man as hero eminently suits the novel's allegorical purpose, for Clarence's plight is no longer purely African and local; his quest for salvation and purification is applicable to the whole human race. Clarence, in fact, is everyman.

Even an allegorical novel must be interesting and meaningful on a literal plane, although a literal interpretation may not exhaust its meaning. Consequently, I shall begin this discussion of the novel by giving a literal interpretation. Clarence, the European, has to discover that once he has crossed into an independent African state, he is no longer the boss, and his colour gives him no advantages. He has to redefine his position relative to the confident people of Aziana, accept their customs, live like them, and become one of them; he must be completely stripped of his European personality.

The choice of Kafka as a model was perhaps inevitable. The theme of adjustment and growth towards self-knowledge, necessarily involves initial bewilderment and isolation. In Kafka's novels nameless individuals, at the mercy of hostile forces, struggle for identity. Groping their way painfully, they come not only to understand their surroundings, but also to self-knowledge.

The Radiance of The King reproduces most of the features of Kafka's novels. Like Kafka's heroes, Clarence is a puzzle. All we know about him is that he is white, has lost all his possessions through gambling, and is now determined to retrieve his fortunes by begging for the King's favour. However, Clarence has not fully realized the change in his situation, and behaves initially with the arrogance normally associated with a white man in more prosperous circumstances. He expects his colour to influence the King to grant him an immediate audience, and when the beggar says, 'young man do you think the King receives just anybody?' he replies: 'I am not "just anybody", I am a white man.' Only after a rebuff does Clarence really begin to grasp the change in his circumstances. But he has a long way to go before achieving full humility, for he still considers himself superior to the blacks, and is appalled at the beggar's 'impertinence' when he offers to intercede with the King on his behalf:

'A fine advertisement you would be!' thought Clarence. If the guards were going to stop him, a white man, from approaching the King, with all the more reason they would stop this black man in his disgusting rags from addressing him. The man was obviously nothing more than an old fool.*

In this Clarence demonstrates not only conceit, but also ignorance of local custom, which accords the beggar a position of privilege denied to others.

From now on, however, the painful growth towards self-knowledge and adjustment begins. In the face of his growing isolation, bewilderment, and helplessness (all of them recurrent themes in Kafka's novels) Clarence is forced to acknowledge the beggar's cunning and superiority, and accepts his offer to intercede with the King on his behalf. When that fails, he entrusts himself to his care in the long journey to the south.

The growth towards self-knowledge is in three stages, corresponding to the three sections of the novel. At the start Clarence's arrogance is obvious, but as the section progresses, he realizes that he is little better than an out-cast, cast off by his country-men, ignored by the indigenous people, and increasingly dependent on, of all people, a beggar, for sustenance and pro-

* Laye, C., *The Radiance of the King*, trans. Kirkup, J., Fontana, 1970, pp. 12–13. All further page references are to this edition.

tection. In the second section Clarence discovers that in spite of his lofty
aspirations, he is nothing but a sensual animal, wallowing more and more
deeply in lust. Finally, in the third section, Clarence fully realizes the kind
of person he is, and has become, and in abject humility he prostrates him
self at the feet of the King. The exposition of bewilderment, isolation, and
subsequent enlightenment and assimilation, also follows three stages. In
the first section Clarence is increasingly mystified by an environment which
is not only incomprehensible, but also overpowering. In the second section
he begins to grope his way to an understanding of his surroundings and of
what has been done to him. In the final section Clarence is no longer bewildered; he knows.

The note of isolation, bewilderment, and estrangement is struck very
early in that magnificent first chapter:

> He made very slow progress. The black people whom he was shoving
> aside made no protest, but neither did they make any effort to clear a path
> for him: they seemed to be unaware of his presence, or pretended to be;
> and Clarence would find himself held up for minutes on end by some
> strapping torso round which it seemed impossible to work his way, or
> wedged as if in a vice between two great hips. At such moments it seemed
> to him as if he was trapped in this crowd as in a liquid that had suddenly
> congealed, or in a slowly-shifting sand, and he felt unable to breathe, or
> maybe he was simply falling asleep. An odour of warm wool and oil, a
> herd-like odour that seemed to dull the senses into a kind of trance,
> emanated from these men packed tightly together under the African
> sky. (p. 7)

This passage, which reminds one of some of the best things in the novels of
D. H. Lawrence, is most brilliantly executed. It gives a glimpse of Camara
Laye's power, and mastery of his art, of his great intelligence, and sensitivity. So much of the novel's meaning and atmosphere is compressed into
it. The scene comes to life largely because of the wealth of detail and the
liveliness and appropriateness of the imagery: the strapping torso, and the
powerful visual and tactile image of Clarence 'wedged as in a vice between
two great hips'. One almost feels their force! The sense of utter helplessness
even of asphyxiation, is most vividly conveyed in the images of Clarence
caught in congealing liquid or in slowly shifting sand, insignificant and
alien. This is the reversal of the colonial situation where Clarence's presence
would have been acknowledged immediately because of his colour.
Clarence has to learn some lessons in humility, among others that he is only
one member of ordinary, frail humanity, subject to the same passions as

other human beings, and that to exist at all, he will have to adjust to his new situation.

The oppressive force of everything is evident in this novel. Clarence's senses, and ours, are subjected to a barrage of impressions – to the heat, the sun, the dust, the crowd, the odour of the forest, and the shapes of women. The novel is rich in sensuous images and Clarence will eventually succumb to their lure. For the moment he experiences nothing worse than torpor:

> He felt at the end of his strength; his patience was running out. Those cries, and this argument on top of everything! He stopped his ears: he did not want to hear anything more. He shut his eyes, too, so that he would not see the vultures. But the screams went on echoing through the very depths of his being, and although his eyes were shut, he could still see the vultures, he could see the King's hands, he could see the knife, he could see the blood spurting from the victims' gaping necks, he could smell the odour of blood, and he could taste this odour on his lips, the taste of blood, a little sugary, a little insipid, as if his own lips or his gums had begun to bleed . . . No! . . . as if it were his own blood spurting up into his mouth from his slit throat! . . . He spat; he felt sick . . . He was shaking more than ever. In an attempt to stop his shaking, he let his head fall on the heads of the two boys; but then a heavy fetid smell rose from them, strong and overpowering, and he felt he was going to faint, he was actually fainting . . . He was suddenly jolted out of this state of torpor: the two boys were pulling at his arms. (p. 35)

In this passage Clarence is not only at the mercy of his enemies, but also of his imagination and all his senses – sight, taste, hearing, and smell. The reader is treated to a detailed account of Clarence's thought processes, and of the impressions floating through his mind. It is another mark of Laye's artistic skill that the story emanates from Clarence's consciousness, so that we are forced to empathize with him through every scene, as we must, to see him painfully groping towards self knowledge and enlightenment.

The note of isolation is also struck early in the novel:

> 'Alone!' he thought. 'I am alone!' And he forced himself not to shout. 'Are you still there?' he asked.
> 'We have not stirred an inch from your side,' replied the two boys.
> 'No, I see you haven't,' thought Clarence. 'But what are you? Two kids! Two kids, that's all! . . . I am alone, just as much alone as when the white hotel-keeper showed me the door.' (p. 38)

The more Clarence gets into company and loses himself in the crowd, the more surely does his isolation increase. On the very next page he exclaims 'each time I find myself a little more alone'. His isolation is intensified by the atmosphere of impenetrable mystery. Clarence does not understand the meaning of the sacrificial paintings on the walls of the palace and the screams of terror he thinks he hears. The boys' explanation merely deepens the sense of mystery. Their very names, Nagoa and Noaga, and their seemingly interchangeable identities, plunge Clarence into even greater confusion. Then, there is the mystifying affair of the coat. Clarence, who had been forced to give the inn-keeper his coat in lieu of payment of his hotel bills is now accused of having stolen the coat again, and the beggar, who could certainly vouch for his innocence, completely lets him down. His isolation, bewilderment, and persecution are most convincingly dramatized in the hall of justice, which is the most Kafkaesque of all the scenes that Camara Laye has created in this novel. The novels of Kafka, particularly *The Trial*, have accustomed us to the enormous hall of justice with the isolated, but innocent prisoner confronting a prejudiced judge at the opposite end. The element of injustice, which is central to Kafka's work, is also present in *The Radiance of The King*. It had already occurred in that first scene, where the strong giants at the front of the crowd forced the smaller and weaker men to the back: in an unjust world men do not get their deserts and the best they can hope for are favours. Here, in the hall of justice, injustice is even more explicit:

> The corridor was narrow and as tortuous as the alleys of the town, but it was extraordinarily quiet, and a great number of doors gave on to it at one point or another. All these doors were ornamented with illegible and pretentious inscriptions – at least, they appeared to be pretentious, for Clarence could only judge by their great length and by their elaborately-formed characters; but these indications were enough, more than enough; they were more eloquent than if the characters were decipherable. It was obvious that these wordy inscriptions and the great number of doorways belonged to a building used for administrative purposes. They made one think of an army of scribes bent over tables or desks, furiously scribbling away in registers or composing forms to be filled in quadruplicate. The doors, of course, remained stubbornly closed, but the very last one, at the end of the corridor, opened as if by its own accord, to admit the little procession. Clarence found himself in a vast hall, vaster than any he had seen since he landed on these shores. At the far end of the hall, a man crouched over a table was telling his beads. This man stared at Clarence a long while.

'So this is the culprit,' he said at last.

'I am not guilty!' cried Clarence.

The man raised his hand.

'They all say that when they're brought here. You can't *think* how sick I am of hearing it! . . . The great thing is that you are here, and that no time has been lost in catching up with you . . . And this person,' he said, pointing to the beggar, 'who may you be?'

'His accomplice,' said the inn-keeper.

'I was not addressing you,' the man said. 'You will speak when you are spoken to. And so far there's no reason to suspect – no reason at all, mark you – that I shall want to speak to you. I shall interrogate you if I see the need for it . . . Well, who is this person?' he asked again.

'It is the beggar who was with the white man,' replied the guard with the girdle round his tunic. 'I thought I would be doing right in bringing him along.'

'You have done well to bring him to me,' said the man. 'He shall act as a witness to the crime.'

'Sir . . .' began Clarence.

'Address me as "my lord president",' ordered the judge.

'My lord president,' said Clarence, 'this man, who is a beggar, has not left my side all evening. He will tell you that I gave my coat to the inn-keeper in payment for the debts I incurred at his hotel, and that at no time have I regained possession of the coat.'

'No! No!' said the judge. 'This man,' he went on pointing to the beggar, 'is here as witness for the prosecution; you cannot transform him into a witness for the defence. It would be against the law . . . you must find some other . . .'

'But what do you expect me to find?' interrupted Clarence.

'The coat, my man, the coat!' said the judge. 'That's all we're asking of you.'

'The inn-keeper's got it,' Clarence replied.

'Come, now!' the judge protested. 'Think well before you speak. Why should the inn-keeper have run all that way after you, if you hadn't taken the coat from him? . . .' (pp. 74–75)

Camara Laye packs in not only resentment against the perversion of justice, but also against the inefficiency of the entire bureaucratic process. Corridors, which abound in Kafka's work, are used here to express man's bewilderment in a hostile world, and the tortuous and seemingly unending process of justice. Significantly, the corridors lead nowhere, and Clarence is later to feel that he was to dash through the same rooms and corridors again and again. Similarly, the filth and debris he sees along the corridors as he dashes for freedom, symbolize the corruption of justice in Adrame.

When Clarence escapes from the hall of justice, he is pursued by the guards in another nightmarish, Kafkaesque passage, in which the great hands of the guards, grown suddenly enormous, reach out to seize him. Escaping once again, his confusion deepens when he is led into a room only to find his friends – the beggar and the two boys – in company with the judge, who turns out to be the father of the woman who helped him to escape. However, he recovers his coat and the long trek to the south commences.

The dominant impression of the south is one of drugged languor. It is important to realize that in this section Clarence completely loses both his original personality and his will. Clarence, once the proud and arrogant European, is now without any power of choice, and has to be borne along by the two boys, literally a man in a dream. The journey to the south is an essential part of the process of adjustment; it marks the transition between Clarence's early arrogance and the readiness with which he later settles down to African life. If he is to be assimilated to village life, and play his new rôle unquestioningly, both his European personality and his will must be eroded. In a sense, the journey through the forest represents a process of initiation.* Certainly the ritualistic overtones of Clarence's wandering in circles around the forest, making no progress, put one in mind of the initiation practices of several societies. In the forest Clarence is completely subdued and paralysed by his surroundings:

> Yes, perhaps this inferno of the senses is everywhere. Clarence suspects it is true, he has a presentiment of bondage; he senses, rather than feels it, but already he is in a state of subjection. He dozes; and in spite of himself the perfumes of the forest are working within him, the poisonous bloom is opening slowly. There is a slackness in the muscles of his legs and in his spirit, while the rest of his body – but he won't admit it, even to himself . . . Perhaps if the clearing were a little broader . . . But Clarence had no sooner taken a breath of fresh air than the clearing had been passed; and again the green tunnel of the forest opens and swallows him up. And the sea stretches away, the musty smells of earth and the poisonous smells of flowers roll endlessly towards him, and he feels the unthinkable fire stirring again in his loins . . . (p. 100)

The odour of the south plays a very important part in the dissolution of Clarence's original personality, and his assimilation into his new environ-

---

* Brench, loc. cit., p. 21.

ment, since it induces a state of perpetual torpor, and physical and spiritual laxness. The odour is interesting in another way. Under its influence Clarence not only abandons himself to his environment, but also senses that 'indefinable something' that 'unthinkable fire stirring in his loins'. Clearly then, the odour of the south is associated with sexuality. That it arouses sexual desire is made more explicit in Aziana where, under its influence, Clarence demonstrates the most remarkable sexual prowess. We have already seen him humiliated, isolated, persecuted, and bewildered. Now we see him drifting into the very last stages of degradation and animalistic sexual indulgence.

Clarence's drift into sexual indulgence is linked quite smoothly with the theme of assimilation and adjustment. There are few sexual inhibitions in Azianan society.* To become fully assimilated, Clarence must shed the northern reticence about sex. The journey through the forest prepares him for this, as well as for the sexual rôle he is to play at the Naba's court. Significantly one of the passages demonstrating Clarence's transformation in Aziana, begins with a reference to his heightened sexuality:

> 'You have Akissi now,' said the boys.
> They laughed, and Samba Baloum laughed too; they were laughing as if the joke they had made were in the very best of taste . . . 'Yes, I have Akissi . . .' Clarence said to himself. '. . . changeable as she is; I have a different Akissi every night.'
> He puffed fitfully at his pipe. His thoughts began to dwell on his past life. If anyone who had known him in those days could have seen him now, smoking and drinking, crouching in the manner of black men under the arcade, and dressed in a *boubou* like a black man, he would have appeared quite unrecognizable. (p. 159)

In Aziana, Clarence's complete loss of personality and freedom of choice is most convincingly registered when the beggar sells him to the Naba, as if he were just a possession, to be used for breeding mulattoes in the harem. Although faintly aware that something is wrong, Clarence does not immediately realize that he is being used for the most sinister ends. That Akissi seems to be a different woman each night, he attributes to her sexual skill. However, through the Master of Ceremonies' imprudence, Clarence realizes the truth of his position, and consciousness of guilt replaces his obsession with sex. Recognizing now that he is as degraded and sinful as any, he can only wait patiently for the coming of the King, in the hope that in spite of his unworthiness, he will be taken into his service.

* See Brench, loc. cit., p. 17.

Clarence has come quite a long way in the process of self-knowledge and adjustment. From the superior, arrogant European of the first chapter, he has come to realize his kinship with ordinary humanity around him. The process of change is fully documented, and in particular it is signalized by a number of important events. The first is Clarence's open confession (p. 48) that the beggar knows the customs of the land better than he does, indicating that he is willing to be educated about local lore and custom. A little later (p. 49) he is prepared to imitate the beggar's table manners. Earlier, he had been contemptuous of the beggar throwing his bones about on the floor, but quite unconsciously Clarence himself extracts a bone from his mouth, and holds it in his hand: 'is it any better to keep it in one's hand and then to put one's fingers in the pot? He abruptly threw away the bone on the rest of the rubbish littering the floor.' Next we see him (quite consciously this time) imitating the beggar's movements while drinking. Then having vowed to have palm-wine with every meal (pp. 58–59) he unreservedly entrusts himself to the beggar and asks him to guide him on the journey to the south. Next the beggar suggests that he should give his jacket to the inn-keeper in lieu of payment (p. 63). This is significant, for the beggar is compelling him to dress like the natives, or, in other words, to modify his European personality: 'Where we are going, it is not necessary to wear such complicated garments, and if you gave some of them up, you would at once be dressed in a style suited to the country you're in.' In Aziana he is ready to perform the tasks normally performed by men: 'but when the cotton had finally been transformed into great hanks of coarse thread, he had begun to work, for at that moment it had been man's work: he had woven the cotton, and had even become expert at it.' Finally, Clarence himself realizes that he has become like a black man in a *boubou*, though he detests this person he has become.

It is important to grasp that clothes are symbols of assimilation. When Clarence agrees to give the inn-keeper his clothes, he indicates his willingness to change, while the *boubou* he adopts indicates his complete transformation. But clothes are also symbols of morality and personality. The inn-keeper's ill-fitting jacket, filched from Clarence, exposes his pretentiousness and cupidity; Clarence's tawdry saffron *boubou*, with its pattern of red roses reflects his sordid new rôle, just as his delight in appearing in the nude reveals his moral decadence. Finally, the Naba indicates his displeasure and his assessment of Clarence's character, by offering him a green *boubou* with a pattern of pink flowers.

This interpretation is interesting but not completely satisfactory. In the first place it takes no account of the third section of the novel where Clarence, increasingly guilt-ridden, waits for the arrival of the King.

It also ignores the important fact that although Clarence is assimilated, he detests the kind of man he has become. For instance, during the Master of Ceremonies' punishment, just as he is becoming fully integrated, he is once more reminded that he is different, and reacts with the strongest revulsion to the natives' cruelty, calling them 'nothing but savages'.

There are still a number of important problems unresolved in our discussion. Why is the figure of the King shrouded in so much mystery? Why does no one know exactly when the King will come? Why does the beggar say that the south is everywhere? Why is the beggar, in Clarence's imagination, brought up short each day against a wall of thorns, from which he just as ritualistically retraces his steps? Why does Nagoa urge Clarence not to mention their lies in the forest? Why does the beggar say that there are many paths through the forest, though Clarence is incapable of seeing them? What is the significance of Dioki, and what does Clarence's vision of the King's departure mean? Why does the forest open up in front of the King as he moves towards the south? These, and certain other passages clearly invite a symbolic rather than a literal interpretation. Look at: 'but he knows what he really wants, which is to be able to sleep until *the day of deliverance*, until the day the King comes on a visitation to his vassals in the south' (my italics). (p. 103) The literal and allegorical interpretations of the novel are not necessarily mutually exclusive. On the allegorical level, Clarence's quest is not merely for self-knowledge and adjustment, but for God. For ultimately, the novel is about sin, temptation, grace, redemption, and salvation. Many of the apparent problems disappear once one realizes that the king is God.

> 'Will the King be here soon?' asked Clarence.
> 'He will be here at the appointed time,' answered the black man.
> 'What time will that be?' asked Clarence.
> 'I've just told you: at the appointed time.'
> 'Yes I know. But exactly what time will that be?'
> 'The King knows!' replied the black man. (p. 10)

If we think in terms of *the second coming* the religious overtones of phrases like 'the appointed time' and 'the King knows' should be obvious. They are even more explicit in the third section. Perhaps I am stretching the point, considering that Camara Laye is not a Christian but a Muslim, but one cannot help being reminded of the biblical references to Christ's second coming, the exact timing of which is equally obscure.

The exact nature of the King is just as mysterious as the time of his arrival; significantly, no one can find words to describe him. Here is the beggar's attempt:

> 'The King . . . But how could anyone fail to recognize the King! . . . He is . . .'
> 'He was at a loss for words. Perhaps he realized that here are no words to express what the King is.
> 'He is . . .' the beggar began again.
> But a sound of drums and trumpets drowned his voice. (p. 17)

On his arrival, the King is announced as the 'King of Kings'. He is dressed in white – the symbol of purity – and gold, the symbol of royalty; and the dancers spread out in the pattern of a star around him. Again I would suggest that there are explicit associations with the Christian story, specifically the birth of God the Son, the 'King of Kings'. Clarence had expected the King to be a magnificent personage, just as the Jewish elders had expected a magnificent Messiah, but when the King appears he is a slender, painfully young adolescent:

> But it was his fragility that was most striking; it was even more striking than his youth, and painfully so. One wondered how the King, such a slender boy, could bear the weight of all those bracelets, why his arms were not broken by such a load; and one understood that he could not have taken a single step without the support of his pages. He was so extraordinarily frail that he seemed utterly defenceless – yes, defenceless, in spite of his innumerable pages and drummers and trumpeters, in spite of the superb warriors who had ridden so proudly before him, in spite of the reverence of the immense crowd that stood all round him. (p. 21)

The beggar informs us later that although the King is young and frail, he is at the same time very old and very strong. Only if we recognize that the King is part of the God-head and in a sense transcends all barriers, can we reconcile the paradoxes which a completely literal translation does not account for. The beggar also says that the King, who was not intended 'for the likes of us', is only kept captive down here by the weight of gold. But he explains that gold is regarded as a sign of love: 'that is the sort of gold that holds the King a prisoner, and that is why his arms are so heavily laden.'

The features of the King are obviously Christ-like:

> As for the features of the King . . . It seemed as if there could be nothing to say about those features: they were regular, and, apart from an almost

imperceptible smile that hovered round the lips, they were quite impas-
sive. But was it really a smile that played round the lips? Was it not
rather . . . And Clarence was afraid to pursue the thought: it was the sort
of smile which one sees on the faces of idols – remote, enigmatic – and
which is composed perhaps as much of disdain as of benevolence; the
reflection of an inner life, no doubt, but – what sort of inner life? Perhaps
of that very life which lies beyond death . . . 'Can that be the sort of life I
have come here to find?' wondered Clarence, Yes, perhaps it was that
life. 'When all is lost, and everything departs out of our hands . . .' (p. 22)

It is amazing how the features of the King resemble the features of the
Christ on several medieval paintings – regular, remote, enigmatic, impas-
sive. Certainly, to Clarence's eyes, the King's appearance is God-like, with
intimations of immortality, 'that very life which lies beyond death'. A
literal interpretation can make no sense of the comment about finding a life
'when all is lost and everything departs out of our hands'. But on an
allegorical level Clarence is wondering whether he is not seeking ultimate
peace with God.

There is plenty of evidence that the King is not an earthly King, but the
heavenly one. Clarence is the abject, ordinary man, his misery emphasized
because he was once prosperous and proud. Now, stripped of all his
worldly goods, but for his clothes, which he will shortly lose too, he realizes
in a flash of insight that the only life which holds out a ray of hope is a
spiritual life, in the service of God. He *must* be taken into the service of the
King. Thus Laye stresses the ordinary man's need for God in a hazardous
world.

But Clarence discovers that it is not so easy to gain access to the King, or
to enter into his service. Before heavenly peace can be attained, he must
triumph over sin and temptation, repent, confess, and eventually achieve
redemption and salvation. At the end of the first scene, Clarence is still very
far from his goal, and the King disappears for an unpredictable length of
time. Characteristically, no one knows when he will return. But in the
meantime Clarence must prepare himself to be acceptable to the King on
his second coming. Hence the significance of the arduous journey through
the forest.

The importance of the beggar in the novel's pattern must not be overlooked. On a literal level he is clearly an old rogue, a cantankerous and arrogant liar. He may be useful, but his lechery and ability to wheedle money
and food out of people remind one of Chaucer's Pardoner and Summoner.
But on the allegorical level he is Clarence's spiritual mentor, and one of the
means of access to the King. He also seems to have supernatural powers

with his ability to read people's minds. He points out Clarence's spiritual blindness when he remarks that although there are paths through the forest, Clarence is unable to see them. The beggar occupies a position which is both culturally and spiritually privileged. Most religions accord positions of privilege to beggars and small children. In the biblical parable the beggar Lazarus is taken into Abraham's bosom, and the rich man pleads with 'Father Abraham' to send Lazarus to dip his finger in water and cool his tongue. Christ's statement – 'suffer little children to come unto me and forbid them not, for of such is the kingdom of heaven' – is also explicit on this point. To Clarence's credit he is kind to the little boys Nagoa and Noaga, who are eventually taken into the King's service; and significantly at the end, it is they who urge Clarence with meaningful looks to advance into the presence of the King. Appropriately, the beggar and the boys guide Clarence through the forest.

The journey through the forest represents not only initiation, but also preparation for entry into the service of the King. It can even be regarded as an allegorical presentation of man's spiritual life, for it symbolizes the entanglements, difficulties, and frustrations that must be encountered and overcome before heavenly peace can be attained. In the course of the religious life it is essential not to evade these difficulties, but to meet them head-on and surmount them:

> What he means is, he would like to sleep far longer than any one night, he would like to sleep a whole day and a whole night, or two days and two nights, perhaps even longer . . . Who knows? . . . But *he* knows what he really wants, which is to be able to sleep until the day of deliverance, until the day the King comes on a visitation to his vassals in the South.
>
> But perhaps that is exactly the sort of favour which cannot be granted if one sleeps all the time. Perhaps it is a favour which can only be granted after one has wandered for a long time in the forest. And perhaps it is not even a real favour, since it has to be paid for. (p. 103)

Clarence clearly wants to have his cake and eat it. He wants to achieve heavenly peace and be taken into the service of God, but at the same time he wants to live a life of spiritual inactivity. However, access to God's presence comes only after strenuous toil and stoical endurance in the forest of life. The wall of thorns is a concrete symbol of the obstacles which have to be encountered and overcome, and the beggar's practice of inspecting it every day, is a demonstration of what is expected of the ordinary man.

Much more important, however, the individual must meet and resist temptation. The journey through the forest is an endurance test of Clarence's ability to surmount difficulties and resist temptation. The seductive, alluring odour of the south, with its mingling of a thousand perfumes, invites the individual to abandon himself to a riot of the senses:

> However, the odour fascinated him at first, for it is not the crowd's herd-like odour, and it is not just an odour of decaying vegetation; it is subtlety itself, a seductive perfume, or rather the seductive mingling of a thousand perfumes, almost too many perfumes, yes far too many perfumes, all of them far too heady, disturbing, caressing, far too . . . But how can he express it? Clarence hardly knows whether he ought to say it . . . He makes a compromise, and says, under his breath: 'far too delectable'.
> It's not quite the right word, but it has some of the quality he wants, and it is certainly the right word to describe the outermost reaches of this perfumed gulf that is like a real sea: . . . an ocean with its own currents and its secret tributaries, an ocean that nourishes its hidden life with the breath of flowers and the exhalations of the fermenting earth. Yes, it is like a ferment! A fermentation and an insistent calling, an eternal rising of sap and that most irresistible of all appealing invitations, the appeal of flower-pollen! . . . the forest, where everything attracts and is attracted, where everything is split open like a ripe fruit bursting with warm and heavy juices, where everything opens itself to every other thing, where everything is penetrated by everything else. (pp. 98–99)

The Keatsian sensuousness of the passage with its perfumery, fermentation, flower-pollen, and the eternal rising of sap, extols the voluptuous luxuriance of the forest. But this luxuriance is related to corruption and decadence, associated with decaying vegetation and complete abandonment. The sensual temptation of the forest is undoubtedly strong, and the beggar's remark that the south is everywhere, points to the universal presence of temptation, and the need for spiritual alertness.

Does Clarence's emergence from the forest suggest that he has resisted the power of temptation and is now ready for the arrival of the King? All the indications are that the forest does not really end at Aziana, which is merely intended to be a pause. But Clarence deliberately chooses to remain in Aziana rather than go on wandering through the forest. In doing so he is taking the soft option already indicated in his wish to sleep until the day of deliverance. The Master of Ceremonies, who has a crucial rôle to play in the novel, as we shall see shortly, says very succinctly to Clarence: 'If you had continued your journey, you would have something to show for it

today – feet bruised with treacherous roots, and hands torn by cruel
thorns. Nothing much, I grant you; these are small things. But you haven't
even that to show – not the smallest scratch or bruise: you have no claim to
any kind of merit.' Clarence ought to have persevered in the journey
through the forest: consequently, his decision to stay in Aziana represents
not a triumph over temptation, but a capitulation. Inevitably, Clarence
drifts further into sexual indulgence and bestiality, and becomes nothing
but a stud. The Master of Ceremonies, spiteful, arrogant, and contemptuous though he is, is the voice of religious orthodoxy, upbraiding Clarence
for his laziness and pointing out his unworthiness to meet the King.

Nevertheless, in spite of his descent into sin, the foundations are being
laid for Clarence's eventual redemption. In the first place, he is really
morally superior to most of the people he comes across in Aziana. It must
not be supposed that Camara Laye idealizes Aziana simply because it is a
traditional African society, even though Clarence's assimilation into it is
necessary on both the literal and allegorical planes. The entire village displays the most appalling cruelty during the Master of Ceremonies' punishment; the Naba is a scheming and vindictive old man, and his government
is immoral; the women are promiscuous, and even Samba Baloum, the
most genial and easy-going member of this community, can be vindictive
and cruel. The villagers of Aziana are very much like the rest of us – poor
and sinful. Among them, Clarence's magnanimity is outstanding; he is
generally considerate towards Akissi, kind to the two boys, and is the only
one who shows some pity for the Master of Ceremonies, although the latter
characteristically repays him with contempt and abuse.

Secondly, Clarence reveals a capacity for contrition, in that, even before
he becomes fully aware of what he is being used for, he is full of a sense of
guilt:

> There were nights, those nights when the odour of the forest filled the
> hut, when he *was* simply a foul, filthy stallion . . . One day, the King
> would come and sit under the arcade, he would come and sit in the very
> place where they were sitting now, fragile and pure, and strong with a
> strength that was drawn from that purity, so indescribably pure, so
> rare! . . . Clarence heaved a sigh . . . Could a stallion approach the
> King? . . . He sighed again . . . Oh, how long these days of waiting
> seemed, waiting for the King's coming! And how heavy! These days were
> a great void, and a terrible burden; they were . . . One couldn't say what
> they were . . . They were messy and glutinously filthy . . . Would the
> King be able to see anything else but this filth? He would see nothing but
> the filth, the foulness, and he would draw in disgust, he . . . (pp. 165–6)

Finally when Clarence realizes the nature of his services to the Naba, he reacts with tremendous revulsion. Sick with guilt, he wonders whether the King will not turn away from such an unclean beast, and he even longs for death. But the forces of temptation are not so easily beaten. Clarence is still aware of the omnipresence of the odour – the symbol of temptation – as it grows denser and stronger; 'this odour lies upon me like a winding-sheet'. At this stage he sees the *manatees*, or fish-women, in the river. The appearance of the fish-women shows that sexuality continues to tempt Clarence powerfully. He momentarily succumbs to the odour, forgets his revulsion, and swims towards the fish-women. For a few agonizing moments it seems as if Clarence is going to succumb completely and finally be overpowered: 'Clarence had fallen with his face flat in this fetid mess, and he breathed in the poison through his mouth as well as his nostrils. He tried to rise, but the efforts he made seemed to suck him even further down into the hotbed of putrefying leaves.' However, by a sudden tremendous effort of will, he fights free from the temptation of the odour and the fish-women, and the triumph is finally his:

If Clarence had at first been attracted and at the same time revolted by these ambiguous creatures, it was now only revulsion he felt for them, all the more so since the fish-women had interrupted their peaceful grazing and were staring fixedly at him as he went gliding by. He felt a kind of awful anguish at the thought that some unconsidered movement might cause him to brush, in passing, against the glittering opulence of those dead white breasts. . . .

Clarence tried to fight against the current. But was it any use now? The water no longer had the same density; it was now a sort of mud that sucked in the feet – a gluey clarts from which it became easier and easier to lift the feet; a sort of pitch or bituminous substance that was as heavy as lead. . . .

Clarence kept his arms pressed tightly against his sides. In this way perhaps he would be able to glide past without brushing against them. But almost immediately he had to abandon this rather feeble hope; the corridor had become so ridiculously narrow, and the fish-women were obtruding their great pointed tits with such a shameless lack of decorum that he could not help brushing against them.

He began to fight against the mud and the current again; but this time the fish-women took his despairing efforts very badly. Their calling voices became more imperious and they seemed barely able to keep a note of irritated impatience out of their cries; moreover, they were thrusting out their breasts at him with an even greater lack of decorum than before. . . . He uttered a loud cry, he made a supreme effort, and disengaged his feet so forcibly from the mud and the current that he felt a great shock, a curious feeling, as if, in falling, he had struck the very bottom of the river, the pebbly bed of the stream itself. (pp. 223–5)

Clarence's initial attraction now changes into complete revulsion against sexuality, and the fish-women's breasts now become 'dead white breasts'. Once Clarence feels this revulsion, it becomes easier for him to lift his feet out of the gluey clarts, which represent the last attempt of sexuality and corruption to engulf him. The fish-women, symbols of sexuality themselves, are determined to claim Clarence for their own; but with one supreme effort Clarence breaks through to final freedom.

Having triumphed at last over the forces of temptation, Clarence is still conscious of the sinfulness of his former life, and he now thinks of the King as the only means of deliverance. In his desperate need for assurance, he calls on Dioki for news about the exact time of the King's second coming. The Dioki episode is one of the scenes in the novel to which some readers react with revulsion. There seems to be some justification for the view that in his handling of the occult and macabre Camara Laye shows some lack of restraint, witness his accounts of the Master of Ceremonies' punishment, Clarence's encounter with the fish-women and Dioki's encounter with the snakes. Many readers are likely to be repelled by the picture of an ageless woman apparently having intercourse with snakes. However, the Dioki episode has its importance. In the first place it finally cures Clarence's lechery. The loathsome spectacle of 'the ignoble fumblings and penetrations', 'orgiastic writhings and groanings' of an old woman and her serpents, nauseates Clarence beyond bearing. Secondly, Dioki is a sort of prophet-figure, forecasting the exact time of the King's second coming. On a literal level this episode is not credible. Both Dioki's sexual experience with the snakes, and Clarence's vision of the King's departure for the South are improbable.

After Clarence's vision at Dioki's, he meets the blacksmith, Diallo, who is also an important element in the allegorical pattern of the novel.

The blacksmith, who has always been highly regarded in Camara Laye's society, features prominently in the whole of his work. In this novel, Diallo is presented as the most religiously sincere and perceptive person in Aziana. Where the Master of Ceremonies is the voice of religious orthodoxy, the concept of Divine grace and forgiveness is present in Diallo's religious philosophy. Shortly before Clarence paid his visit to Dioki's, he had called on Diallo, who during the short interview, expressed essential religious truths. Talking about the King's second coming he had said:

'It's like this: we are waiting for him. Every day and every hour we wait for him. But we also get weary of the waiting. And it is when we are most weary that he comes to us. Or we call to him – every moment we are calling him; but however hard we try, we do not call to him all the time – we keep forgetting to call to him; we are distracted for a fraction of a second – and suddenly he appears, he chooses that very fraction of a second in which to make his appearance . . .'

'Will your axe be ready by the time he comes?' asked Clarence.

'Probably,' Diallo replied. 'Anyhow, I hope it will be. But what is an axe? I have forged thousands of them, and this one will undoubtedly be the finest of them all; the others will have been no more than experiments I made in order to forge this one perfect axe. So that this will be the sum of everything I have ever learnt; it will be like my life, and all the effort I have made to live it well. But what does the King want with an axe? . . . he will accept it and admire it only in order to give me pleasure . . . Yet I go on forging it . . . Perhaps I can do nothing else, perhaps I am like a tree . . . And perhaps, in spite of having so many faults . . . in spite of everything, the King will give me credit for my goodwill . . .' (pp 210–11)

Diallo is expressing man's unworthiness and unpreparedness for God. His statement that God comes to us not in our moments of strength and prosperity, but of weakness and adversity will prove true in Clarence's own situation. Diallo's industry and patient devotion are meant to be contrasted with Clarence's earlier idleness. Unlike Clarence he spends the period of preparation making an axe for the King which will be the culmination of his life's work, the sum of all his professional experience.

Now, after the vision at Dioki's, Clarence has another interview with Diallo. Earlier, he had been despondent because, in his vision, the King's eyes seemed to be turned inward hardly noticing him. But during this second interview he is encouraged by Diallo's simple faith, and he prepares for the arrival of the King in a mood of exhilaration and rapture. However, the Master of Ceremonies dampens his enthusiasm by reciting a long catalogue of his misdeeds, convincing Clarence of his unworthiness to meet the King. When Clarence suggests that the King might give him credit for his goodwill in spite of his unworthiness, the Master of Ceremonies replies: 'What use is your goodwill to you if you never make use of it? Only those who deserve it are allowed to have access to the King.' Orthodox though he is, the Master of Ceremonies errs because he is unaware of the change that has taken place in Clarence, through his repentance. He also ignores the importance of 'goodwill' and the power of Divine grace.

E

At this stage one should perhaps consider the importance of favours, which are mentioned so often in the novel as the King's special gift. Although Samba Baloum refers to them as 'luck', the more perceptive Diallo is probably closer to the truth with 'pity'. 'Favour' is nothing less than Divine grace, which is defined in doctrinal terms as 'that which God grants to us unmerited'. The Master of Ceremonies seems unaware of the concept of grace, and does not believe that the King grants favours to the undeserving.

For the time being Clarence is convinced that the Master of Ceremonies is right, and that the King could not possibly see such a foul stallion, a mere cock. He is conscious of his unworthiness more than ever, and decides to stay in his hut, instead of taking the opportunity of going up to meet the King. 'Don't you understand', he says to Akissi, 'I am impure.' Nagoa's and Noaga's 'fecundity mime' only reminds Clarence all the more of his recent indulgence in indecent orgies. When the boys come and question him about his reluctance to present himself to the King, he replies: 'Can you not smell the odour that clings to me?' Echoing the Master of Ceremonies, whose religious position he has now completely accepted, he remarks: 'Everyone according to his merit. Everyone has the fate he deserves'. Like the Master of Ceremonies, he ignores the concept of Divine grace. Diallo points to his error when he says, 'An axe, Clarence, a simple axe, that is all I possess.' The worldly Samba Baloum, in his brusque way states the true religious position even more explicitly: 'If all those who present themselves to the King had to be worthy of him, the King would live alone in the desert.'

And so the King arrives. Although Clarence is urged by the boys to approach, he is so dazzled by the King's fragility, strength, and immaculate purity, and so conscious of his own bestiality, that he cannot bring himself to go up to him. Yet he is now more contrite and repentant than he has ever been:

'And yet . . . My goodwill . . .' he thought. 'It is not true that I was lacking in goodwill . . . I was weak, no one has ever been as weak as I am; and at nights, I was like a lustful beast . . . Yet, I did not enjoy my weakness, I did not love the beast that was inside me. . . .'

But at that very moment the King turned his head, turned it imperceptibly, and his glance fell upon Clarence. That look was neither cold, nor hostile. That look . . . Did it not seem to call to him?

'Alas, lord, I have only my goodwill,' murmured Clarence, 'and it is very weak! But you cannot accept it. My goodwill condemns me: there is no virtue in it.'

Still the King did not turn his eyes away. And his eyes . . . In spite of everything, his eyes seemed to be calling . . . Then, suddenly, Clarence went up to him. . . .

He went forward and he had no garment upon his nakedness . . . And that look . . . That look still did not turn away from him. 'My lord! My lord!' Clarence kept whispering, 'is it true that you are calling me? Is it true that the odour which is upon me does not offend you and does not make you turn away in horror?' . . .

'Yes no one is as base as I, as naked as I,' he thought. 'And you, lord, you are willing to rest your eyes upon me!' Or was it because of his very nakedness? . . . 'Because of your very nakedness!' the look seemed to say. 'That terrifying void that is within you and which opens to receive me; your hunger which calls to my hunger; your very baseness which did not exist until I gave it leave; and the great shame you feel . . .'

But presumably he had still not come quite near enough; probably he was still too timid, for the King opened his arms to him. And as he opened his arms his mantle fell away from him, and revealed his slender adolescent torso. On this torso, in the midnight of this slender body there appeared – at the centre, but not quite at the centre . . . a little to the right – there appeared a faint beating that was making the flesh tremble. It was this beating, this faintly-beating pulse which was calling! It was this fire that sent its tongue of flame into his limbs, and this radiance that blazed upon him. It was this love that enveloped him.

'Did you not know that I was waiting for you?' asked the King.

And Clarence placed his lips upon the faint and yet tremendous beating of that heart. Then the King slowly closed his arms around him, and his great mantle swept about him, and enveloped him for ever. (pp. 282–4)

The religious overtones in this very important passage should be obvious. Significantly, it is when Clarence is most conscious of his weakness and unworthiness, that God calls to him, and he goes abject, naked, stripped of all his possessions, and aware of his baseness. But the King grants him pardon and grace. Indeed, he welcomes him precisely because of the baseness and nakedness, and envelops him in his love for ever. The final picture of the King is not unlike the figure of Christ on a number of icons; certainly paintings of Christ with a flaming heart are familiar features in Catholic societies.

The Radiance of The King celebrates profound religious truths. Whether the final movement is meant to suggest Clarence's eventual death, when he is taken into God's bosom and enveloped in his love for ever, is not completely clear. What is certain, however, is that after a life of sin and guilt,

Clarence, the representative of everyman, is granted grace and pardon, redeemed, and enveloped in God's love. Camara Laye pursues his allegorical theme at every point with consummate skill, so that every episode, almost every statement has a bearing. The blending of the literal with the allegorical also deserves praise. The theme of assimilation is properly part of the higher allegorical theme, for Clarence, in adjusting himself to life in Aziana, sinful as it is, is being forced to recognize his kinship with sinful humanity. The literal interpretation, far from being an alternative, reinforces the truer, allegorical meaning. Tribute must also be paid to Laye's superb descriptive skill, which can bring the forest, Clarence's apparently drunken reveries during the journey through the forest, Dioki's orgy with the snakes or Clarence's experiences with the fish-women completely to life. This for instance, is an account of the beggar drinking:

> He looked at the old man's neck: in front, between his chest and his chin, there was like a skein of slack strings – muscles, nerves, sinews, God knows what – and whenever the beggar threw back his head to drink, the skin which only an instant before had been dangling rather dismally was suddenly tightly stretched, and the Adam's apple would give a great jump. It kept jumping at every mouthful, running joyfully to greet it and accompanying it all the way, guiding it into the right channels, and then rushing back to greet the next arrival. (p. 53)

The technique is cinematic – the close-ups magnifying every detail. The concentration on detail is also applied to Clarence's thoughts, giving us superb passages of interior monologue.

The Radiance of The King is a rare achievement. Camara Laye has demonstrated metaphysical and religious truths with brilliance, but also drawn a concrete and powerful picture of a society.

4: Elechi Amadi

▼▼▼▼▼▼▼▼▼▼▼▼▼▼▼▼▼▼▼▼▼▼▼▼▼▼▼▼▼▼▼

THE CONCUBINE

ALTHOUGH many readers applaud Elechi Amadi's *The Concubine*, quite a few have grave reservations about the novel. While praising the novelist's presentation of his society and his powers of characterization, they are unable to accept his portrayal of the supernatural. They compare him with Hardy, and deplore his attempt to attribute responsibility to the gods, when their experience shows that the motivations of conduct and the agents of destiny are strictly sociological. On the other hand, I have met many students who frankly admitted that of all the African novels they have read, *The Concubine* was the only one they could respond to fully, because it presented an almost exact copy of village life as they knew it. This conflict of opinion presents a very interesting problem. On the one hand, the strictures against the novel are honest and serious, and have to be seriously considered; but on the other hand, one has to be careful about denigrating a work which elicits such a powerful response, precisely because of its especial relevance to people's lives. I rather suspect that some people condemn the novel as a reflex action, simply because they do not believe in the supernatural at all, and not because of any stylistic defect. I intend to show why I feel Amadi's achievement is significant, paying attention to his treatment of the supernatural.

The Concubine is a powerful love story, written with effortless ease, in lucid and beautiful prose. The author examines the problems of young love and of man's relationship with the gods, and presents a society whose stability rests on tradition and the worship of the gods. It is not difficult to see why many students feel that the novel reflects the life of their villages. For, of all African novels, including those of Achebe, Amadi's *The Concubine* conveys most truthfully the quality of life not just in one particular region, but of most African societies. The activities he describes – daily excursions to the farm, setting traps for hunting, singing and dancing in the evenings, the effortless musical improvisation, the marriage customs, divinations, and fear of the gods – are all integral to numerous African villages. Here is a description of an evening dance:

> For a time they moved round and round swaying to the rhythm in a half-stoop. Suddenly the soloist stopped and the instruments took over completely. No one talked, not even the old men who sat around the arena on their three-legged chairs. This was the time to know the top dancers. Everyone bent low. Faces were as rigid as masks. The men moved their backs and shoulders but the women moved only their waists and every bit of their energy seemed to be concentrated there. The vibrations were extremely rapid. It was admirable how they maintained the rhythm at such high speeds. For several seconds tension was at fever pitch. Then one by one the men straightened out and watched the women admiringly. They danced so well. It was difficult to choose between them. Adiele belaboured the short high-pitched end of his oduma, Mmam caressed the crazy edge of his female drum with his crooked fingers, and the women nearly sobbed with enthusiasm. At last the deepest okwo beat out a peculiar sequence and the instruments came to a neat and abrupt stop.*

We saw in our study of Achebe that descriptions of sociological phenomena can become tedious, unless they are relevant and handled with great skill. In this novel there are numerous descriptions of sacrifices, dances, and even cooking processes, but they are handled so competently that they hardly attract attention as sociological data. They are always subservient to some larger concern. For instance, when Madume consults the *dibia Anyika*, and subsequently collects the various items for the sacrifice, we are much more aware of the young man's fear of death and his anxiety to placate the gods, than of the phenomenon of sacrifice. In describing the cooking at Ihuoma's mother's home, the sociological detail is introduced casually:

> There are certain critical moments in the preparation of soup when constant attention is vital for a good result. This was what kept Okachi in the kitchen behind the house when Ihuoma arrived. Ihuoma did not wait for her to appear but went to the kitchen with her youngest child. (p. 46)

The conversation which follows between mother and daughter leads quite naturally to comments on the soup and to a description of the cooking process:

---

* Amadi, E., *The Concubine*, African Writers Series, Heinemann Educational Books, 1966, pp. 35–36. All further page references are to this edition.

At last vegetables went in, closely followed by okro and a delicate species of mushroom reputed to taste like chicken. Other condiments followed, in their proper order. An expert knowledge of this order was necessary for real success in soup making, and every mother made sure that her daughter understood it thoroughly. Experience had shown that it was no good putting all the items in at once and letting them boil for the same length of time. Some melted on prolonged heating; others lost their taste or even acquired a positively nauseating taste. On the other hand meat and other items required prolonged boiling to bring out their taste and soften their texture. Timing therefore was most important. At this Okachi excelled and Ihuoma took after her.

'Nne, where did you get this mushroom? It is a long time since I tasted it last. This soup will be really tasty.'

'Chikwe the hunter brought some back from the forest. You will take some back with you.'

'Indeed I must. It is so rare. I wonder why we hardly ever see it at Omokachi.'

'Well, your men don't go far enough into the forest.'

'They do. Ekwueme is a good trapper, for instance.'

'Yes and he is good in many things. He sings so well. I rather like him.' (pp. 47–48)

The description of the cooking modulates quite easily into the comments on the mushroom and this in its turn leads unobtrusively to the mention of Ekwueme, who is Amadi's real concern in the passage. Through techniques such as this we get a credible picture of Omakachi society, without the novel seeming to be just a sociological document.

However, Amadi's main concern in this novel is not the presentation of Omakachi society, powerful though his portrayal is, but the story of the life and loves of Ihuoma; in particular her relationship with Ekwueme, and the terrible fate which the gods have ordained for her. Ihuoma, who is admired by all in the village, loses her first husband, the popular and exemplary Emenike, a few years after their marriage. Then Madume, the blustering village bully, presses his unwelcome attentions on her, is blinded by a spitting cobra when he tries to steal plantains from her farm, and commits suicide. But Amadi reserves much of his narrative skill and psychological insight for the treatment of the next phase of Ihuoma's fortunes – the relationship with Ekwueme. Ekwueme, who has been pampered and spoilt by his mother, falls in love with Ihuoma, but his parents force him to marry the childish Ahurole, to whom he had been betrothed from an early age. The marriage ends in disaster, and everyone now consents to Ekwueme's marriage to Ihuoma, who had played a major rôle in curing his madness. However, the *dibia* reveals that this marriage too will end in disaster, for Ihuoma used to be the wife of the powerful sea-god, and against the wishes of her husband, sought reincarnation, and came to live among human beings. Although the sea-god was furious, he agreed to allow her to live her human span, reserving his vengeance instead for any man who dared to make advances to her, or marry her. It is revealed that this was the cause of Emenike's and Madume's deaths. Since Ekwueme is determined to go ahead with the marriage, his parents consult another *dibia* who promises to bind the sea-god and make him powerless. However, in the process of collecting the items for the sacrifice which would bring this about, Ekwueme is killed by an arrow shot by Ihuoma's little son.

The creation of perfect or near-perfect characters is a task of considerable difficulty, which Amadi has undertaken with great success. Ihuoma's goodness, politeness, courage, chastity, modesty, good sense, selflessness, and beauty, are not only commented on but demonstrated. We actually see her selfless efforts to cure Ekwueme; her good sense in deciding to visit Ekwueme's young wife Ahurole in spite of everything; her concern for decency in warning the ardent Ekwueme that his attentions might expose both of them to scandal; her polite and tactful response to Wigwe's unreasonable visit and proposal. If we have any complaints about Ihuoma, it is not that her perfection is not demonstrated, but that she is too good to be true. Amadi, who is himself aware of the difficulty, attributes her perfection to her being a sea-goddess.

Although Ihuoma is the heroine, Ekwueme is the centre of the novel, and the study of his character demonstrates Amadi's keen psychological insight and knowledge of human nature. We see a lot more of Ekwueme than of the other men in the novel, but he never really strikes one as a forceful young man, even though everyone is agreed about his exemplary character. Although he is about twenty-five, he has an air of immaturity, an impression which is later confirmed by information about his early life. Ekwueme's character and attitudes are readily understood if one realizes that he is a *mother's boy*, who measures other women against the standards set by his mother, and wishes, subconsciously, to marry a woman like his mother.

Ekwueme had been an only child for twelve years, petted and spoilt by his mother. To prevent him getting hurt she discouraged him from all masculine activities, keeping him constantly in her company. Here are the roots of those rather feminine characteristics, and that indifference to women which appear more openly in his later life:

In his early years Ekwe was often jeered at by his fellow boys because he was slow and clumsy and could not do many of the things which boys in his age group could do. He could not make thatches, he was poor with bows and arrows; he was well beaten in the few fights he was ever involved in; he could not wrestle. Each time he came home crying, Wigwe would try to send him back into the streets to fight it out, but Adaku's pleading always prevailed. She was sure the child was not weak. It was because he was growing too fast. One day he would be able to beat back his assailants. Wigwe accused his wife of trying to make a woman out of a man. She in turn accused him of setting too high a standard for a very young child. She pointed out to Wigwe's amusement that at Ekwe's age he himself could not even walk, let alone talk of wrestling and fighting. (p. 171)

The admiration for his mother is so strong that even when Ekwueme begins to take an interest in more masculine activities, it is purely in order to please her.

Ekwueme grew to be good in many things. But all his efforts were directed towards pleasing his mother, to justify her confidence in him. He valued her praise more than anything else. His relationship with his father was cordial but he preferred his mother's company to his father's. He would sit in the kitchen with her after his trapping and watch her cook. He would chat with her for hours in the evening while his father dozed off by his lonely fire in the reception hall. (p. 172)

Men who show such devotion for their mothers tend to have difficulty in forming lasting relationships with other women, for they are always comparing their girl friends and wives with their mothers. Ekwueme is never sexually aroused by girls, although there must have been several beautiful ones in the village. The only woman he ever has any sexual feelings for is Ihuoma, who, although she is only about twenty-three, behaves like a much older woman. Ihuoma is, in fact, rather motherly, and it is obvious that Ekwueme's ideal is a 'mother figure'.

However, he reluctantly marries Ahurole, since his parents have chosen her for him. From the start this match is doomed to disaster, because both, in spite of their ages, are just overgrown adolescents. Ahurole, a peevish, moody girl, bursts into tears at the slightest opportunity, the result, it is believed, of having a bad *agwu*:

Wonuma soothed her daughter, but not without some trouble. Ahurole had unconsciously been looking for a chance to cry. For the past year or so her frequent unprovoked sobbing had disturbed her mother. When asked why she cried, she either sobbed the more or tried to quarrel with everybody at once. She was otherwise very intelligent and dutiful. Between her weeping sessions she was cheerful, even boisterous, and her practical jokes were a bane on the lives of her friends, particularly Titi. But though intelligent, Ahurole could sometimes take alarmingly irrational lines of argument and refuse to listen to any contrary views, at least for a time. From all this her parents easily guessed that she was being unduly influenced by agwu, her personal spirit. (p. 128)

Marriage changes neither Ekwueme nor Ahurole. *He* continues to be 'mother's boy', and expects every day to get the food at the bottom of his mother's pot. *She* continues her crying fits and nags her husband into uncontrollable fury. Their moments of happy domesticity are characterized by childish pranks. When smoke from her fire worries Ahurole, she employs a childish charm to drive it away:

'Ah, it is annoyed with me,' she said.

'No, it likes you,' her husband retorted.

'I shall drive it towards you again.'

'Let's see you do it.'

'I shall employ a charm I used to know when I was a child,' Ahurole said smiling.

'And what are you now?'

'An old woman of course.'

'Fine. Go ahead with your charm, anyway.'

Ahurole cleared her throat. 'You see,' she said, 'it is in the form of a song.'

'Go on,' Ekwueme urged. She half sang, half said the incantation.

> 'Smoke go, go away,
> Smoke go, go away,
> I haven't got your broken pot,
> Ekwe has your broken pot;
> Smoke please go to him.'

'That is exactly what my little sister does when the smoke worries her,' Ekwueme said. (pp. 174–5)

In a happier mood she wrestles energetically in the bedroom with her husband, amidst tumbling chairs. This is a marriage of two immature people, both lacking in tact, and unwilling to make compromises. Ahurole needs a

man who is capable of handling difficult women, and Ekwueme needs a
woman who is capable of looking after men:

> Ahurole expected far more gentleness than her husband could give. On
> the other hand Ekwueme's ideal wife was a composed stable woman who
> could get on without too much help from him. More, he wanted a
> woman who would not only receive praise and encouragement but also
> give them in return; a mature woman, soothing and loving. A woman
> who would act for him in an emergency if he were away. A woman . . . a
> woman . . . well, something like his mother. (pp. 179–80)

Ihuoma of course is such a woman and, with his marriage on the brink
of failure, Ekwueme turns increasingly to her. Inevitably Ahurole's jealousy is aroused, and on the advice of her mother she gives Ekwueme a love
potion which makes him insane. The scenes describing Ekwueme's madness are some of the most powerful in the novel. The pace of the narrative
visibly quickens, conveying the suspense, the misery of Ekwueme's parents
– Adaku and Wigwe – and Ahurole's agonizing sense of guilt. We also feel
the village's helpless paralysis at the prospect of losing a good young
man – the third in two years. Amadi has also captured accurately and convincingly the workings of a madman's mind, without resorting to grotesque
sensationalism, melodrama or the macabre:

> 'What about your traps, Ekwe?' he asked.
> 'Doing fine.'
> 'It doesn't look as if you have inspected them for some time.' Ekwueme
> laughed outright. His father was terribly shocked.
> 'What are you laughing at?' he asked timidly. His son looked at him
> and laughed still more.
> 'Ekwueme!' Laughter greeted his call.
> 'Ekwueme!!' His son only laughed more loudly.
> Wigwe turned round and sought for his wife. She had gone to the
> farm. He was nearly frantic. He went back to take another look at his son.
> He was still in his room, lying on his bed quietly. A contented smile,
> the remnant of the laughter that had frightened his father, still played on
> his face. He was facing the wall and gesticulating with his fingers,
> oblivious of his father's presence. He was mumbling to himself but much
> like someone having an interesting *téte-à-téte* with someone else. (p. 215)

Under Ihuoma's influence, however, Ekwueme is eventually cured. He
divorces Ahurole, and resumes the love affair with Ihuoma with everyone's

approval. In spite of Ekwueme's immaturity, Amadi treats this love affair as beautiful and good, and it accounts for some of the most effective and tender passages in the novel. Here, for instance, is Ekwueme's first attempt to declare his love:

'Greet Nkechi and the new baby when you get back,' Ihuoma said a little nervously and turned back into the house.

'Ihuoma!'

She turned and faced him.

'I have something important to say to you.'

'Say on.'

'Let us go into your sitting-room.'

'Why not here?'

'Too many sand flies.'

Ihuoma led the way into her sitting-room. Nwonna came and sat beside her. Ekwueme sat opposite, his arms folded across his breast. For a moment he eyed Nwonna and fidgeted uneasily.

'Nwonna, go and warm the soup in the kitchen,' Ihuoma ordered.

'Ihuoma,' Ekwueme began, 'I really don't know how to begin.'

She kept quiet. Looking at her well-scrubbed floor. Ekwueme's perplexity grew. He began to trace figures on the floor with the point of his knife.

'You are digging up my floor,' Ihuoma protested.

'You can always scrub it again.'

'I have other things to do.' She did not smile.

There was another pause, a little more uncomfortable than the first. Ekwueme felt that somehow the woman sitting in front of him had suddenly grown a little detached. And yet she was just the same. She did not press him to unburden his mind. She just sat there quiet and contemplative. He played on for an opening.

'I like your ways,' Ekwueme began again.

She said nothing.

'You understand me, don't you?'

Still no answer.

'Ihuoma, are you ignoring me?'

'No, I am listening.'

'But you say nothing.'

'You haven't said much yourself.'

'I have more to say.'

'Go on.'

Ekwueme studied her for a moment. It appeared her mind was far away. But there was no knowing since she looked down and her long eye-lashes completely obscured what the lids failed to cover. Ekwueme thought that perhaps sitting beside her might help him make his point. He made up his mind to cross over to her. As he drew in one leg prepara-tory to rising, Ihuoma raised her head and looked at him fully in the face. He winced, then tried to smile but failed. His attempt to talk ended in a stammer. Clumsily he stretched out his hand to hold her but in his con-fusion he misjudged the distance and his hands failed to reach her. (pp. 59–60)

This passage perfectly describes the fumbling attempts of an immature and sensitive young man to express his love for a woman he really considers superior. The lyrical quality of their relationship after Ekwueme's madness is itself a hint that it cannot last; it is too idyllic and the all-power-ful sea-god's vengeance in having Ekwueme accidentally killed by an arrow, is a logical, not an illogical climax.

This brings us to a discussion of the rôle of the supernatural. First, one or two preliminary points. We should not judge works dealing with the supernatural by our own personal feelings about its rationality or scientific basis. Secondly, an author is open to criticism if he brings in the super-natural as an easy way to round off a story which he cannot conclude satis-factorily; or if, after demonstrating that certain events are caused by social factors, he contradicts himself by bringing in the supernatural. This would be superimposing an unproven supposition.

The supernatural does have a place in literature, but the novelist must show that the events cannot be entirely explained by social, or other factors; secondly, he must persuade the reader to suspend his disbelief. This implies that in order to determine whether certain things could happen in a novel, we must look for the answer, not to the scientist, philo-sopher or social anthropologist, but to the resources available to the novelist. The question must be whether he has convinced us of the reality of the incidents he is describing or the world he is presenting. Does Amadi manage to do this?

First, can events in the novel all be explained by social or scientific factors? It would be a simple way out to say that Emenike, Ihuoma's hus-band, dies, not through the malevolence of the gods, but of lock-chest, the consequence of the fight with Madume. But Elechi Amadi is much more skilful than some of his critics give him credit for. He has deliberately left a question mark hanging over the circumstances of Emenike's death. Emenike does not die after the fight; indeed he recovers completely from the illness which follows it, and, with profound shock one learns of his

death at the start of chapter five. The mystery surrounding his death is
powerfully conveyed. Here is part of a conversation between Ihuoma and
her mother:

> 'Kaka, do you think that that fight caused his death?' Ihuoma asked in
> an undertone.
> 'What else caused it?'
> 'I thought it was "lock-chest".'
> 'But what brought about the lock-chest?'
> 'He worked too hard in the rain.'
> 'Was that the first time he had worked under the rain? No my child,
> we know what happened to him. Amadioha will kill them one by one.'
> (p. 27)

So even the inhabitants of Omochaki are puzzled about the causes of
Emenike's death. Similarly, Madume apparently meets his fate by being
blinded by a spitting cobra, but isn't it rather a coincidence that the cobra
is there at precisely the moment when Madume tries to cut down the bunch
of plantains? Why does no spitting cobra attack Ihuoma when she cuts
down *her* bunch of plantains? Why do spitting cobras attack no one else? If
Amadi had attributed Madume's death to the spitting cobra and left it at
that, it would have been a crude device to get him out of the way, and few
sensitive readers would have accepted it. Actually, Madume's death has
been carefully prepared for. We see him cutting his toe when attempting
to make advances to Ihuoma, and we are also informed that several spirits
swore to kill him there and then. Even before Anyika's explanation about
the sea-king's hostility, we already have more than a faint suspicion that
Madume's death is connected with his attitude to Ihuoma.

Finally, it is difficult to see what social forces are responsible for
Ekwueme's death. It can be explained as an accident. But Amadi is enough
of an artist not to contrive a mere accident at this stage, which would appear
as a crude attempt to impose a tragic conclusion to finish off the novel. It is
too coincidental that Nwonna should release his arrow just as Ekwueme
leaves Ihuoma's room. Also, we were prepared in the previous few pages
for Ekwueme's doom. During the discussion of the sacrifice, Ekwueme
knew that he was fighting for his life; we saw the wave of despair that swept
over him; and even the lyrical conversation with Ihuoma forbodes the
end:

> 'Ekwe, I am sorry about all this trouble on my behalf,' she said.
> Ekwueme suppressed his fears and put on a more cheerful expression.
> 'Just tonight and then we shall be married.'
> 'Yes.' (p. 275)

After this, Ekwueme's death does not come as a surprise; it is a logical climax. A successful outcome to the sacrifice, and a conclusion showing the couple living happily ever after, would have been an anticlimax. Sometimes it is said that Amadi 'kills' Ekwueme prematurely, to avoid the technical problems involved in capturing the sea-god. But Amadi knows that the sea-god's power would be all the more forcefully demonstrated, if he kills Ekwueme even while the latter is making plans to bind him.

Amadi forces us to suspend our disbelief by using so much detail in his supernatural scenes that he gives the illusion of truth. During the various divination scenes, for instance, one's attention is so engrossed by the cowries chasing each other across the floor, by the anxiety shown by the *dibia*'s clients, by the urgency of the superb dialogue, and by the *dibia*'s own movements, that one does not question the scientific or rational validity of the process. Let us take an example:

> Anyika cast his cowries to and fro for some time. Then he chewed some alligator pepper and spat it out in a fine spray in front of his temple. Madume watched him keenly, wondering what pronouncements he had up his sleeve. He thought himself clever to have come to Anyika to know the true story behind what he thought of as his toe disaster. He had not been mistaken. The gods were behind it. It was certainly a premonition.
>
> 'You were lucky,' Anyika said slowly, 'to have come out alive from Emenike's compound.'
>
> 'Ojukwu forbid!' Madume stammered.
>
> 'Several spirits swore to kill you there and then.' . . .
>
> 'What is to be done, dibia?'
>
> 'There will be several sacrifices to appease Emenike's father and his train.' . . .
>
> 'Let me know the various items involved in the sacrifice.'
>
> 'Here they are: seven grains of alligator pepper, seven manillas, an old basket, three cowries, a bunch of unripe palm fruit, two cobs of maize, a small bunch of plantains, some dried fish, two cocks, one of which must be white, seven eggs, some camwood, chalk, a tortoise (or the shell) and a chameleon.'
>
> 'Hei, this is a costly sacrifice. Can we not omit a few items?'
>
> (pp. 74–75)

The use of detail is impressive; we note especially the detail of the sacrifice – the palm fruit must be unripe, one of the cocks must be white, and if a tortoise is not available, its shell will do – and finally there is Madume's all too-human response. It is by using such devices that Amadi induces us to suspend our disbelief. We can do this without necessarily changing our scepticism about the existence of the supernatural. Amadi is not conducting a rational argument to prove the existence of supernatural forces. He may not even believe in the supernatural himself; there is no evidence in the novel that he does. He merely presents to us a group of people for whom the supernatural is important, and he tries to make their way of life as realistic as possible.

It now only remains to comment on a few more aspects of Amadi's technique. We have already referred to the realism of his descriptions, and his keen psychological insight. The way, for instance, in which Ekwueme vents his fury on his younger sister Nkechi, after his discomfiture at Ihuoma's house, shows great psychological understanding. Similarly, Madume's ill-tempered bullying of his wife when he is faced with the hopelessness of blindness, is plausible and convincing, and the immature Ekwueme's attempt to play the married man at every possible opportunity is exact and true to life. There are numerous human touches such as Ihuoma's reaction to Ekwueme's gift of venison, after his father's brutal treatment of her, and the old women's chatter during the second burial ceremonies for Ihuoma's husband. Elechi Amadi's prose is exhilarating, lucid and fresh, as is evident in this passage:

> Ihuoma received these attentions gracefully. She relaxed and let the gossips say what they would. At first people raised their eyebrows and whispered furtively but soon her growing intimacy with Ekwueme became a stale subject for gossip. She carried herself proudly and gracefully and a new radiant form of beauty suffused her face. (p. 249)

The plot is well-constructed, with every episode relevant and duly related to the others. The only significant weaknesses are the sudden introduction of Ahurole, and the rather sluggish pace of the first few pages. But these are small faults compared with the quality of Amadi's achievement.

5: Ayi Kwei Armah

▼▼▼▼▼▼▼▼▼▼▼▼▼▼▼▼▼▼▼▼▼▼▼▼▼▼▼▼▼

THE BEAUTYFUL ONES ARE NOT YET BORN

THE DECOLONIZATION of African Literature is already in progress. Novelists are becoming less preoccupied with cultural and sociological matters, and more concerned about exposing the corruption and incompetence which are so widespread in African political and governmental circles. Ayi Kwei Armah's first novel – *The Beautyful Ones Are Not Yet Born* – is one of the most successful results of this exercise.

The Beautyful Ones Are Not Yet Born is a symbolic moral fable. What strikes one most forcefully, is the strength of the author's moral earnestness. On almost every page, in unusually vigorous and realistic language, Armah expresses his nausea at the corruption he sees everywhere. The symbolic nature of the characters and the vagueness of the setting reinforce the impression of a moral fable. Indeed, the temptation to compare this work with *Everyman* or Bunyan's *Pilgrim's Progress* is very strong. The characters are important not for what they are in themselves, but for what they represent. Most of them are very vaguely particularized and indicated by generalized names. The hero himself is known only as 'the man', and is referred to variously as 'the watcher', 'the giver' and 'the silent one'. His immediate dependants are called 'the loved ones', and one of the most important characters is called 'the teacher'. Although Maanan, Oyo, and Koomson have names, it is clear that their function is mainly symbolic. Ghana is itself symbolically presented, one of the consequences being that Accra is much less vividly described than the Lagos of Achebe or Ekwensi. But this deliberate vagueness makes it similar to *Everyman's* 'Field Full of Folk'* or Tutuola's 'Land of the Deads'. Most of the inhabitants of the

---

* See Jones, Eldred, 'The Beautyful Ones Are Not Yet Born', *African Literature Today 3*, Heinemann Educational Books, 1969, pp. 55–57, in which he points to the similarity between the novel's setting and 'the field full of folk'.

country walk like dead men in a land which is morally and spiritually dead. The passengers in the bus are described as 'walking corpses'. Home is called the 'land of the loved ones' but there is a suggestion later that 'the loved ones are dead, and their embrace will be a welcome unto death'. Clearly, Armah sees Ghana as a land of the spiritually dead. The symbolism is strengthened by numerous religious references. During the week before pay-day (the most difficult period of the month) called 'passion week', the man himself, like Christ, is exposed to various humiliations. Maanan is often called Sister Maanan, and two characters appear briefly called Zacharias Lagos and Abednego Yamoah. There are also references to 'Jesus Wept' and 'Onward Christian Soldiers'.

Armah expresses his disgust for corruption by exploiting the potential of a central symbol – that of filth, putrefaction, and excreta. Throughout the novel the reader's nose is, so to speak, rubbed in spittle, or in the phlegm from somebody's chest or a little child's nostrils. The odours of excreta, effluvia, and vomit assault his sense of smell.

All these aspects of the novel are present in the first powerful scene in the bus. It is passion week, and the conductor knows that it will be virtually impossible for him to make large profits out of his usual corrupt practices. His passengers seem like walking corpses or sleepwalkers. The man gives him a cedi and, as usual, he gives short change. Immediately, corruption and foul smells are associated:

> The cedi lay there on the seat. Among the coins it looked strange, and for a moment the conductor thought it was ridiculous that the paper should be so much more important than the shiny metal. In the weak light inside the bus he peered closely at the markings on the note. Then a vague but persistent odour forced itself on him and he rolled the cedi up and deliberately, deeply smelled it. He had to smell it again, this time standing up and away from the public leather of the bus seat. But the smell was not his mistake. Fascinated, he breathed it slowly into his lungs. It was a most unexpected smell for something so new to have: it was a very old smell, very strong, and so very rotten that the stench itself of it came with a curious, satisfying pleasure. Strange that a man could have so many cedis pass through his hands and yet not really know their smell.*

Only when the conductor's satisfaction is tinged with shame does he turn round and notice the man staring at him. He is immediately overwhelmed

---

* Armah, A. K., *The Beautyful Ones Are Not Yet Born*, African Writers Series, Heinemann Educational Books, 1969, pp. 3–4. All further page references are to this edition.

by fear of exposure and in a desperate bid to save himself, attempts to bribe the man. Again, nauseating images suggest the repulsiveness of bribery: 'An important bargain was hanging in the air. The conductor cleared his throat and ate the phlegm.' When the conductor realizes that the man is actually sleeping rather than watching, and that his spittle is soiling the bus, a wave of indignation fills him:

> Then a savage indignation filled the conductor. For in the soft vibrating light inside the bus, he saw, running down from the left corner of the watcher's mouth, a stream of the man's spittle. Oozing freely, the oil-like liquid first entangled itself in the fingers of the watcher's left hand, underneath which it spread and touched the rusty metal lining of the seat with a dark sheen, then descended with quiet inevitability down the dirty, aged leather of the seat itself, losing itself at last in the depression made by the joint. (p. 6)

What happens in the bus is a parable of what happens in the country as a whole. The bus, like the State, is in a state of decay, its pieces only held together by rust. The passengers represent the ordinary citizens, and the driver and conductor are authority, conniving to defraud the citizens and, if caught, to bribe them into silence.

At the centre of the novel is the hero – the man – whose anonymity represents everyman, the ordinary Ghanaian citizen. He is a man of unquestioned integrity. Although he and his family are living in the most abject poverty, and he constantly has to endure the silent accusation of his wife and children, and the open hostility of his mother-in-law, yet he resolutely refuses to accept bribes and thus take the easy way out, which seems to be universally accepted in Ghana as the only way to prosperity. Nevertheless, Armah, far from idealizing his hero, demonstrates his passive impotence, and weakness. In spite of his high ideals the man could not champion an anti-corruption movement, or even explain convincingly why he refuses to accept bribes. He drifts aimlessly through a colourless life of poverty, unrelieved by any bright spot. Each day he makes the dreary journey from his loveless home through filth, slime, and insults, to his tedious job in the decaying Railway Administration Block. Far from being heroic, the man is a pathetic figure plagued by consciousness of failure. He lacks the guts to reply or defend himself even against the worst insults. Here is his encounter with the taxi driver:

> There, away from the overpowering glare of the headlights, he saw the dim outline of the taxi driver's head as it thrust itself out through the

window. For long moments of silent incredulousness the taxi driver
stared at the man, doubtless looking him up and down several times.
Then in a terrible calm voice he began, 'Uncircumcised baboon'. The
taxi driver spoke as if the words he was uttering expressed the most
banal of truths. 'Moron of a frog. If your time has come, search for
someone else to take your worthless life.'

The man took a step forward in order to be closer to the taxi driver,
and said apologetically, 'I wasn't looking. I'm sorry.'

But the apology only seemed to inflame the taxi driver's temper.
'Sorry my foot,' he said with a cutting softness in his voice. 'Next time
look where you're going.' He started his engine running again, and as the
car began to ease itself forward, he exploded in a final access of uncontrollable ire, 'Your mother's rotten cunt!' (pp. 10–11)

Several other people – the bus conductor, the merchant with the wolfish
teeth and the mother-in-law – insult the man, but he does nothing. Furthermore, he himself is conscious of his impotence and lack of will: 'I have been
walking along paths chosen for me before I had really decided.'

One might excuse all these faults if the man showed conviction and made
a resolute stand against corruption. But he is continually plagued by doubts
about the course he has chosen. Even when he rejects the temptation offered
by the timber merchant, he is unable to muster enough courage to say why
he must refuse the bribe. When one would have expected a tirade on the
evils of corruption, or at least a rebuke to the merchant for doubting his
integrity, his reply to the merchant's question, 'but what is wrong?' is a
weak 'I don't know'. He becomes increasingly conscious that the world
regards him as a fool, and there are moments when he is inclined to agree:

> For the man sitting on the desk opposite, all the cool sadness seemed able
> to do was to raise thoughts of the lonely figure finding it more and more
> difficult to justify his own honesty. How could he, when all around him
> the whole world never tired of saying there were only two types of men
> who took refuge in honesty – the cowards and the fools? Very often these
> days he was burdened with the hopeless, impotent feeling that he was
> not just one of these, but a helpless combination of the two. (p. 59)

Time and time again the man wonders whether everyone and everything
does not inevitably succumb to the power of corruption. During his walk
towards the Teacher's house, he becomes conscious of the power of night to
call every sleeping thing to itself. Suddenly he feels that he is the only one
who does not answer this call. The darkness is a moral darkness – the cor-

ruption prevalent in contemporary Ghana. And just as little lights here and there emphasize the night's power, so little spots of honesty call attention to the widespread corruption. In this scene the man is the only honest creature – 'the only thing that had no way of answering the call of the night' – everything else succumbs eventually.

> . . . and it was all the same in the end. Was there not something in the place and about the time, everything, in fact, that sought to make it painfully clear that there was too much of the unnatural in any man who imagined he could escape the inevitable decay of life and not accept the decline into final disintegration? Against the all too natural, such scruples – could they be anything but the perverse attempts of desperate hedonists to perpetuate their youth against the impending rot of age? (p. 55)

At this stage the man remembers a Ghanaian friend who had taken the name Rama Krishna. Horrified by the threat of decay he saw around him, he had withdrawn into the spiritual life, practising yoga, and living on a frugal vegetarian diet. In a frantic attempt to avoid corruption and decay, he decided never to touch a woman, but to save his semen, and rejuvenate his brain by standing on his head. In spite of his efforts, corruption and decay overtook him:

> It was of consumption that he died, so very young, but already his body inside had undergone far more decay than any living body, however old and near death, can expect to see. It was whispered – how indeed are such things ever known? – that the disease had completely eaten up the frail matter of his lungs, and that where his heart ought to have been there was only a living lot of worms gathered together tightly in the shape of a heart. (p. 56)

The man's lack of conviction about the wisdom and rightness of his stand is powerfully communicated here. He wonders whether he is not fighting an impossible battle. In striving so earnestly to avoid corruption and decay, would he not, like his friend, inevitably end up more corrupt and decayed than he had feared? This uncertainty makes him such a weak, unheroic opponent of corruption. He is no watchdog: in the bus scene, the conductor, almost paralysed with fear at being found out, discovers him drowned in the most swinish sleep. It is only towards the end, when the terrible consequences of corruption are demonstrated in Koomson's ruin, that the man feels his position finally vindicated.

The power of this novel derives partly from the consistency with which
Armah exploits the central symbol of filth to articulate his revulsion against
corruption. This alleviates the didactic quality of the novel's preoccupation
with political and social corruption. On the way to work the man passes a
waste box with the caption in bold, shiny, red capitals: KEEP YOUR
COUNTRY CLEAN BY KEEPING YOUR CITY CLEAN. Immedi-
ately the association between filth and moral squalor, cleanliness and moral
purity, is registered. Ironically, however, the box which was supposed to
symbolize the people's determination to preserve certain standards of
decency and purity, attracts the worst kinds of filth, and within a very short
time the shiny red capitals reflecting the optimism of a few idealists, can no
longer be seen. Like the all-powerful night, corruption and filth draw everything to themselves, and smother even the very best of intentions. The
Railway Administration Block where the man works is a mass of decay,
putrefaction, and filth, reeking of putrid turpentine. The banister is like a
long piece of diseased skin, and the character of the wood itself has been
changed by the accretion of excreta over the years:

> Apart from the wood itself there were, of course, people themselves,
> just so many hands and fingers bringing help to the wood in its course
> towards putrefaction. Left-hand fingers in their careless journey from a
> hasty anus sliding all the way up the banister as their owners made the
> return trip from the lavatory downstairs to the offices above. Right-hand
> fingers still dripping with the after-piss and the stale sweat from fat
> crotches. The calloused palms of messengers after they had blown their
> clogged noses reaching for a convenient place to leave the well-rubbed
> moisture. Afternoon hands not entirely licked clean of palm soup and the
> remnants of *kenkey*. The wood would always win. (p. 15)

Armah insists on the realistic details of urine, faeces, and snot, to shock
us into a realization of the repulsiveness of corruption. In his view, the
whole of Ghana, buildings as well as people, stinks of corruption. Later,
Armah focuses on the bubbles of yellow, filmy saliva playing around the
wolfish timber merchant's mouth. The following nauseating passage is
hard to beat:

> Walking with the slowness of those whose desire has nowhere to go,
> the man moved up the road, past the lines of evening people under the
> waning lamps selling green and yellow oranges and bloated bread
> polished with leftover oil, and little tins and packets of things no one was
> in any hurry to buy. Under a dying lamp a child is disturbed by a long

cough coming from somewhere deep in the centre of the infant body. At the end of it his mother calmly puts her mouth to the wet congested nostrils and sucks them free. The mess she lets fall gently by the roadside and with her bare foot she rubs it softly into the earth. (p. 41)

The passage recalls a similar one quoted on p. 67 from *No Longer At Ease*, in which Achebe exposes the moral and physical squalor of Lagos life. Here, as in that passage, the juxtaposition of filth and food is an implied comment on the negligence and lack of concern shown by the authorities towards the lower classes. Armah forces us to feel disgust as the woman sucks her child's nostrils, not to arouse our indignation against her, but against the authorities who allow her to languish in poverty, squalor and ignorance, while they fatten themselves on their country's riches.

For obvious reasons the image of the latrine is a recurrent one in this novel:

The man leaps up on the cleanest he can find, near the far end of the long latrine, passing his eyes over the row of cans encrusted with old shit. When he chooses the one he will use he is careful, in letting down his trousers, not to let the cuffs fall into the urine grooves in front. The thing that makes this place better than home is that here there is air, even if this air also rises from the holes below and is misty with the presence of familiar particles suspended in it. Squatting up there, he lets the air from below blow a cooling draft against his buttocks, and he looks at the crowded wall opposite, with the bright light of the big bulbs bouncing off it. Up near the ceiling the wall is still a dazzling white where there are no webs to hide the paint. The colour does not really change until about the level of the adult anus. There the wall is thickly streaked with an organic brown, each smear seeking to avoid older smears, until the dabs have gone all round the wall. There are places where, it seems, men have bent down to find an unused spot to use, and in a few incredible places men seemed to have jumped quite high and then to have accomplished a downward stroke. There must have been people who did not just forget to bring their paper, but who also did not bother to drop their loads, for the wall has marks that are not mere afterpieces, but large chunks of various shit. (pp. 123–4)

Armah is completely frank in describing the bodily functions. Undoubtedly, a large number of readers will wish he had not resorted to such coarse language. However, it does make its point very effectively. The latrine becomes another symbol for the Ghanaian body politic – decayed, uncared-for and stinking with corruption, just as the latrine reeks of excrement. And just as each user leaves his own dark smear on the walls, so each minister or official befouls his already ill-used country with his own corrupt acts. Armah also insists on the juxtaposition and association of excrement and sex: (there are sexual drawings on the walls of the lavatory) in the country as a whole the most corrupt men are notable for their sexual activities.

Occasionally, however, a few bright spots appear amidst the engulfing filth, like the little pool of clear water the man sees under the bridge: 'and yet here undoubtedly was something close enough to the gleam, this clearness, this beautiful freedom from dirt'. The purity is only momentary, for a little farther down the stream the water is clouded with 'the mud of its beginnings'.

The novel as a whole reveals the contemporary condition of Ghana, and parallels that of many independent African countries, where independence has propelled a new set of masters, black this time, into the seats the colonial bosses used to occupy. These new masters have acquired the same status symbols, and behave with the same arrogance and condescension as the old bosses. Armah's satire is especially vitriolic when directed against the grotesque attempts of this new class to behave like Englishmen. There is, for instance, the intolerable snobbery of Koomson's wife, Estella, who is endlessly pushing an imaginary curl back into the mass of her false hair with the languidness of a Hollywood film star; top civil servants scramble to convert genuine Ghanaian names into grotesque English-sounding concoctions like Binful, Fentengson and Kuntu-Blankson; the black golfers show their gratitude for being admitted into the golf club by imitating English mannerisms, English accents, and the nuances of English speech; inefficient civil servants stretch thirty minutes' work over a whole day; there is the irresponsibility of the ministers whose main preoccupations are night clubs, parties, and girls, and there is the contrast between the opulence of the popularly elected ministers and the squalor of the people who put them in power.

Over the entire country broods a mood of hopeless gloom. The prospect for most of these people is bleak. Their lives are marked by spiritual sterility, boredom, and loneliness; from the night clerk's cry of anguish: 'but I sat here alone, and I was wishing somebody would come in, and all night long there was nobody. Me alone,' to the man's realization at the end of the novel that the remainder of his life could offer him nothing but this aching emptiness. The soul-destroying monotony of colourless jobs, in oppressive offices is hardly more endurable because home is much worse. The optimism of bright young hope is all too easily replaced by cynicism and consciousness of failure: 'but along the streets, those who can, soon learn to recognize in ordinary faces beings whom the spirit has moved, but who cannot follow where it beckons, so heavy are the small, ordinary days of the time'. Despair is written on the face of almost every character.

Corruption is accepted as inevitable, or even necessary, and even those adversely affected by it, are prepared to bear patiently, in the hope that their own turn to 'eat' will come. Ministers and other authorities carry on their fraudulent practices without interference largely because corruption is virtually accepted as the legitimate means of enhancing one's prosperity. For instance, the man's wife, struggling under the weight of poverty is convinced that he should accept bribes to supplement his meagre salary. She uses this striking analogy: 'Those who wanted to get far had to learn to drive fast . . . Accidents would happen . . . but the fear of accidents would never keep men from driving, and Joe Koomson had learned to drive.' The claims of the loved ones and the silent accusation in the eyes of relatives, help to wear down the resistance of men of honesty and integrity. Everywhere, men had become accustomed to the darkness 'and they would laugh with hate at the bringer of unwanted light if what they knew they needed was the darkness'. The teacher's story of the myth of Plato's cave emphasizes this. The story tells of a group of people who had been bound in chains, in a cave of impenetrable darkness, for ages. At last one of them breaks his chains and wanders to the world of light outside:

> With the eagerness of the first bringer the wanderer returns into the cave and into its eternal darkness, and in there he shares what he has, the ideas and the words and the images of the light and the colours of the world outside, knowing surely that those he had left behind would certainly want the snapping of the ancient chains and the incredible first seeing of the light and the colours of the world beyond the eternal cave. But to those inside the eternal cave he came as someone driven ill with the breaking of eternal boundaries, and the truth he sought to tell was nothing but the proof of his long delusion, and the words he had to give were the pitiful cries of a madman lost in the mazes of a mind pushed too far out and away from the everlasting way of darkness and reassuring chains. (pp. 93–4)

The insidious power of corruption, and the difficulty of avoiding being engulfed by it, are suggested in the novel by a number of powerful images and analogies. The first of these is the rot on the banister of the Railway Administration Block. The banister was continually polished to get rid of the rot, but in the end it was the rot which won: 'It would always take the

newness of the different kinds of polish and the vaunted cleansing power of
the chemicals in them, and it would convert all to victorious filth.' Then
there is the reference to the *chichidodo*. This bird which 'hates excrement
with its soul', feeds nevertheless on maggots which grow best inside the
lavatory. The story of the *chichidodo*, like that of Rama Krishna, demonstrates the people's conviction that the more earnestly one tries to avoid
corruption, the more surely does one become involved in it. Finally, there
is the proverb of the healthy green fruit, healthy only for a brief spell.
When it decays, the only life that emerges from it comes from the seeds
feeding on their own rotten fruit. 'What then, was the fruit that refused to
lose its acid and its greenness? What monstrous fruit was it that could find
the end of its life in the struggle against sweetness and corruption?' This
proverb shows that most men not only see the descent into corruption as
natural, inevitable, and in a sense beneficial, but regard all those who resist
it as selfish and unnatural; they are 'monstrous fruit'. The novel also
demonstrates, by means once more of significant images, that almost everyone, those who wish to resist, as well as those who welcome it, are involved
in messy corruption. In the Railway Administration Block for instance, the
stewy atmosphere is compounded from the salt from the sea and the sweat
of every office worker. Subsequently, we see in one of the lavatory scenes
that 'all around decaying things push inward and mix the body's juices
with the taste of rot'. Near the lavatory, an old man, conscious that he and
everyone else is enveloped in corruption, in spite of all possible efforts to
avoid it, sleeps with his mouth wide open, thus allowing particles of excreta
to rush in. 'Why should he play the fool and hold his breath?'

However, some manage to rise above involvement in corruption, although only at tremendous cost to themselves. One of them is the man, the
other is the teacher. The teacher's rôle in the novel is central. He is the
upright man who has resisted temptation. When we first meet him, he is
absolutely naked, his nakedness symbolizing his absolute purity. Far from
being ashamed of his nakedness, he deliberately flaunts it. In spite of his
isolation and idealism, the teacher is a realist, who sees with great clarity
what is going on in society. He sees that in Ghanaian society anyone who
wants to be happy, and give his loved ones the things they desire, will sooner
or later have to compromise himself. He has realized that the land wants a
man 'not honest and living, but completely like its dead self'. The only
way to rise above it, and still maintain one's dignity, is to run away from
the situation. The man, on the other hand, has tried to rise above it, while
remaining within the situation. Consequently, he has merely exposed himself to perpetual humiliation. The teacher's story and conduct unwittingly
vindicate the belief that remaining happily within the Ghanaian situation

inevitably supposes being drawn into corruption. The teacher has obtained freedom, but only at the terrible price of condemning himself to a half-life of loneliness. And he is not really free, because he still longs to meet the loved ones, to touch them, and be touched by them. The memory of those dear ones, and his consciousness of the way in which he has abandoned them, constantly prey on his mind, and they even visit him in his dreams:

> There is my mother. Now at last she leaves me alone, but two nights past she was with me in a dream full of guilt and fear and loneliness . . . The castle, in my dream, belonged to my mother. With a companion who shared all my soul's desires I had come from a long way off, seeking refuge with my mother in her house. The mansion was very large. There was room, lots of room, in it, but when I spoke to my mother she seemed torn within by an impossible decision. But then she made up her mind, and out of her ran a stream of words, every drop filled with all the resentment and the hate of her long disappointment with me. 'Yes, you have come to rest here, you who have put nothing here at all. So how much money have you given me in all your life, and how much help? And now you come here, here, here.' When her anger grew unbearable she drove me out into the street outside. (pp. 69–70)

The teacher then, is far from a happy man. In spite of his outer calm and nakedness, he is a man in pain. The tragedy of his situation, and of the whole of Ghana, is summed up in his discovery that there is no salvation anywhere.

Half-way through the novel the teacher launches into an account of his past experiences. This account, in the first person, constitutes one of the novel's weaknesses, for it holds up the narrative and some readers may well feel that it shatters the illusion of reality. Also, in this section one becomes most uncomfortably aware of the didactic quality of the novel. However, the purpose of the teacher's narrative is clear. It powerfully communicates the reasons for his present disillusionment. The picture he paints of life in the pre-independence period is one of despair, suffering, disillusionment, and death. In their emptiness he, Maanan, and Kofi Billy resort to taking the drug *wee*. Under the influence of the drug their eyes are opened and they see the truth; they become aware of the ghastly smell of their environment and Kofi Billy gets a vision of the aimlessness of life: 'It is not at all possible to come out and see where we are going. I am just going.' Returning from the beach after one of their *wee* sessions they see a young girl leaning against a pole, waiting for someone: 'She looked more like some insect lost in all the vastness of the world around it.' The figure of the girl reinforces their vision of universal gloom and aimlessness, and after this frightful vision Kofi Billy kills himself. But suddenly their hopes are raised by the new politicians agitating for independence and promising them the millennium. Maanan, roused as never before, responds to the new men and their compelling rhetoric, with her body and soul. However, it does not take them long to discover that they have been used by unscrupulous men. The disillusionment comes all too quickly.

Maanan is a symbol of patient suffering. She represents the millions of Ghanaian women betrayed by husbands who have failed them and politicians who have exploited and then destroyed them. Kofi Billy's vision of universal despair and aimlessness leads him to suicide; Maanan's disillusionment drives her to insanity. When we last see her she looks 'like something that had been finally destroyed a long time back'. She is sifting the fine sand through her fingers and muttering: 'They have mixed it all together! Everything!'

The men who are responsible for this inextricable confusion of good and evil, are represented by the minister, Koomson. His career shows how the originally well-intentioned politician can be seduced by the fruits of office. Koomson is not really a bad man. During his visit to the man's home, we see the marked contrast between his behaviour, and that of his repulsive wife, Estella. Where she is condescending, ill-mannered, and snobbish, he is jovial and expansive, and does his best to put his host and hostess at their ease. Where she mutters some incomprehensible nonsense about refrigerators which are full to bursting, he gets out of his car and buys some bread from a pleading old woman, although he already has more than enough. He is an example of a will perverted by the prevailing temper of the times. However, he is now thoroughly corrupt, and his spiritual rottenness is indicated by the foul smells emanating from his body as he cowers in the man's bedroom in his attempt to escape from the police:

He waited for Koomson to say something now, but only the subdued breathing of the frightened man, punctuated with increasing rapidity by half-audible rumblings from his belly and full, loud farts from below, destroyed the peace of the room. When the man's eyes had again adjusted to the darkness, he could see the vague luminosity of Koomson's eyes in the black space of his face . . . His mouth had the rich stench of rotten menstrual blood. The man held his breath until the new smell had gone down in the mixture with the liquid atmosphere of the Party man's farts filling the room. At the same time Koomson's insides gave a growl longer than usual, an inner fart of personal, corrupt thunder which in its fullness sounded as if it had rolled down all the way from the eating

throat thundering through the belly and the guts, to end in further silent
pollution of the air already thick with flatulent fear. (pp. 190–2)

And yet, although we are aware of the extent of Koomson's corruption and
of his spiritual rottenness, we do feel some sympathy for him as he cringes
like a frightened animal, and finally squeezes his enormous bulk through
the lavatory hole used by the nightsoil man. The gruelling struggle through
the putrid lavatory has two functions. In the first place it enables Koomson
to experience the conditions of life of ordinary men and women – the men
and women whose trust he has betrayed; but also the lavatory is really the
place where Koomson belongs in the end; its putrefaction mirrors his spiritual rottenness:

'Push!' the man shouted, before he had thought of the nearness of the
searchers, or of the fact that his companion could not hear him anyhow.
Quietly now, he climbed on to the seat, held Koomson's legs and rammed
them down. He could hear Koomson strain like a man excreting, then
there was a long sound as if he was vomiting down there. But the man
pushed some more, and in a moment a rush of foul air coming up told
him the Party man's head was out. The body dragged itself painfully
down, and the man got ready to follow into the hole. (p. 198)

By following Koomson into the hole, the man finally vindicates the view
that everyone, innocent as well as guilty, is involved in the effects of corruption.

The novel's title – *The Beautyful Ones Are Not Yet Born* – is endorsed
by its bleak conclusion. The coup occurs, but corruption continues, and
although the man undergoes a symbolic cleansing in the sea before turning
in the direction of home, it is only a personal cleansing, unrelated to what
goes on in the larger world around.

Although there can be little doubt that Armah makes his point about corruption in Ghana, the novel is not without its weaknesses. *The Beautyful
Ones Are Not Yet Born* consists largely of the man's reflections, and the
various impressions which impinge on his senses. But these impressions and
reflections are about one thing and one thing alone – corruption and the
rottenness that goes with it. Consequently, the novel seems to have a
peculiarly theoretical and didactic quality, with the doctrine about corruption being persistently hammered into the reader's brain. The teacher's
lengthy narrative is also rather pedantic. The best method to preach a
doctrine in a novel is to evoke a quality of life over and above the doctrine,

but in which it is implicit. In Armah's novel, however, very few scenes are vividly realized. Its vagueness may have been deliberate, to accord with the symbolic intention, but it means that few scenes are brought to life, and few characters powerfully presented. Most of the characters are types, or symbolic figures, who do not seem to have transcended their theoretical conceptions; it is a pity that in a novel about corruption, Armah has not put them in interesting situations in which corruption is demonstrated. Instead, he has chosen to rely on his (admittedly powerful) exploitation of certain symbols. Perhaps the criticism of this novel relates to moral fables in general. In the moral fable the message is, of necessity, insistent, since almost every other aspect of the novel has to be subordinated to the message.

It is a tribute to the author's skill that *The Beautyful Ones Are Not Yet Born* survives its flaws, largely because of the way in which Armah exploits symbols, and because of the strength of his indignation against the parasites who live off their country's fat. In the entire corpus of African literature it remains the most thoroughgoing exposé of corruption. Armah has performed a very vital and necessary service for Ghanaians in particular, and Africans in general.

6: Mongo Beti

▼▼▼▼▼▼▼▼▼▼▼▼▼▼▼▼▼▼▼▼▼▼▼▼▼▼▼▼▼▼

MISSION TO KALA

MONGO BETI'S *Mission to Kala* tends to elicit two responses. Some applaud the author's celebration of African rural values and his rejection of modern, urban traditions. These readers see Mongo Beti as rebelling against the French educational system and calling for the preservation of pure African traditions. On the other hand are those who see the idealization of African tribal life in the novel as phoney and affected. I intend to demonstrate, *inter alia*, that both sides are wrong, and fail to respond to the novel's complexity and irony.

The misconceptions stem from too facile an identification of the author, Mongo Beti, with the narrator-hero, Jean-Marie Medza, that silly, posturing, opinionated schoolboy. It is quite easy to see what kind of boy Jean-Marie is, but it does not necessarily follow that he is Mongo Beti. One cannot assume that *Mission To Kala* is autobiographical. Apart from the fact that both Jean-Marie and Mongo Beti were born in the Cameroons, and attended Lycées there, there is very little evidence in the book or in the details of Mongo Beti's life as we know them, which indicate without question that the novel is autobiographical.

Far from identifying himself with Jean-Marie, Mongo Beti presents him ironically, subjecting his views and actions to the most critical scrutiny. The relationship between author and hero is almost exactly the same as that between Achebe and Odili, which has been already discussed in chapter two. In *Mission to Kala*, as in *A Man of the People*, the first-person hero's views are not endorsed by the author. Either there is a gap between the author and the narrator-hero, or we must conclude that Mongo Beti is as irresponsible, snobbish, and deluded as his schoolboy hero. In spite of his endearing wit, there are several reasons why readers might dislike Jean-Marie. He is stupid, condescending, and untruthful. Mongo Beti must distance himself from Jean-Marie to expose these qualities in him. Accordingly, Jean-Marie, like Odili in *A Man of the People*, becomes not so much

a spokesman, as a *persona* or mask, to be manipulated at will, to be deliberately put in a number of embarrassing situations and laughed at; at times
he himself actually joins in the laughter at his own expense. Irony, is the
dominant mode in *Mission to Kala*.

As in *A Man of the People*, the irony is primarily reflected in the nature
of the hero's language. Even a superficial analysis of Jean-Marie's style
reveals that he is very much addicted to clichés and stock-phrases:

> My God, how lovely she was! Her cheekbones stood out just far enough;
> her nose was small and pert, her mouth proud as well as sensual. Her
> whole personality breathed that air of calm, detached assurance which is
> only to be found in those girls who know what they want and can reflect
> on many past occasions when they got it . . .
>
> She seemed to be waiting for something; but the longer I watched her,
> the less certain I became of just what it was. All women spend their lives
> waiting for something, I thought – probably I'd read that somewhere –
> and they only differ in the degree of their foreknowledge.*

This is surely not Mongo Beti's own style; it is more reminiscent of tenth-
rate American 'sex-and-crime' fiction. In fact Beti must be applauded for
very subtly moulding the style to suit the character. Take another example:

> My heart began to beat violently. I was as nervous as a partisan about to
> raid a strongly-held enemy position. (p. 93)

The truth is that Jean-Marie's style has been affected by his reading of
cheap fiction, and his uncritical assimilation of random phrases from his
masters' lessons and conversation; hence the clichés and stock-phrases.
The clichés expose the essential hollowness of Jean-Marie's mind, a point
which will be of great significance as we follow the story. This is all part of
the ironic technique by which Beti manipulates the reader's responses
towards Jean-Marie, even though he is himself telling the story.

Irony is also effectively indicated by the tone of voice, and the vehemence
or the illogicalities of the speaker's arguments. For instance, Jean-Marie
describes a meal:

> This was, according to local custom, an enormous meal, chiefly because
> they only had two meals a day. The women went to work in the fields
> early in the morning, and only returned late in the afternoon . . .

* Beti, Mongo, *Mission to Kala*, African Writers Series, Heinemann Educational
Books, 1964, p. 70. All further page references in this chapter are to this edition.

The table was loaded with food. My uncle was distinctly lacking in table manners: he crammed his mouth so full that a great bulge appeared in each cheek, and I was afraid he might burst. I trained myself not to catch his eye during meals, so as to avoid betraying my astonishment at his feeding habits. His son, on the other hand, shot constant glances of shame and reproach at him. (p. 57)

Jean-Marie's condescension towards the people of Kala is surely exposed in his contemptuous reference to their 'two meals a day' and in the obvious exaggeration about his uncle's table manners. But the author does not share it. To take another example:

Is there, as I am inclined to suspect, a kind of complicity, an unspoken agreement between even the severest examiner and any candidate? But if so, does this complicity not rest on the implied assumption (which the professor, at least, is consciously aware of) that all they both know is, in differing degrees, illusory and insubstantial? Pursuing this sour train of thought, I asked myself how many geography teachers in Western Europe and the areas under European influence, such as Central Africa, had any real or precise information about contemporary conditions in Russia? It was a depressing state of affairs if countless poor little bastards were forced to sacrifice their youth in assimilating a lot of fairy tales. (pp. 67–8)

Failure to appreciate the distance between Mongo Beti and his hero in a passage such as this leads to the view that Mongo Beti is a rebel against European values. But Jean-Marie is just inventing face-saving excuses for his inability to talk about Russian conditions. The passage is full of illogicalities and *non-sequiturs*. Jean-Marie assumes that since he survived an 'extra-mural' session in Kala, he would have passed an oral in Russian geography. But, he suggests, his lecturers would have demonstrated, not only their incompetence, but also the general complicity between examiner and examinee, made necessary by the ignorance of the examiners themselves. He then concludes that most European geography teachers are ignorant of Russian conditions, and refers to the facts of geography as 'fairy tales'. And all this because he was able to deceive the people of Kala with his lies about Russia. However, the readers know that Jean-Marie has failed not only his oral, but his entire baccalauréat. It is not college learning which is being criticized, but Jean-Marie's imperfect assimilation of the syllabus.

Mongo Beti is looking at Jean-Marie with a critical eye, and so should we.

F

It is important to establish at the outset that Jean-Marie's judgements should not be accepted at face value. We can now proceed with a detailed examination of the novel.

The first point is that *Mission to Kala* is not about a mission to recover Niam's delinquent wife. Rather it is a story of growth and discovery, during which the hero is forced to acknowledge many truths about himself, his education, and his so-called rustic cousins. As is usual with the picaresque novel, interest lies less in the hero's adventures during his travels, than in his moral, emotional, and psychological development. Like all picaresque heroes, Jean-Marie starts off in a state of innocence, and has to be exposed to external experience to learn more about life.

At the start of the novel Jean-Marie is himself under no illusions about his actual position and achievement. His full consciousness of his failure is the reason for his depression. It is his fellow Vimilians who persist in regarding him as an educated man, who possesses certificates and know-ledge of the white man's secrets; 'he only has to make the trip there and put the fear of God into those savages'. This is why a sixteen-year-old boy is sent on an errand to recover the wife of a thirty-five-year-old man. Mongo Beti rises to the occasion and exploits the tremendous comic potential to the full.

At this stage of the proceedings there are only two sane people: Aunt Amou, that self-effacing but very perceptive widow, is the voice of reason and sanity, seeing with amazing clarity that the Vimilians are attributing to Jean-Marie a whole scale of values that he quite patently does not possess: 'Aren't you ashamed to drag this poor boy into your dirty lies? He's just a child.' The second is Jean-Marie himself, who is quite properly appalled at the nature of the task.

But from now on a change occurs in Jean-Marie. As soon as it becomes clear that the Vimilians are determined to send him on this mission, he becomes infected with their enthusiasm for the task, and their condescension towards the people of Kala: 'An *easy* adventure, among comparatively simple people, is the secret wish and aim of every adventurer. When you come to think of it, the very existence of adventurers is only made possible by the survival of primitive simpleminded tribes.' Jean-Marie is already demonstrating an acceptance of other people's values which will make him an unreliable narrator.

Jean-Marie now begins to have delusions of grandeur, regarding himself not just as a missionary taking light to the barbarous people of Kala, but as a conquistador, about to engage on a mission of conquest. He thinks of a means of transport in terms of a richly caparisoned horse, and he refers to his bicycle as a 'splendid machine', an 'aristocrat among bicycles':

Occasionally I stopped, and with one foot just touching the ground while the other remained, as it were, in the stirrup, I gazed at the vast panorama lying open to my future exploits. (This 'vast panorama' was for the most part restricted to a seedy vista of tree-trunks lining the road, oppressive in the most literal sense.) Then there was this strange name of mine, Medza. If I added one tiny syllable, only one, it would be transformed into a real Conquistador's name. Medzaro! – just like Pizarro, or near enough, anyway. (pp. 19–20)

Jean-Marie comes to Kala with preconceived ideas about the people, but he will gradually be forced to change them. In the first place, his arrival is unnoticed, since the village is preoccupied with its own pastimes, and he fails to get a conquistador's welcome. Here is his reaction to the game he finds in progress:

I was astonished by the whole thing, though in the end I remembered that when we were about six or so we used to play a similar sort of game at home. But in our case it was a childish pastime, a mere survival from former times, and not taken in the least seriously. At Kala, to judge by this match, it was still going very strong indeed. (p. 22)

Jean-Marie's condescension is striking in this passage. In his view, the people of Kala are at the emotional and mental level of children of 'six or so'. Subsequently he sees Zambo:

Having first taken a bird's-eye, panoramic view of the scene, I now began to examine it in detail. The first thing that caught my eye was a great hulking devil in the Kala team, who had such enormous muscles that I concluded he must have bought them on the instalment system. There was simply no other explanation possible. He was tall and flat-footed, with a disproportionately lengthy torso which, nevertheless, he carried very badly. His buttocks were incredibly slender, yet he retained the country native's slight pot-belly, due to a habitually rough and meagre diet. He was like a kind of human baobab tree . . .

I found it hard to convince myself that this monster was really my cousin, the young man from whom old Bikokolo had promised me so wonderful a reception. By what miraculous process, I asked myself, could this man be related to me in any way? (p. 23)

Zambo emerges from Jean-Marie's description as a clumsy brute. But as the novel progresses, we begin to entertain doubts about the accuracy of the description, for the Zambo we come to know is no brute. Indeed, all the girls seem to be in love with him, and a little later Jean-Marie himself calls Zambo his handsome cousin; on yet another occasion he calls him a Greek demi-god. Jean-Marie's initial picture of Zambo is a cruel distortion, as we can see if we look again at the passage. First Jean-Marie makes a comment which is to Zambo's credit, but then he proceeds to denigrate him; he takes away with one hand, what he gives with the other. He ridicules Zambo's impressive muscles and tries to detract from the favourable impression of his height with the contemptuous 'flat-footed'. In conjunction with his long torso and incredibly slender buttocks, we are told of his cousin's pot-belly. We may well ask how Jean-Marie knows about the country native's 'rough and meagre diet' seeing he has never been in Kala before? We ourselves are soon to see that the Kalans' diet is anything but 'rough and meagre'.

Jean-Marie is deliberately forcing Zambo to fit his preconceived image of the rustic Kalan. However, from now on the position is reversed, and Jean-Marie has to laugh at himself, as he discovers his inferiority in many respects to the Kalans. His first surprise comes with the hospitality of his welcome. His cousin Zambo, from whom he expected nothing but savagery, behaves with such marked courtesy, that he almost passes out.

At Kala, Jean-Marie discovers what had been so conspicuously lacking in Vimili – the strength and warmth of personal relationships. Those four 'irresponsibles' – Zambo, Petrus Son-of-God, Abraham the Boneless Wonder, and Duckfoot Johnny – cling to each other with an almost religious devotion. Zambo enjoys the most cordial relations with his father, who even allows him to keep his mistress in the house. (We can imagine how Jean-Marie's father would react to his son's girl-friend living with them.) Indeed the Zambo–Mama relationship is the exact antithesis of Jean-Marie's with his father, who rules his household with a mailed fist, and hardly communicates with his sons. In his family there was continual fighting: 'there was never any peace or sense of security; nothing but rows, reproaches and fear'. The father scolded everyone, the mother scolded the children, the boys beat the girls, and the elder sister bullied the younger. It was a home calculated to produce juvenile delinquents, and it is hardly surprising that both Jean-Marie and his elder brother show delinquent tendencies in the end.

In Kala Jean-Marie discovers a spontaneity he never thought existed. When, during the swimming party the other boys strip and plunge in naked, Jean-Marie, conditioned by the restrictive morality of his environment, rather self-consciously keeps his pants on, until he is shamed by the others into removing them.

In Kala Jean-Marie is first introduced to the pleasures of alcohol. But by far the most important of his discoveries is sex. Sexual experience is the watershed between youth and manhood. So it is not surprising that much of the novel consists of attempts to get Jean-Marie into bed with a girl. Here in 'primitive' Kala, the supposed experienced 'city slicker' is initiated into manhood. At the start, Jean-Marie, who is a virgin, is scandalized by his cousin's offer to find him a girl, but the urge grows on him. Yet when he is confronted by the most beautiful and sophisticated girl in the village, his feeling of inadequacy makes him frigid and impotent. Later, still pretending to be the city slicker with lots of experience, he tries to cover up his inadequacy with scandalous allegations about the girl's health. Fortunately for him, however, he is finally able to make love with the equally inexperienced Edima, the chief's daughter.

Increasingly, Jean-Marie the conquistador, finds himself at a disadvantage and is forced to admit his inferiority to the other boys: 'I'd have given all the diplomas in the world to swim like Duckfoot Johnny, or dance like the Boneless Wonder; or have the sexual experience of Petrus Son-of-God.' Despite his various set-backs, in the field of learning Jean-Marie ought to be the incontestable champion. After all he is the only person in Kala with any education worth talking about, and he had been deliberately selected for this mission by Vimili, because of his learning and his certificates. The Kalans respect him because they are convinced that he knows the white man's secrets. But this is just where Jean-Marie's inferiority is most glaringly exposed. He who had intended to bring light to the barbarous savages, finds out that he can't hold a candle to them, in knowledge of basic facts and native intelligence.

Since the Kalans, like the Vimilians, wrongly regard Jean-Marie as a scholar, they organize 'extra-mural' sessions at which he is supposed to answer their questions and talk to them about the white man's secrets. Before the first of these sessions Jean-Marie behaves with his characteristic condescension and conceit. His hostess asks him what he has been taught at school and he says:

I wanted to be kind to this woman; she meant well enough; but how on earth was I to give her the most elementary notion of such things as geography, advanced mathematics or the social sciences?
... I honestly believed that the old lady was suffering from the effects of senility. (p. 48)

Jean-Marie later wishes he had not been so condescending and conceited:

Scarcely was dinner over when my hostess began to fire a whole fusillade of questions at me. She sat next to me and went on absolutely ruthlessly, dragging detailed explanations out of me, and going back over muddled points with a needle-sharp clarity. She obviously was aware of all my weaknesses and shortcomings; she was equipped to give me the most humiliating oral I had ever been through in my life. To think that there are people like me whose job is passing exams all their life. (p. 62)

The woman is not an isolated case; the entire audience direct the most penetrating questions at Jean-Marie, probing his weaknesses and exposing his ignorance. As his embarrassment increases he wants 'to yell for mercy, to throw in the sponge, anything'. Even the 'bright definitions' he had prepared to answer possible questions fail to help him. He has to tell lies about Russian geography and the problems of New York, and is quite unable to talk about his own prospects and those of other members of his generation.

And this is not all. Far from educating the Kalans, they educate him in such matters as village economics and tribal customs during his stay in Kala. Moreover, he is hardly what one might call a bright student. Indeed, on many occasions, Zambo and his father are almost in despair at the impenetrable stupidity of the boy. For instance, this is how his uncle reacts after a characteristic howler from Jean-Marie, during the celebrated discussion on blood relationships:

> He stooped down to his work again, his face twisted into a kind of despairing grimace. It was just such an expression as is common among classics masters in the provinces, indicating that their pupils are incurably third-rate and will never be any use at anything, let alone classics. Then he stood up once more, with an air of conscientious determination. *Nil desperandum* was written all over him. (p. 89)

On one occasion Zambo exclaims: 'Don't you know anything in your part of the country?'

We witness the complete reversal of Jean-Marie's initial relationship to the people of Kala and, in particular, his relationship with Zambo. As we have seen, he is quite convinced at the start of Zambo's barbarity and stupidity. As far as he is concerned, Zambo is mule-headed and uncritical. But increasingly the would-be conquistador is forced to rely on the dull-witted savage for security and support. Moreover, as we get to know Zambo, we fail to see any evidence of dullness or neurosis; on the contrary, he seems a highly imaginative and resourceful young man, far more quick-witted and perceptive than his 'educated' cousin. It is Zambo who first realizes that the whole episode in which Edima and Jean-Marie are discovered in bed together, is a carefully-planned farce, designed to bolster the ego of the mother and improve Edima's matrimonial chances. When Niam's delinquent wife returns and treats Jean-Marie with studied indifference, it is Zambo who points out the real reasons for her strange behaviour, and Jean-Marie is eventually forced to admit:

> There was a good deal of common sense in Zambo's remarks: he was more level-headed about the whole thing than I was. (p. 145)

Although in many ways the Kalans treat Jean-Marie as a superior they also exploited him as if he was an inferior. Even Zambo uses him to bolster his prestige. Jean-Marie, in his simplicity, supposed that the four friends, Zambo, Duckfoot Johnny, Abraham the Boneless-Wonder, and Petrus Son-of-God, had invited him on their groundnut-scrounging enterprise as a mark of friendship; but it turns out that he was merely being used as a mascot: 'you've got to admit it, we've our little city mascot to thank for this haul. If he hadn't been there, no one would have taken any notice of us at all . . . That's why we invited him to come along.'

But it is his uncle, Mama, who exploits Jean-Marie most of all. He farms him out every evening to the highest bidder, with complete lack of consideration for his health or convenience. On one occasion Jean-Marie had spoken contemptuously of those people who were 'entirely innocent of modern notions concerning economies and capitalism', but his uncle demonstrates that he has a very good notion of both. He knows very well that he has a commodity which is in demand, and the collection of sheep and poultry (the fee for hiring out Jean-Marie) continues unabated. Subsequently, his uncle calmly proceeds to appropriate half the sheep and poultry for his own use after lulling Jean-Marie into a false sense of security.

By this time any notion of Jean-Marie as a competent negotiator who could put the fear of God into those Kalans, and recover Niam's wife, has disappeared. Not surprisingly, the negotiations are largely conducted by Mama and Zambo, and Jean-Marie, the real emissary, hardly plays a significant rôle at all.

Finally, in some brilliantly comic scenes towards the end of the novel, the 'city slicker' is tricked into marrying Edima, the chief's daughter. A dreamlike quality dominates the work at this stage; Jean-Marie has been overwhelmed by forces that have proved too strong for him. The supreme irony is that the educator has become the educated, and the conquistador has become the 'conquered'.

In the meantime, Jean-Marie is himself aware of the change in his circumstances. Bullied, exploited, tricked, exposed, and faced with the superiority of these rustic Kalans, he rebels against his background, his education and his father. He feels that it is these factors, rather than any defects in his own character, which are to blame for his débâcle at Kala:

> Looking back, I suspect Eliza had become my symbol of absolute liberty, the freedom enjoyed by country boys like Duckfoot Johnny, the Bone-less Wonder, Son-of-God, and the rest. I saw this freedom as the most precious possession I could acquire, and realized at the same time that in all likelihood I should never have it. Without being aware of it, I was no more than a sacrifice on the altar of Progress and Civilization. My youth was slipping away, and I was paying a terrible price for – well, for *what*? Having gone to school, at the decree of my all-powerful father? Having been chained to my books when most children of my age were out playing games? (p. 63)

Similar sentiments are expressed towards the end of the novel with much greater vehemence:

> Fathers used to take their children to school as they might lead sheep into a slaughterhouse . . . We were catechized, confirmed, herded to Communion like a gaggle of holy-minded ducklings . . . What god were we being sacrificed to, I wonder? (p. 165)

One might take statements such as these quite literally as part of the message of the novel, and see Jean-Marie Medza as the white-man's 'representative', who, having been exposed from an early age to Western education and civilization, is at a loss in his own tribal culture. One might feel that Mongo Beti is suggesting that being exposed to an alien system of education cuts a boy off from his roots, robs him of all that is good, beauti-ful, and valuable, and makes him unfit, not only for tribal life, but for any kind of life at all. But this kind of judgement simplifies Mongo Beti's meaning; identifies him wrongly with Jean-Marie; does less than justice to the subtlety and complexity of his technique; and fails to see passages such as those quoted above as the culmination of the ironic process which has been going on all along.

We have already seen that Jean-Marie's judgement is unreliable. We have seen irony also operating in another passage (quoted on p. 145) in which he discusses education with characteristic vehemence. In these passages the generally vehement tone indicates irony too. Is Jean-Marie's youth really slipping away? Isn't he exaggerating in calling this freedom the most precious possession he could ever acquire, and over-simplifying in describing himself as a sacrifice on the altar of progress and civilization? Jean-Marie is just wallowing in self-pity and giving vent to personal antagonism for his father, whom he sees lurking behind all his troubles. Mongo Beti does not give him his endorsement, and must not be identified with him here.

No doubt there are valuable things in Kala society, and Jean-Marie is the worse for not possessing them. But the text does not warrant the suggestion that Mongo Beti is decrying education or Western civilization. In the first place, Jean-Marie is not the representative of the white man. The Kalans and the Vimilians, not Mongo Beti, attribute white values to him, that we can see he does not possess. In the second place, Jean-Marie is not the embodiment of Western education. In spite of all the talk about his learning and certificates, we know he has failed his baccalauréat and is only half educated. Indeed, at Kala, his inability to assimilate his teacher's lessons is all too clearly revealed. At best, Jean-Marie's attitude to his studies was perfunctory; he tells us so himself:

> I had really only applied myself to my studies at all because my father was ambitious on my behalf. He wanted me to get more and more diplomas and certificates, without bothering his head overmuch as to where they would get me. In short, I had been made to go to school, and then arranged things as best as I could to suit myself: I had turned the whole thing into a game, something to pass the time away and amuse me. (p. 79)

Since this is Jean-Marie's attitude to his education, how can we blame his education for his reverses at Kala? How can we say he is made impotent at Kala because he has been transformed by Western education into the 'white man's representative'?

Partly because of his antagonism to his father, and partly because of his discomfiture, Jean-Marie comes to regard Kala society as the ideal. We said before that he is too ready to accept other people's values uncritically. Now we must question the Utopian values that he attributes to Kala. In the first place, the marvellous Kalan freedom can easily degenerate into licentiousness, as in the case of Zambo himself, who cannot go to sleep so long as 'there is a girl to screw somewhere in the world'. Moreover, death is ever-present in this society, as the case of Elias Messi proves, and there is something rather pathetic about the 'togetherness' which binds Zambo and his three friends. The orphans, Endongolo and his sister, show that life in Kala is not entirely free from misery.

Mongo Beti is much too intelligent to idealize the Kalans. They can be vulgar, like Petrus Son-of-God, or the girls who watch the boys bathing in the river, generous like Zambo, self-effacing like Zambo's mother, petty like the chief, mean and calculating like Zambo's father, friendly like Endongolo, flirtatious like Edima, and sluttish like Niam's wife. Jean-Marie mistakenly regards them as the ideal, and rebels so violently against his education and background, that he becomes a juvenile delinquent and a vagrant.

Mission to Kala is neither an attack on education nor on Western civilization; rather, it is a brilliant satire directed against all those half-baked young men who feel that a partial exposure to Western ways makes them superior to their countrymen who still live the tribal life. Mongo Beti subjects Jean-Marie's personal weaknesses – his condescension, arrogance, and stupidity – to rigorous criticism by means of his comic art.

7: Gabriel Okara

▼▼▼▼▼▼▼▼▼▼▼▼▼▼▼▼▼▼▼▼▼▼▼▼▼▼▼▼▼▼▼▼▼▼

THE VOICE

GABRIEL OKARA'S haunting novel, *The Voice*, has received much less attention than it deserves. Within one hundred pages or so the Nigerian poet has blended a number of literary influences, created some memorable characters, painted some vivid scenes, and achieved effects that other African novelists have unsuccessfully striven after in much more voluminous works. Unfortunately, the way the novel has sometimes been recommended, does it a disservice. For instance, the inside cover of the Panther edition declares that '*The Voice* is the painful story of a student, Okolo, his desperately acquired, and sadly superficial formal education completed, returning to his native village bursting with energy and optimism, and determined to sweep his country into the twentieth century'. There is nothing in the novel to substantiate any of this. Nor is Okolo's catastrophe caused wholly, or partly, by the inadequacy of his education. The blurb on the back cover of the same edition declares that Okolo, determined to live a life unfettered by tradition, heads up river to the fleshpots of the nearest town. Because of an unwitting indiscretion on the way, he is accused of violating a powerful taboo. However, a careful reading of the novel reveals few signs of fleshpots, and the episode referred to is only one of a number in which his innocent integrity is contrasted with the world's wickedness. Such comments do a very grave disservice to the novel for by presenting it as 'sociological' and sensational they may well frighten off a number of readers. In fact the mainsprings of Okolo's actions in this novel are religious and moral, rather than social, technological, or political.*

* See Dathorne, O. R., 'The African Novel: Document to Experiment', *Baale*, no. 3, 1965, pp. 18–39; and Anozie, S. O., 'The Theme of Alienation and Commitment in Okara's *The Voice*', *Baale*, no. 3, 1965, pp. 54–67.

Dathorne attacks Okara's use of language and accuses him of sacrificing plot and character development to moral preoccupation. Anozie sees Okolo's alienation from his people as a fault which Okara should have recognized. Both critics misconceive Okara's purpose and the meaning of his novel.

At the African-Scandinavian Writers' conference held at Stockholm in 1967, Wole Soyinka called on the African writer to abandon his preoccupation with the past, and face up to the threat of disintegration in present-day Africa. As we have seen, his call had been anticipated by Chinua Achebe and Mongo Beti, and has subsequently been heeded by Armah. But in 1964 Okara had already gone well beyond these writers, who, while shedding their romantic and sociological preoccupations, still concentrate on the social and political corruption of modern Africa. Okara blames the disintegration of modern African society on spiritual sterility and materialism, and uses age-old myths to relate a local, African situation to the universal one.

A number of literary influences have gone into the making of this small but complex novel. Firstly, Okara has relied rather heavily on the oral tradition, reproducing the rhythms and sentence patterns of Ijaw speech, so that the story seems to emerge from the ballad or folk tale. Although the references to political independence and modern education are contemporary, the strange linguistic rhythms and the indeterminate setting are reminiscent of ancient myths:

> The engine canoe against the strong water pushed and slowly, slowly it walked along the wide river with the tall iroko trees, kapok trees, palm trees, standing on its banks, the sky's eye reaching. Soon, the day's eye became bad. It became so bad and black and closed that it could not be looked at. And soon lightning flashed in the day's eye and the thunder sounded like the sound of one hundred cannons going off near your ears. All the passengers woke up with a shout. Thunder had torn their sleep and deafened their ears. Then they feared and shouted and spoke, not hearing each other.*

In the following passage we can almost hear the story-teller's accents as he tries to recreate Izongo's movements:

> As Izongo was thinking thus his eyes were moving from Abadi to Otutu and from Otutu to Abadi. Then as Otutu sat down muttering to himself he got up and spoke standing straight. (p. 126)

The peculiarly rural quality of the images, analogies, and proverbs suggests that they come direct from the oral tradition. The plot and structure of the novel correspond to, and have probably been determined by an important

* Okara, G., *The Voice*, African Writers Series, Heinemann Educational Books, 1970, p. 61. All further page references are to this edition.

characteristic of the oral tradition – the circular passage of the hero through a series of adventures involving a departure, initiation, and return.* During the journey he normally achieves emotional equilibrium and maturity. Okolo's experiences – the departure from Amatu, the sojourn in Sologa, and the decision to return to Amatu, correspond to this pattern.

Secondly, *The Voice* has affinities with symbolic religious fables such as *The Pilgrim's Progress* or *Everyman*: In this it resembles Armah's *The Beautyful Ones Are Not Yet Born*. Just as Christian in *The Pilgrim's Progress* is engaged in a search for salvation, so Okolo is ultimately searching for spiritual values. All the characters play symbolic roles, representing forces and ideas much larger than themselves. The symbolic nature of the novel is strengthened by the vagueness of the landscape and by the use of symbolic names such as the Big One, The Listeners, and the Watchers. The absence of landscape description helps to convey the impression of a spiritual wilderness, rather like the Field Full of Folk in *Everyman*. In spite of the vague setting the novel is not didactic, because Okara quite skilfully and imaginatively creates his characters, and evokes situations and scenes.

The theme of a quest is central, and the similarity between this novel and such works as Eliot's *The Waste Land* is very marked. Okolo wanders through a spiritually dead society, a kind of 'Waste Land', devoid of spiritual values and dominated by materialism. The search for the Holy Grail as the means of purging the 'Waste Land' finds its counterpart here in Okolo's search for *it*. Okolo's persecution by hostile, incomprehensible forces in Sologa and Amatu is reminiscent of Kafka. In Sologa, like Kafka's heroes, or Clarence in Part I of *The Radiance of the King*, he is lost and out of his depth. A number of other scenes have a macabre and nightmarish, Kafkaesque quality:

> The people snapped at him like hungry dogs snapping at bones. They carried him in silence like the silence of ants carrying a crumb of yam or fish in bone. Then they put him down and dragged him past thatch houses that in the dark looked like pigs with their snouts in the ground; pushed and dragged him past mud walls with pitying eyes; pushed and dragged him past concrete walls with concrete eyes; pushed and dragged him along the waterside like soldier ants with their prisoner. They pushed and dragged him in panting silence, shuffling silence, broken only by an owl hooting from the darkness of the orange tree in front of Chief Izongo's house. (pp. 38–9)

* See Campbell, J., *The Hero With a Thousand Faces*, Pantheon Books, New York, 1949.

Finally, Okolo, like Cervantes' picaresque hero Don Quixote, is an innocent idealist let loose in a corrupt, materialistic world. Like Don Quixote he is regarded as insane. The world exposes his naïvety, but his very innocence acts as a catalyst precipitating the hypocrisy, spiritual sterility, and materialism of the people he meets.

The message of *The Voice* is pessimistic in the extreme. Although at the end there is a suggestion that Okolo's and Tuere's 'spoken words' have begun to take root, and that Ukule the cripple will go on preaching the message, the dominant impression is of bleak hopelessness. *The Voice* is a cry of protest against the spiritual sterility, inhumanity, and materialism that Okara sees everywhere about him, and it is a message of an obviously universal relevance. The 'voice' is Okolo's, crying in the spiritual wilderness, and calling for a restoration of traditional integrity and moral purity.

> 'If you put a black paint over a white paint, does it mean there is no white paint? Under the black paint the white paint is still there and it will show when the black paint is rubbed off. That's the thing I am doing – trying to rub off the black paint. Our fathers' insides always contained things straight. They did straight things. Our insides were also clean and we did the straight things until the new time came. We can still sweep the dirt out of our houses every morning.' (p. 50)

The novel is of course dominated by Okolo's search for *it*. What is *it*? *It* is that indefinable something which gives integrity, honesty, spiritual values, faith in God and man, and a sense of purpose. Some call it God, or the Holy Spirit, others the grace of God. *It* comprehends everything which is opposed to the present tendency to a sterile materialism. On one occasion Okolo says:

> 'All I want to do in my search,' Okolo spoke out at last, 'is to revitalize my flagging faith, faith, in man, belief in something,' he said with all his inside and his shadow. 'Belief and faith in that something we looked up to in times of sorrow and joy have all been taken away and in its stead what do we have? Nothing but a dried pool with only dead wood and skeleton leaves. And when you question they fear a tornado is going to blow down the beautiful houses they have built without foundations.' (pp. 88–9)

The conflict is not between traditionalism and modernism, as some critics imply, but between spiritual sterility and materialism on the one hand, and a concern for moral values on the other. Okolo's call for spiritual revitalization threatens the very basis of his amoral society. Although not politically motivated, his call does have political implications. Izongo and his elders realize that they can only retain power as long as their message 'of you never had it so good' continues to be credible and the people continue to ignore moral and spiritual values. Hence their violent reaction to Okolo's activities. Behind the simplicity of the arguments used on both sides, really big issues are at stake. Okolo is, in a sense, calling for a revolution and, like Christ and other prophets who question the basis of their society, he has to be destroyed. Early in the novel there is a menacing image forecasting Okolo's ultimate destruction:

> To the window he went once more and looked at the night. The moon was an about-to-break moon. A vague circle of light surrounded it, telling a dance was going on up or down river. Across the moon's face and the dance circle, menacing dark clouds idled past, casting shadow after shadow on the river. Larger and darker clouds, some to frowning faces, grimacing faces changing, were skulking past without the moon's ring, suffocating the stars until they too lost themselves in the threatening conformity of the dark cloud beyond. (p. 26)

The moon and the stars are Okolo and his supporters, and the frowning, grimacing, dark clouds Izongo and his elders, threatening to suffocate them, and envelop them in the darkness.

Okara insists on the spiritual sterility of Izongo's society. On page 34 Tuere says to Okolo: 'How do you expect to find *it* when everybody has locked up his inside?' The word 'inside' is used several times in the novel to refer to the heart or conscience; when men no longer have a conscience how does one discover honesty and integrity? A number of telling phrases also suggest a spiritual vacuum: early in the novel the footsteps of the people who come to seize Okolo are described as 'bad footsteps', and 'knowing-nothing footsteps'. Later, as they drag him through the town, their feet are described as 'blind feet'; the cripple says of them: 'they are singing with voices like a piece of earth, and drinking with throats that pick nothing, and shaking the world with their looking-at-nothing feet.' People are often described as having no shadow, referring both to their hollowness and to lack of spiritual strength. Significantly, Tuere, one of the strongest people in her society, has a clearly defined shadow. A very important passage concentrates this sense of spiritual nothingness:

> So his inside many questions asked. Faith and faithlessness adding up to nothing. Belief and unbelief adding up to nothing. Man has no more

shadow, trees have no more shadow. Nothing has any more meaning but
the shadow – devouring trinity of gold, iron, concrete. (p. 89)

In modern society everything is robbed of value; faith and faithlessness
add up to nothing; one is momentarily reminded of the caves' echo in
A Passage to India, where everything – filth as well as the most glorious
poetry – is reduced to an appalling nullity. Only the materialism associated
with spiritual emptiness has meaning – the shadow-devouring trinity of
gold, iron, and concrete. The passage ends with a grotesque parody of the
trinity, suggesting that materialism has replaced concern for spiritual
values, and has created a sterile society.

Amatu society is dominated by material considerations: Izongo can persuade his people by bribery not to sacrifice their newly-found prosperity by
listening to Okolo. Sologa, too, is preoccupied with cars, food, and concrete
houses; the slogans painted on the walls of the eating house – eat and drink
O, die one day we go – are significant. But a number of allusions and
images suggest that this code has very fragile foundations. The houses are
built without foundations; the Chief's laughter is described as a 'surface-
water laugh'; and on page 34 Tuere asks Okolo, 'How or where do you
think you will find *it* when everybody surface-water-things tell, when things
have no more root?' This is a world in which people are content with the
superficialities 'that fly off the surface of things'. Okolo is one of the few
who sense the disintegration lurking behind the apparent prosperity. At the
start he is one of the few not to join in the general rejoicing, for 'what was
there was no longer there and things had no more roots. So he started his
search for it'.

Political corruption is one aspect of Amatu and Sologa society, although
the political material is unobtrusive and subservient to the plot. Izongo's
régime is clearly totalitarian. Lip-service is paid to the idea of democracy,
but everyone is expected to conform to Izongo's wishes and opinions:
'We are in a democracy and everyone has the right to express any opinion.
But we have to think what our leader has done for us.' Several images
suggest the sinister implications of Izongo's leadership. We are told of his
messengers who 'Willingly or unwillingly had their insides put in his
inside'; people look at Okolo 'with Chief Izongo's eyes', and Okolo's friends
walk 'with Chief Izongo's feet'. The people have been brainwashed to
conform to Izongo's personality and opinions. Sologa, too, is a police
state where the secret police are constantly on the alert for nonconformers.

Like Achebe, Armah, and other African novelists who have dealt
with the disintegration of modern African society, Okara realizes that
Izongo's success is partly the result of the indifference, or even the tacit

acquiescence of the people themselves. The second messenger, for instance, is representative of those who unwittingly support the system by their complaisance.

'As for me (shrugs his shoulders), if the world turns this way I take it; if it turns another way I take it. Any way the world turns I take it with my hands. I like sleep and my wife and my one son, so I do not think.' (p. 25)

Others, like Tebeowei, recognize the moral decadence of the times, but they choose the path of political expediency rather than integrity:

'But there is nothing I alone or you and I can do to change their insides. It is a bad spirit that is entering everybody and if you do not allow it to get you, they say it's you that has it. So I just sit down and look. If they say anything, I agree. If they do anything, I agree, since they do not take yam out of my mouth.' (pp. 48–9)

People tend to vegetate, letting everything slide on around them: 'the people with the sweetest insides are the think-nothing people'.

Okolo the Christ-like figure is precipitated into this atmosphere. We know very little about Okolo's past, and next to nothing about his physical appearance and personal habits, a deliberate vagueness reinforcing the impression of a symbolic prophet-like figure; but his courage, idealism, and moral purity are undeniable. Having decided to embark on his search for *it*, he single-mindedly pursues the task, never allowing himself to be deflected from his goal by fear of any kind, including the fear of death. When he fails to find faith and a concern for spiritual values in Amatu, he decides to go and search for them in Sologa. Discovering that Sologa is even worse than Amatu, he decides to return to inspire his people with a spiritual ethos. But like all idealists, Okolo combines great courage with a certain naïvety, which threatens to lead him into some embarrassing situations.

Great play is made of the sanity-insanity theme. Almost everyone in Amatu is convinced that Okolo is mad, and at Sologa they come very close to committing him to a lunatic asylum. Is Okolo actually mad? Dorothy Van Ghent, in her discussion of *Moll Flanders* in *The English Novel: Form and Function*, gives this definition of sanity, which is helpful in deciding Okolo's case:

A person is sane who is socially adapted in his time and his place, in tune with his culture, furnished with the mental and moral means to meet contingencies, accepting the values that his society accepts, and collaborating in their preservation.*

Since Okolo is socially maladjusted, out of tune with the prevailing culture, and neither accepts the values of his society nor collaborates in their preservation, he could be considered insane according to the standards of this society. But by any normal, decent, humane standards he is quite sane. Throughout the ages, various societies have been quick to call those insane who do not conform to their conventions. In the amoral world of Amatu, the morally strong are either regarded as insane or are outcasts. For instance the young boy, admirably determined to marry the unhappy Ibiere, is told by his mother that his head 'is not correct'; Tuere is regarded as a witch for daring to tell Izongo some home truths; and Ukule is a cripple. Okolo's society stigmatizes him because he threatens the basis of their society.

The novel divides quite clearly into three parts. First, the scenes at Amatu record Okolo's maladjustment, and culminate in his expulsion. Then Okolo journeys to Sologa hoping to find the spiritual values which were lacking in Amatu; finally he returns to Amatu. In the second section of the novel the influence of Cervantes and Kafka is apparent. Okolo is humiliated, persecuted, and overwhelmed by his surroundings, but he gradually grows to understand their real nature, gains maturity, and returns to Amatu a much wiser man. His innocence is most glaringly exposed and ridiculed by the people he meets, but this very innocence shines out in contrast with the world's vice. The first episode of the second section, in the boat, demonstrates Okara's powers of vivid realization:

Okolo opened his eyes and looked in front of him. The people were sleeping. He looked towards his left. The people were sleeping. He looked towards his right. The people were sleeping. A man was snoring, and saliva flowing like an Okra soup out of his mouth's corner. A woman, wearing an accra suit, though sleeping, held firmly her playing child sitting astride her lap. She was going to Sologa to meet her husband. A fat man with a belly like an oil puncheon, was breathing like a man blowing a fire, with his mouth open wide. He wore a dark singlet reaching down to only his navel and the sides were bursting. His boasting gone, by sleep taken. He was a whiteman's cook, so he said. He had told everybody loudly that he had, with his cooking, sent his son to college.

* Van Ghent, D., *The English Novel: Form and Function*, Harper and Row, New York, 1953, p. 38.

His son would soon finish and join the Council and then money 'like water flow' he had said, rubbing his hands, and laughed a laugh which made the groaning engine sound like the feeble buzz of a mosquito. Okolo at the rising, falling, rising, falling cheeks, looked. They were rising, falling, rising, falling like the cheeks of a croaking frog. He was returning to Sologa from leave to meet his master. Okolo thus remembered the whiteman's cook's spoken-out words. (pp. 58–9)

Okara creates Breughel-like portraits with bold and sure touches, reminiscent in some respects, of the prologue to Chaucer's *Canterbury Tales.* The canoe is a microcosm of Amatu and Sologa society, and the sleeping passengers symbolically demonstrate the spiritual lethargy and complacency of that society. Okara sketches in their qualities, presenting the unattractive, unpleasant people as braggarts with hard, loud, voices, and the honest ones – Okolo and the sixteen-year-old girl – as silent. As they sleep the unattractive qualities smoulder beneath the surface; but when the storm breaks out, like the storm in *King Lear*, it unleashes hidden passions and shows this society up in its true light. Okolo's goodness and innocence, and the world's malice are most vividly demonstrated. The sixteen-year-old girl huddles close to Okolo, for protection against the driving rain, with innocent, trusting faith and Okolo, pitying her, offers her protection. They are contrasted with the malicious mother-in-law, the white man's cook, and the policeman, who suspect Okolo of having violated the girl. Okolo's action may be indiscreet, but it stems directly from the spontaneity and unworldliness of his impulses. Quite literally it is his goodness which brings out his society's brutality and malevolence. Okara's ability to bring a scene to life is apparent in this episode. First there is the drama of the storm itself, then there is the human comedy as the passengers range themselves on Okolo's or the mother-in-law's side, and the various personality clashes find expression in other 'sub-disputes'. However, the comedy does not inhibit a serious moral judgement: the boat episode expresses Okara's pessimistic view that the good and innocent are normally persecuted by an ungrateful, insincere, and hypocritical majority.

In the next scene Okolo has his first experience of the city, and encounters the policeman:

Okolo found himself standing in daylight in a street, hither and thither turning his eyes. He stood turning his eyes this way and that way in the street. Thus he stood with the crowd passing him by: cars honking, people shouting, people dying, women delivering, beggars begging for alms, people feasting, people crying, people laughing, politicians with grins that do not reach their insides begging for votes, priests building houses, people doubting, people marrying, people divorcing, priests turning away worshippers, people hoping, hopes breaking platelike on cement floors. Thus Okolo stood watching the crowd pass him by until he saw a constable approaching with eyes that nothing saw and feet that did not touch the ground. (pp. 77–8)

This passage communicates Okara's resentment at the muddle in the world. The scene gives the first of the many shocks Okolo experiences, in his bid to find in Sologa the spiritual strength lacking in Amatu. Instead of spiritual values, however, he discovers in Sologa the same decadence as in Amatu, and his experience with the policeman just confirms his growing suspicion of universal duplicity and corruption.

If the street scene shows the world as a muddle, the eating house presents the world as a madhouse:

'He is the expected one.'
As he who owned the eating house said this they stopped eating and laughed aloud, some with food dropping from their mouths, others with drink going down the wrong side of their throats, choking, coughing, tears in their eyes appearing. The floor held Okolo's feet and he tried to run out. He who owned the eating house held him and into his ear spoke. (pp. 81–2)

Assessed by any decent human standards Sologa society is insane, but by the conventions of this society, it is Okolo who is mad. The eating house is a symbol of the world's materialism, and the slogans expressing this also convey a mood of despair, pessimism, and resignation: 'Even the white man's Jesus failed to make the world fine. So let the spoilt world spoil.' The owner of the eating house expresses a mood of resignation in telling Okolo of their own fruitless search for spiritual values. This society has relegated spiritual grace to rubbish heaps and night-soil dumps. He tries to tempt Okolo to give up the search and conform to the materialistic ethos of his society, but Okolo refuses and leaves.

Now Okolo encounters the only spot of brightness in the enveloping gloom, a carver proclaiming his faith in God by carving heads out of wood. Like Diallo in *The Radiance of the King*, the carver is inspired by religious faith and he achieves peace of mind. Okolo's conviction that his own peace of mind also depends on his finding *it* is strengthened, and he continues resolutely with his search.

The final scene is Okolo's encounter with the white official. Now Okolo receives his biggest shock. He had mistakenly assumed that since the white man came from another society, he would be a man of honesty and integrity and would understand his search for *it*. But the white man also believes in political expediency:

'Look, my son, life isn't that way,' the whiteman started with a quiet teaching voice. 'Life's like playing checkers. If you make the wrong move you are finished. There are some to whom you can tell the truth, however unpleasant, about them to their faces and you get away with it. But the same won't be true of others. They may make things very, very unpleasant for you. See?'

'You don't believe in truth and honesty, then?'

'Look, my lad, these things simply don't exist in real life, if you want to get anywhere, if you want to make good. But mind you, I am not saying I do not believe in them. All I am saying is, you have to be judicious.' (p. 88)

With his eyes opened by his stay in Sologa, Okolo now decides on a different course. *It* does not seem to exist in the world as it is, so he resolves to return and create it in the minds of the people: 'If the masses haven't got *it*, he will create *it* in their insides. He will plant *it*, make *it* grow in spite of Izongo's destroying words.' Yet this determination is undermined by a haunting fear of failure, for Okolo unconsciously realizes that the time is not yet ripe; and when he looks outside he sees only darkness, 'the kind of darkness you see when you close your eyes at night'.

The journey back to Amatu by canoe parallels the earlier one to Sologa, and again the canoe becomes a microcosm of the world. This time, however, Okolo is no longer an innocent: the change is reflected not only in his decision to return to Amatu, but also in his determination not to allow his body to touch any other. More mature ideas pass through his mind during the journey. He ponders that his 'spoken words', his philosophy, will not die, but will enter some people's hearts. Considering the cross-section of the world in the canoe, he reflects that wars and quarrels are caused by selfishness and lack of consideration for others. He realizes also that everyone has, or ought to have, a purpose in life, although these may all be different. The trouble with people like Izongo is that their lives lack meaning; like people lost in a fog, they lack a sense of direction. Perhaps God is the only meaning to life and people try in their various ways to reach God, a goal that he refers to as *it*.

Back in Amatu there are signs that Okolo's words are already taking root. One messenger refuses to be as materialistic as the others, and another finds his new black shoes, bought with Izongo's bribe, are becoming uncomfortable. The final scenes are dominated by Tuere's tenderness and loyalty, and Okolo's determination and courage. One is reminded of the scenes in Golding's *Lord of the Flies*, where the frenzied excitement of those celebrating the triumph of evil takes on a ritualistic aura, and the good boy, stumbling into the centre of the arena, becomes a sacrificial victim. Both Abadi and Izongo are quick to realize that some people are already responding to Okolo's message: although Abadi would have spared him, Izongo resolves to destroy Okolo. The note of pessimism and frustration is sounded in the last line of the novel: 'And the water rolled over the top and the river flowed smoothly over it as if nothing had happened.' Perhaps one day the seeds Okolo has sown might grow and produce fruit, but for the moment life goes on as though he had never existed.

Okara's language deserves special attention. One can only speculate about his intentions in emulating the rhythms of Ijaw speech. Several critics say that unless African literature is written in an African language it lacks immediacy and power. On the other hand such works would obviously reach only a limited audience. Perhaps Okara was trying to get the best of both worlds – reach a wide audience by writing in English, while simultaneously achieving immediacy by using the rhythms and sentence patterns of Ijaw speech. Whatever his purpose, the experiment is quite successful. In the first place *The Voice* has the directness of folk-lore, the mystery of a fairy-tale and the symbolism of a fable or religious quest. Secondly, by capitalizing on the strange Ijaw rhythms, Okara infuses a certain poetic quality into his style, enhanced by the vivid imagery:

> When Okolo came to know himself, he was lying on a floor, on a cold cold floor lying. He opened his eyes to see but nothing he saw, nothing he saw. For the darkness was evil darkness and the outside night was black black night. Okolo lay still in the darkness enclosed by darkness, and he his thoughts picked in his inside. Then his picked thoughts his eyes opened but his vision only met a rock-like darkness. The picked thoughts then drew his legs but his legs did not come. They were as heavy as a canoe full of sand. His thoughts in his inside began to fly in his inside darkness like frightened birds hither, thither, homeless. . . . Then the flying thoughts drew his hand but the hands did not belong to him, it seemed. So Okolo on the cold cold floor lay with his body as soft as an over-pounded foo infoo. So Okolo lay with his eyes open wide in the rock-like darkness staring, staring. (p. 76–7)

One notices the repetition, the rhythmic prose, and the images. The images

are all associated with village activity and must have come to Okara from
the oral tradition – proverbs and sayings familiar in Ijaw speech. Notice
especially, the use of certain recurrent images: for instance, Okara always
refers to purity of thought or of heart through a water image, for example,
Okolo's head 'was clear and his inside was unruffled as water in a glass'.
Later, when Okolo returns to Amatu, his footsteps sound 'like water dropping fast on paper'. Malevolence is always suggested by bad smells;
when Izongo rages his 'inside' is 'stinking', and during the quarrel in the
canoe 'the whiteman's cook's inside boiled and stank more than any odour
that if it were dropped into the river the fishes would die and if it were to be
smelled, the people in the canoe would have been suffocated'.

Of course on occasion Ijaw rhythms sound ludicrous in English, but
Okara turns this to his advantage. Whenever Chief Izongo is speaking, the
occasional awkwardness is fully exploited, to make him sound ridiculous:

> 'If it is man-killing medicine to you, then it is bad more than badness
> which to me is nothing. You cannot fell a fallen tree. I know the world
> is now bad but your coming with me will not make it bad more than
> badness. . . .' (p. 37)

Enough has already been said to suggest Okara's ability to create vivid,
realistic scenes. Quite often one feels as if one were watching a film, for
Okara's descriptive power is almost cinematic. Think of Izongo manipulat-
ing his elders like puppets, of the quarrel between Okolo and the mother-
in-law in the boat, of the street scene in Sologa, of the eating house scene,
of the encounter with the white man, and of the final orgy at Amatu.
Finally Okara draws in his characters with subtlety and skilful economy.
Sometimes a small detail, such as the disharmony of Chief Izongo's appearance at the final celebrations (he wears a black suit with brown shoes and a
white pith helmet in the dark night), sometimes a few words – the young
son's touching 'I will marry her' – stamp a character on the reader's mind.
Even the minor characters are convincing, for instance, the bitchy,
domineering, mother-in-law and her trusting young son. The plot and
structure, disciplined by folk-tradition and by the picaresque influence of
Cervantes, cannot be faulted: every episode is relevant. *The Voice* is
unique; its treatment of a universal theme makes it one of the most significant novels to come out of Africa, despite, or even perhaps because of, its
strangeness.

Select Bibliography

▼▼▼▼▼▼▼▼▼▼▼▼▼▼▼▼▼▼▼▼▼▼▼▼▼▼▼▼▼▼▼▼▼▼

List of Abbreviations

ALT — *African Literature Today*
ASB — *African Studies Bulletin*
BA — *Books Abroad*
BO — *Black Orpheus*
BAALE — *Bulletin of the Association of African Literature in English*
CLAJ — *Commonwealth Languages Association Journal*
JCL — *Journal of Commonwealth Literature*
JMAS — *Journal of Modern African Studies*
JNESA — *Journal of The Nigerian English Studies Association*
JNALA — *Journal of the New African Literature and the Arts*
Pres. Afr. — *Présence Africaine*
REL — *Review of English Literature*
Rev — *Review*

SELECT BIBLIOGRAPHY

Jahn, Janheinz, *A Bibliography of neo-African Literature from Africa, America and the Caribbean*, Andre Deutsch, London 1965.

Lindfors, B., 'Additions and Corrections to J. Jahn's Bibliography', ASB XI, 2, September 1968, pp. 129–48.

Zell, Hans and Silver, Helene, *A Reader's Guide to African Literature*, Heinemann Educational Books, London, 1972.

'American University and Research Library Holdings in African Literature', ASB XI, 2, September 1968, pp. 286–311.

A current bibliography of African Literature is also published in the journal *African Literature Today*, Heinemann Educational Books, London.

ACHEBE 1. *Things Fall Apart. African Writers Series*, Heinemann Educational Books, London, 1962.

Heywood, Christopher, 'Surface and Symbol in *Things Fall Apart*, JNESA, 2, November 1967, pp. 41–46.

Jones, Eldred, 'Language and Theme in *Things Fall Apart*', REL, V, no. 4, October 1964, pp. 39–43.

Mortty, G. A., Rev. BO, 6, 1959, pp. 48–50.

Speed, Diana, Rev. BO, 5, 1959, p. 52.

2. *No Longer at Ease. African Writers Series*, Heinemann Educational Books, London, 1963.

Aragbabalu, O., Rev. BO, 8, 1960, pp. 51–52.

Riddy, Felicity, 'Language as Theme in *No Longer at Ease*', JCL, no. 9, July 1970, pp. 38–47.

3. *A Man of the People*. African Writers Series, Heinemann Educational Books, London, 1966.

Dathorne, O. R., Rev. BO, 21, 1967, p. 61.
Nwoga, Donatus, Rev. JCL, 4, 1967, pp. 21–24.
Okpaku, Joseph, Rev. JNALA, 2, 1966, pp. 76–80.

4. *General*

Gleason, J., 'Out of The Irony of Words', *Transition*, 18, 1965–66.
Irele, Abiola, 'The Tragic Conflict in Achebe's Novels', BO, 17, 1965, pp. 24–32.
Killam, G. D., *The Novels of Chinua Achebe*, Heinemann Educational Books, 1969.
Lindfors, Bernth, 'Achebe's African Parable', *Pres. Afr.*, 66, 1968, pp. 130–6.
 'The Palm Oil with which Achebe's Words Are Eaten', ALT, no. 1, 1968, pp. 3–18.
Ogundipe, Abiodun, 'Some Aspects of The Technique of Chinua Achebe', JNESA, 1969, pp. 160–2.
Shelton, Austin, 'The Offended *Chi* in Achebe's Novels', *Transition*, III, 13, 1964, pp. 36–37.
Stock, A. G., 'Yeats and Achebe', JCL, 5, 1968, pp. 105–11.

AMADI *The Concubine*. African Writers Series, Heinemann Educational Books, London, 1966.

Jones, Eldred, Rev. JCL, 3, July 1967, pp. 127–31.
Palmer, Eustace, Rev. ALT, 1, 1968, pp. 56–58.

ARMAH *The Beautyful Ones Are Not Yet Born*. African Writers Series, Heinemann Educational Books, London, 1969.

Jones, Eldred, Rev. ALT, 3, 1969, pp. 55–57.
Apronti, J., Rev. *Legon Observer*, IV, 6, 1969, pp. 23–24.

BETI *Mission To Kala*. African Writers Series, Heinemann Educational Books, London, 1964.

Moore, G., Rev. BO, 9, 1969, pp. 68–69.
Palmer, Eustace, 'Mongo Beti's *Mission To Kala*: an Interpretation', ALT, 3, 1969, pp. 27–43.

EKWENSI
Lindfors, B., 'Cyprian Ekwensi: An African Popular Novelist', ALT, 3, 1969 pp. 2–14.
Povey, John, 'Cyprian Ekwensi and Beautiful Feathers', *Critique*, VIII, 1, 1965, pp. 63–69.
Shelton, Austin, '"Rebushing" or Ontological Recession to Africanism: Jagua's Return To The Village', *Pres. Afr.*, XVIII, 46, 1963, pp. 49–58.

LAYE 1. *The African Child*. Fontana Books, William Collins Ltd, London, 1959.
Ramchand, K. and Edwards, P., 'An African Sentimentalist: Camara Laye's *The African Child*', ALT, 4, 1970, pp. 37–53.

2. *The Radiance of The King*. Fontana Books, William Collins Ltd, London, 1970.
Cook, David, 'The Relevance of The King', JNESA, December 1968, pp. 163–4.

Ramsaran, J. A., 'Camara Laye's Symbolism', BO, 3, 1958, pp. 55–57.

Jahn, Janheinz, 'Discussions on Camara Laye', BO, 6, 1959, pp. 35–38.

3. *General*

Brench, A. C., 'Camara Laye: Idealist and Mystic', ALT, 2, 1969, pp. 11–31.

NGUGI 1. *Weep Not Child. African Writers Series*, Heinemann Educational
  Books, London, 1964.

Carlin, M. M., Rev. *Transition*, IV, 18, 1965, pp. 53–54.

Irele, A., Rev. *Pres. Afr.*, XXIV, 52, 1964, pp. 234–7.

Knipp, T. R., 'Two Novels From Kenya', BA, XLI, 4, pp. 393–7.

2. *The River Between. African Writers Series*, Heinemann Educational Books,
  London, 1965.

Carlin, M. M., Rev. *Transition*, IV, 19, 1965, pp. 52–53.

3. *A Grain of Wheat. African Writers Series*, Heinemann Educational Books,
  London, 1968.

Elders, D., Rev. ALT, 1, 1968, pp. 51–53.

4. *General*

Ikiddeh, Ime, 'James Ngugi as Novelist', ALT, 2, 1969, pp. 3–10.

Reed, J., 'James Ngugi and the African Novel', JCL, 1, 1965, pp. 117–21.

OKARA *The Voice. African Writers Series*, Heinemann Educational Books,
  London, 1970.

Anozie, S. O., 'The Theme of Alienation and Commitment in Okara's *The Voice*'
  BAALE, 3, 1965, pp. 54–67.

SOYINKA *The Interpreters. African Writers Series*, Heinemann Educational
  Books, London, 1970.

Jones, Eldred, 'Interpreting *The Interpreters*', BAALE, 4, 1966, pp. 13–18.

  '*The Interpreters*: Reading Notes', ALT, 2, 1969, pp. 42–50.

Killam, Douglas, 'Recent African Fiction', BAALE, 2, 1964, pp. 1–10.

TUTUOLA

Collins, H. R., 'Founding a New National Literature: the "Ghost" Novels of Amos
  Tutuola', *Critique*, 4, 1960, pp. 17–28.

Jones, Eldred, 'Turning Back the Pages: *The Palm-Wine Drinkard* 14 years on',
  BAALE, no. 4, March 1966, pp. 24–30.

Lindfors, Bernth, 'Amos Tutuola and His Critics', *Abbia*, 22, May, 1969, pp. 109
  18.

  'Amos Tutuola's *The Palm-Wine Drinkard* and the Oral Tradition', *Critique*, XI
  1, pp. 42–50.

Moore, G. M., 'Amos Tutuola: A Nigerian Visionary', BO, no. 1, September 1957
  pp. 27–35.

Obiechina, E. N., 'Tutuola and the Oral Tradition', *Pres. Afr.*, 65, 1968, pp. 85–105.

General Books and Articles

▼▼▼▼▼▼▼▼▼▼▼▼▼▼▼▼▼▼▼▼▼▼▼▼▼▼▼▼▼▼

For list of abbreviations see p. 168.

Banham, M. J., 'The Beginning of a Nigerian Literature in English', REL, III 1962, pp. 88–89.

Banham, M. J. and Ramsaram, J., 'West African Writing', BA, 36, 1962, pp. 371–4.

Beier, Ulli., ed. *Introduction to African Literature*, Longmans, London, 1967.

'The Novel in the French Cameroons', BO, 2, 1958, pp. 42–52.

Brench, A. C., *The Novelists' Inheritance in French Africa*, Oxford University Press, London, 1967.

Writing in French from Senegal to Cameroon, Oxford University Press, London, 1967.

Cartey, Wilfred, *Whispers From A Continent*, London, Heinemann Educational Books and Random House, New York, 1971.

Chukwukere, B. I., 'African Novelists and Social Change', *Phylon*, XXVI, 3, 1965, pp. 228–39.

'The Problem of Language in African Creative Writing', ALT, no. 1, 1968, pp. 15–26.

Crowder, Michael, 'Tradition and Change in Nigerian Literature', BAALE, 3, 1965, pp. 1–17.

Dathorne, O. R., 'The African Novel – Document to Experiment', BAALE, 3, November, 1965, pp. 18–39.

'The Beginnings of the West African Novel', *Nigerian Magazine*, 93, June 1967, pp. 168–70.

Edwards, P., 'The Novel in West Africa', *Overseas Quarterly*, 3, June 1963, pp. 176–7.

'Polemics: the Dead End of African Literature', *Transition*, III, 12, 1964, pp. 7–8.

and Carrol, D. R., 'Approaches to the Novel in West Africa', *Phylon*, 23, Winter 1962.

Hanshell, D., 'African Writing Today', *Month*, XXXII, November 1964, pp. 246–54.

Irele, Abiola, 'In Defence of Negritude', *Transition*, III, 33, 1964, pp. 9–11.

'Negritude or Black Cultural Nationalism', JMAS, III, 3, October 1965, pp. 321–348.

'The Criticism of Modern African Literature', JNESA, II, 2, 1968, pp. 146–8.

Izevbaye, D. S., 'The Relationship of Criticism to Literature in Africa', JNESA, II, 2, 1968, pp. 148–9.

'African Literature Defined: The Record of a Controversy', *Ibadan Studies in English*, I, 7, May 1969.

Jahn, Janheinz, 'African Literature', *Pres. Afr.*, XXXX, 48, 1963, pp. 47–57.

A History of Neo-African Literature, Faber & Faber, London, 1968.

Jones, E. D., 'Locale and Universe: Three Nigerian Novels', JCL, 3, July 1967, pp. 127–31.

'The Decolonization of African Literature', in *The Writer in Modern Africa*, ed. P. Wastberg, Almquist and Wiksell, Uppsala, 1967, pp. 71–77.

Jordan, A. C., 'Toward an African Literature', *Africa South*, I, 4, 1957, pp. 90–98, to IV, 3, 1960. Twelve articles in all.

July, R. W., 'African Literature and the African Personality', BO, 4, February 1964, pp. 33–45.

Kane, M., 'The African Writer and His Public', *Pres. Afr.*, XXX, 58, 1967, pp. 10–32.

Kesteloot, L., 'The Problems of the Literary Critic in Africa', *Abbia*, 8, 1965, pp. 29–44.

Killam, G. D., 'Recent African Fiction', BAALE, no. 2, October 1964, pp. 1–10.

Laurence, Margaret, *Long Drums and Cannons*, Macmillan, London, 1968.

Lienhardt, Peter, 'Tribesmen and Cosmopolitans: On African Literature', *Encounter*, XXV, 5, November 1965, pp. 54–57.

Lindfors, Bernth, 'Five Nigerian Novels', BA, XXXIX, 4, Autumn 1965, pp. 411–13.

'African Vernacular Styles in Nigerian Fiction', CLAJ, IX, no. 3, March 1966, pp. 265–73.

Makward, E., 'Negritude and the New African Novel in French', *Ibadan*, 22, pp. 37–45.

Mazrui, Molly, 'Religion in African Fiction: a Consideration', *East African Journal*, January 1968, pp. 32–36.

McDowell, R. E., 'Four Ghanaian Novels', JNALA, 4, 1967, pp. 22–27.

Moore, Gerald, *Seven African Writers*, Oxford University Press, London, 1962.

'African Literature, French and English', *Makerere Journal*, 8, 1963, pp. 29–34.

ed. *African Literature and the Universities*, Ibadan, 1965.

The Chosen Tongue, Longmans, London, 1969.

Nkosi, Lewis, 'Some Conversations with African Writers', *Africa Report*, IX, 7, July 1964, pp. 7–21.

'Where Does African Literature Go From Here?', *Africa Report*, XI, 9, December 1966, pp. 7–11.

Obiechina, E. N., 'Modern African Literature and Tradition', *African Affairs*, July 1967, pp. 246–7.

'Growth of a Written Literature in English Speaking West Africa', *Pres. Afr.*, no. 66, 1968, pp. 58–78.

'Cultural Nationalism in Modern African Creative Literature', ALT, no. 1, 1968, pp. 24–35.

'Transition From Oral to Literary Tradition', *Pres. Afr.*, no. 63, 1968, pp. 140–61.

Parry, John, 'Nigerian Novelists', *Contemporary Review*, 200, 1961, pp. 377–81.

Pieterse, Cosmo and Munro, Donald, ed. *Protest and Conflict in African Literature*, Heinemann Educational Books, London, 1969.

Povey, John, 'Contemporary West African Writing in English', BA, XL, 3, Summer 1966, pp. 253–60.

'Changing Themes in the Nigerian Novel', JNALA, 11, Spring 1966, pp. 3–11.

'The Quality of African Writing Today', *The Literary Review*, no. 4, 1968, pp. 403–21.

Press, John, ed. *Commonwealth Literature*, Heinemann Educational Books, London, 1965.

Ramsaran, J. A. and Jahn, J., *Approaches to African Literature*, Ibadan University Press, Ibadan, 1959.

Ravenscroft, Arthur, 'African Literature V: Novels of Disillusionment', JCL, no. 6, January 1969, pp. 120–37.

'University Syllabuses and African Literature', BAALE, no. 1, 1963, pp. 1–4.

Redding, Saunders, 'Modern African Literature', CLAJ, VII, 3, March 1964, pp. 191–201.

Reed, John, 'Between Two Worlds: Some Notes on the Presentation by African Novelists of the Individual in Modern African Society', *Makerere Journal*, 7, 1963, pp. 1–14.

Schmidt, Nancy, 'Nigerian Fiction and the African Oral Tradition', JNALA, no. 5/6 Spring/Autumn, 1968, pp. 10–19.

Sterling, T., 'Africa's Black Writers', *Holiday Magazine*, XLI, 2 February 1967, pp. 131–40.

Stuart, Donald, 'African Literature III: The Modern Writer in His Context', JCL, December 1967, pp. 113–29.

Taiwo, O., *An Introduction to West African Literature*, Nelson, London, 1968.

Wake, Clive, 'African Literary Criticism', *Comparative Literature Studies*, I, 3, 1964, pp. 197–205.

Wali, O., 'The New African Novelists', *Freedomways*, VI, 2, 163–71.

Wastberg, P., ed. *The Writer in Modern Africa*, Almquist and Wiksell, Uppsala, 1968.

Wauthier, Claude, *The Literature and Thought of Modern Africa*, Pall Mall Press, London, 1966.

Wright, Edgar, 'African Literature I: Problems of Criticism', JCL, 2, December 1966, pp. 103–12.

Index

▼▼▼▼▼▼▼▼▼▼▼▼▼▼▼▼▼▼▼▼▼▼▼▼▼▼▼▼▼▼▼▼